THE RECEPTION C

THE RECEPTION OF THE FAITH

Reinterpreting the Gospel for Today

G. R. EVANS

First published in Great Britain 1997
Society for Promoting Christian Knowledge
Holy Trinity Church
Marylebone Road
London NW1 4DU

Copyright © G. R. Evans 1997

All rights reserved. No part of this book may be reproduced or transmitted in any form or by any means, electronic or mechanical, including photocopying, recording, or by any information storage and retrieval system, without permission in writing from the publisher.

British Library Cataloguing-in-Publication Data
A catalogue record of this book is available from the British Library

ISBN 0–281–05092–9

Typeset by Wilmaset Ltd, Birkenhead, Wirral
Printed in Great Britain by
Arrowsmiths Ltd, Bristol

CONTENTS

ABBREVIATIONS	vi
PREFACE	viii

Part I *Teaching*

1	Divine pedagogy: the role of revelation	3
2	*Mater et Magistra*: 1 *Mater*	10
3	*Mater et Magistra*: 2 *Magistra*	30
4	Education of the ordinary clergy	55
5	Continuing education	65

Part II *Obedience*

6	Being official	75
7	Defending the Faith	94
8	The anomalous	102

Part III *Participation*

9	Sharing a common mind	109
10	The ebb and flow of influence in the community	120

Part IV *Narrative*

11	Ideas in their context: histories of reception	139
12	Coming out of controversy	155

Part V *The modern ecumenical model*

13	What is 'ecumenical reception'?	165
14	Mutual reception	172
15	Shared reception – your faith or mine?	183
	NOTES AND REFERENCES	193
	BIBLIOGRAPHY	220
	INDEX	225

ABBREVIATIONS

AAS *Acta Apostolica Sedis*
Apologia John Henry Newman, *Apologia Pro Vita Sua* (London, 1900)
BEM *Baptism, Eucharist and Ministry*, the 'Lima' text of the World Council of Churches, 1983
R. W. Blackmore, tr., *The Doctrine of the Russian Church* (Aberdeen, 1845)
CCC *Catechism of the Catholic Church* (London, 1994)
CCCM *Corpus Christianorum Continuatio Medievalis*
CCEO *Codex Canonum Ecclesiarum Orientalium* (Vatican, 1990)
CCSL *Corpus Christianorum Series Latina*
CIC *Codex Iuris Canonica* (Vatican, 1983)
Creeds *Creeds of the Churches*, ed. John H. Leith (Virginia, 1963, rev. edn 1973)
CSEL *Corpus Scriptorum Ecclesiasticorum Latinorum*
Church and Churches G. R. Evans, *The Church and the Churches: Towards an Ecumenical Ecclesiology* (Cambridge, 1994)
De Cat. Rud. Augustine, *De Catechizandis Rudibus*
De Ut. Cred. Augustine, *De Utilitate Credendi*
Duffy Eamon Duffy, *The Stripping of the Altars* (Yale, 1993)
Encounters *Encounters for Unity*, ed. G. R. Evans, Lorelei Fuchs and Diane Kessler (Norwich, 1995)
Examen Martin Chemnitz, *Examination of the Council of Trent*, tr. F. Kramer (St. Louis, 1971), 4 vols.
Growth *Growth in Agreement*, ed. H. Meyer and L. Vischer (Geneva, 1984)
GS *Gaudium et Spes*, Vatican II
Hudson A. Hudson, *The Premature Reformation* (Oxford, 1988)
LG *Lumen Gentium*, Vatican II
Mozley Anne Mozley, ed., *Letters and Correspondence of John Henry Newman during his life in the English Church* (London, 1891)

ABBREVIATIONS

PL *Patrologia Latina*
Porvoo *Together in Mission and Ministry: The Porvoo Common Statement with Essays in Church and Ministry in Northern Europe, Conversations between the British and Irish Anglican Churches and the Nordic and Baltic Lutheran Churches* (London, 1993)
Rogers *Works of Thomas Rogers*, Parker Society edn, 1894
Stormon E. J. Stormon, ed. and tr., *Towards the Healing of Schism: The Sees of Rome and Constantinople* (New York, 1987)
Tanner Norman P. Tanner, ed., *Decrees of the Ecumenical Councils* (Georgetown, 1990), 2 vols.
UR *Unitatis Redintegratio*, Vatican II
WCC World Council of Churches
Whitaker *Works of William Whitaker*, Parker Society edn, 1849

PREFACE

'Reception means a continuing process of reinterpretation or appropriation of the Gospel in new circumstances.'[1] There has never been such high consciousness of the tensions and difficulties inherent in this as is felt today. It has been described as 'one of the hotpoints of contemporary reflection'. Reception is especially topical because it is 'closely related to an ecclesiology of communion', and that has been at the leading edge of recent work on the nature of the Church.[2] In the wider context reception has become a theme of the moment in the history of ideas, of law and literature; and its theological development belongs within that area too.

Few areas of human endeavour have been such fertile breeding-grounds of new and independent thinking as the Christian theology which has dominated Western thought for two thousand years. Century after century Christianity has had at its disposal a high proportion of the best minds of the day in the lands where it has held sway, among them original thinkers whose integrity has forced them to question not only points of detail but also fundamentals. It has had to accommodate their views, either by stating more clearly why they will not do, or by coming to accept them as valuable insights. Yet much of this has been generated in an endeavour to maintain a faith which can recognize itself to be the same as that which was held by the first disciples of Jesus Christ. The new has arisen in the name of the old.

It has also arisen in the context of certain assumptions about the 'giving' of that which reception 'receives'. Houtepen stresses that this process is not merely one of human analysis and judgement of ideas under discussion. On the Christian understanding, the receiving is ultimately from God.[3]

This has been a continuing activity. It has not been enough simply to go on expressing the faith in exactly the same words century after century. Language changes and cultures change. There have to be new sets of words. More is involved than straightforward translation, because the underlying attitudes which form the context of thought and assumptions change too. There has never been a time when things could be said to be finally agreed, although paradoxically, the faith has always been seen as a settled thing, a secure place for mind and heart to rest.[4]

That is the problem with which 'reception' has to deal, and this 'vertical' is compounded by the 'horizontal' dimension of the wide span covered by faith-concepts which can sometimes seem like veritable families of ideas. Every time a new idea or a new formulation is suggested it has eventually (and it may take centuries to work its way through) to be accepted or rejected by the interaction of a more or less 'official' process with something which happens in the whole Christian community. The new *Catechism of the Catholic Church* of 1992 is offered for 'reception' in language which recognizes this 'community' character of the process: 'All the Church's Pastors and the Christian faithful' are asked to receive this catechism in a spirit of communion'.[5]

Over the centuries this process of 'reception' has produced explanations and understandings of the faith which is expressed in the New Testament. In terms of sheer detail much more has become explicit. That does not necessarily mean that there have been additions, though that has been claimed in periods of controversy when some wanted to challenge what were perceived to be illegitimate innovations. But it does mean that there is quantitatively as well as qualitatively a great deal more to be taken into account.

'Reception' has grown yet more complex in the late twentieth century as Christians tackle for the first time the task of 'ecumenical reception' in a divided Church. This involves several interrelated new endeavours: putting together what has been going on in the 'separated' reception processes of the churches which have been divided (in some cases for many generations); learning to take other churches in their present separation as equally churches, so that the task becomes one of synthesis in a common forum, rather than selection and rejection through judgement and mutual condemnation; receiving documents agreed in ecumenical conversation as something to be owned by both or all the participating churches; the 'reception' by separated churches of one another's faith and teaching as authentically apostolic, and of statements agreed between them as also in harmony with apostolic truth; learning to ask again after many centuries not 'is this the faith of *our* church?' but 'is this the faith of *the* Church?'

PREFACE

Any study of the struggle to maintain a single shared faith must also move between the theology and the practice, the elegance of the ideal and the untidiness of the event, the universal and the particular. Something of the sort has had to be attempted here, because at every point in this study this discrepancy presents itself. We may go some way towards resolving the paradox by arguing that the disputes have a 'historical' reality only; they are episodic and particular. That allows us to suggest that the truth of the oneness of the faith is a reality of a different order, which transcends history.[6] Nevertheless, there is a great deal that is very awkward to be accounted for.

This book is about these tensions between individual and community, official and unofficial, the old and the new, continuity and change, and the ways in which they have been, and still are being, accommodated.

The need to synthesize this new endeavour with the lessons of the earlier and continuing 'reception process' makes it sensible to take the whole span of the story as the canvas on which to work. I have attempted here to look at the implications of the principle that the faith is that of 'all Christians', 'at all times' and 'everywhere' (Vincent of Lérins' dictum)[7] for today's ecumenical task of reception. As we shall see again and again, that needs nuancing now. But it is structurally helpful to take it as a starting-point.

It has also been necessary to try to strike a balance in this study between describing what is often on the face of it historically a muddle, and giving an account of the ways in which theologians have sought to make sense of it. That creates a methodological problem. I cannot tell whether I have been successful in resolving it. But I think it is a real difficulty of this kind of work, and one which it is important to strive to resolve.

The Roman Catholic Church speaks recently in terms of a 'harmony' of 'many voices' which 'expresses what could be called the "symphony" of the faith'.[8] This is a useful image, with its connotations of a moving pattern in which discords are relieved by fresh juxtapositions of sounds. It is the governing image of this book, in which I have tried to trace the movements and tensions in search of the harmonies which sound within them.

I
TEACHING

CHAPTER ONE

DIVINE PEDAGOGY: THE ROLE OF REVELATION

It has always been fundamental to the Christian story that God has revealed himself both so as to supplement what human reason can see for itself[1] and so as to bring mankind closer to himself: 'to communicate his own divine life to the men he freely created, in order to adopt them as his sons in his only-begotten Son', as the recent *Catechism of the Catholic Church* puts it.[2]

The New Testament describes the decisive intervention of God in the troubles of the world by sending his Son. The teaching of Jesus himself and the coming of the Holy Spirit are seen in the Christian tradition as direct acts of revelation. Episodes such as the vision which taught Peter that God wanted the gentiles to be reached as well as the Jews (Acts 10) have been read as indicating a continuing active process of revelation on God's part.

But revelation has also been seen as a gradual process, allowing for human limitations; the understanding is that human beings need time; they have to be prepared so as to be able to grasp something which stretches human capacities so hugely.[3] A fine but crucial distinction has to be made here between 'additional' revelation and the unfolding of an existing completed revelation.[4] Christian traditions have distinguished between the two chronologically, usually at the point after the forming of the Canon of Scripture from the New Testament books composed within the early Christian community and accepted by the common agreement of the Church as completed and forming a unique corpus with the books which make up the Old Testament.[5] The Orthodox would perhaps set a different date when revelation ceased to be foundational, including in the special category the utterances of the early ecumenical councils.

That might seem to imply that the divine guidance of 'revelation' became somehow less definitive after that. But there was a confidence in a continuing guardianship of the truth, with God unfolding things further for his people. An English Wycliffite sermon of the fifteenth century describes how people first get a general idea of something and then in due course come to understand it more exactly. In the same way Christ's teaching is unfolded through the work of the Holy Spirit, so that people understand it better and better until in heaven they shall know it fully.[6]

The problem can be crisply stated: 'How do we discern what is within and what is outside of the Church when we meet a movement, denomination, or even a congregation that claims to be inspired by the Spirit?' 'What makes it possible for Christians to recognize each other as Christians, and movements and denominations to recognize each other as being legitimate parts of the universal Church'[7] in the sense that they are all guided by the same Spirit? The existence of the Pentecostalist and Charismatic movements is a particular challenge here, for these feel themselves to be directly Spirit-led. They can also be challenging in their claim to speak at the Spirit's prompting.[8] 'Modern Pentecostalism and the broader Charismatic renewal, confronts us with the need for discernment in much the same way that the early Church was confronted with this need.'[9] One recent list of questions to ask runs like this: What is the source of inspiration? What are the actions of the inspired? What is being said by the inspired? Cecil Robeck, the author of this list, suggests that recognition of the Spirit in others is particularly important. He speaks of the role of experience and 'a recognition or illumination, or an inner testimony that others, too, have the same Spirit and are therefore the children of God'.[10]

Christianity has always made an appeal to the Holy Spirit, both as guide of the whole Church and as the answering confirmation to the individual soul when it asks 'is this right?' Orthodoxy has a powerful sense of this as a working reality. 'We believe no one to be saved without faith. And by faith we mean the right notion that is in us concerning God and divine things, which, working by love, that is to say, by (observing) the Divine commandments, justifieth us with Christ; and without this (faith) it is impossible to please God.'[11] This is rather different from the self-evident truth (*communis animi conceptio*). It is not purely rational. That is to say, it is not a function of reasonable minds. It has to be revealed, implanted. It is to be deemed a gift of God. In addition the Orthodox see 'the Church acting as one' to be a token of the Spirit's presence.[12]

In some communions the 'sense of rightness' implanted by the Holy Spirit is strongly in evidence in the accounts which are given of the process of reception. Roman Catholic teaching can say that:

> The sense of the faithful, that rectitude of judgement, which permits them to 'test and interpret all things in a truly Christian spirit' (Modern World, art. 62), ... is an active thing, a sort of supernatural instinct which aids in discerning the Holy Spirit at work in the church.[13]

For the Roman Catholic Church, 'Ultimately, it is the Holy Spirit that constitutes the essential unity of the Church, the principle of communion that binds all the faithful together.' The Roman Catholic Church also sees the Spirit as 'the principle of catholicity in the Church, that which makes the Church whole throughout the world'.[14]

Among the Society of Friends we find:

> The object of the saints' faith is the same in all ages, though set forth under divers administrations. Moreover, these divine inward revelations, which we make absolutely necessary for the building up of true faith, neither do nor can ever contradict the outward testimony of the scriptures, or right and sound reason. ... this divine revelation and inward illumination is that which is evident and clear of itself, forcing, by its own evidence and clearness, the well-disposed understanding to assent, irresistibly moving the same thereunto; even as the common principles of natural truths move and incline the mind to a natural assent.[15]

Lutherans see the Spirit as 'working through and in connection with the Word of God to guide and empower the Church through those structures to respond faithfully to God's calling'.[16] For Presbyterians 'ultimately it is the Spirit working in and through ... representative councils that exercises true authority in the Church and that is a constantly creative force in the Church's life.'[17]

This is all in keeping with the patterns of collective witness and participation already sketched, but it makes the action of the Spirit as inspiration and guide the test and guarantee of the system.

Nevertheless, it seems that we have to postulate a subtle interactive force between the individual and the community processes, a perpetual mutual tugging and correcting, as a necessary element in any theory allowing for the action of the Holy Spirit in the human community of the Church. Certainly it is clearly visible at the human level.

The Bible has been the central authoritative text of Christian revelation. For our present purposes the text of Scripture is a 'given' of the reception process. Yet reception problems in connection with Scripture have exercised the Church throughout its history, and it is instructive to begin to set the reality of the historical diversity beside the ideal of a shared belief in this context.

The first group of such problems is internal; it is a feature of the Bible texts themselves. Critics have pointed in every age to the possibility that Scripture itself can be said to fail in consensus,[18] when it appears to contradict itself or give different accounts of the same events. For most of the Christian era problems of that sort have been addressed on the assumption that the consensus is there if exegesis can find it, that God, direct inspiration for every word of the text, has merely bent to our human inadequacy by providing a text in such a form.[19] More recent biblical scholarship has leaned towards treating the Bible according to the same criteria as critics would use in working on any other ancient text. Then it becomes in principle possible to think in terms of the human authors of Scripture disagreeing with one another, rather than having been misunderstood or misreported. That leads us to a second group of reception problems to do with Scripture. It is not always obvious what the texts of the Bible mean. Even where there is a plain sense, additional meanings can be read in (but not, of course, into) it. Exegesis has sought out these senses and elicited ever more of them.[20] The place of the Bible as test and reference-point with which the community works, as it generates and judges and receives or rejects new insights, remains imperfectly defined, indeed only partly conscious. Scripture's subtle or more evident presence, in much of what follows by way of illustration, is perhaps our best indication of what has happened in practice on that front. But there is an important theological job still to be done in understanding how it works.

God's teaching and the 'simple faithful'

In addition there is the difficulty that the sense of the faithful cannot depend exclusively upon a 'touchstone' of authority accessible only to the educated. The interpretation of Scripture has been an unfolding, largely by writers and preachers, and thus *by* the educated *for* others. Yet even though everyone cannot be expected to be master of all theological technicalities, Christian theology must assume that everyone can judge whether a doctrine, as explained in non-technical terms, corresponds with his or her own faith.

God's unfolding of the implications of revelation has certainly been widely believed throughout much of Christian history to have taken place in a way even the least educated could understand.[21]

I want to look briefly here at ideas to do with a continuing revelation in the form of divine teaching through the visual aids of miracles,[22] signs and portents. For example, affliction could be held to have the character of providential intervention when it was seen as a mode of teaching used by God:

> Tortgith . . . had lived for many years in the convent, humbly and sincerely striving to serve God. . . . In order that her strength might be 'made perfect in weakness' as the Apostle says, she was suddenly attacked by a serious disease. Under the good providence of our Redeemer, this caused her great distress for nine years, in order that any traces of sin that remained among her virtues due to ignorance or neglect might be burned away in the fires of prolonged suffering.[23]

These 'teachings' could be looked for in small things and in common lives which were dedicated and holy.

> In this convent many proofs of holiness were evident, which many people have recorded from the testimony of eyewitnesses in order that the memory of them might edify future generations.[24]

At the other end of the scale of divine teaching, the extraordinary was instructive because it was striking. The tale is told in Bede's *Ecclesiastical History* of a young man injured in battle. He was captured by the enemy and given medical treatment. When he recovered his captors tried to chain him to stop him escaping, but the chains kept falling off. His brother, a priest, thinking him dead, 'offered many Masses for the repose of his brother's soul. And it was on account of these Masses that . . . when anyone tried to chain him, he was immediately set free'. The ealdorman, whose prisoner he was, was astonished, and asked why he could not be bound, and 'whether he possessed any written charms like those mentioned in fables'. He replied,

> I know nothing about such things, but I have a brother who is a priest in my own province, and I am sure that, thinking me killed, he has said many Masses for me; and were I now in another life, my soul would be freed from its pains by his prayers.

This speech alerted his captors to the fact that he was no mere peasant but of noble birth. He was subsequently sold as a slave, but no one could keep fetters on him. When he reached home at last and talked to his brother

> he . . . realised how he had received comfort and strength from heaven in many other dangers through the prayers of his brother

and his offering of Christ's saving sacrifice. He related his experiences to many people, who were inspired to greater faith and devotion, and gave themselves to prayer, almsgiving and offering the Holy Sacrifice to God for the deliverance of their friends who had departed this life; for they understood how this saving Sacrifice availed for the eternal redemption of soul and body.[25]

The problem with belief in miracle as a revelation-process is its closeness to magic in popular understanding. 'Charms' came naturally to the captor's mind in this story. Christian authors work hard to clear away such misunderstandings. According to William of Canterbury, a knight who lost his horse in the forest of Ponthieu attributed the finding of it to prayers to St Thomas:

> To admit the power of chance in the physical world is to detract from the power of the Creator. . . . If we are to seek the cause of things, we must look for the original cause, which is not itself caused by something else. And the original cause, that is, God, is the true cause of the miracle I have just described.[26]

He tells the story thus:

> Each year God allows this miracle to take place during the days of his passion: when all the lights in the Holy Sepulchre and the church have been put out, he ordains that the extinguished lamps shall be rekindled by divine power. Whose heart is so hard, my brethren, that it will not kindle at so great a miracle?[27]

> But perhaps they say, how shall we know if this word comes from the Lord? What signs have you given that we may believe in you? I do not reply to that, spare my modesty. Reply on my behalf and for yourself also, according to that which you have heard and seen or according as God inspires you to answer.[28]

When evidences for it are clear the authority of holiness is powerful:

> When sound merits come first and are followed by notable miracles, they afford a sure proof of sainthood – to inspire in us a veneration for the man whom God by preceding merits and following miracles presents as worthy of veneration.[29]

Evidences are important if stories of the miraculous are to continue to be edifying, and to have long-term value:

> I will give a true account of the different events, both prosperous and adverse, which have happened in the course of thirty years,

and will record them simply, for the benefit of future generations. For I believe there will be some men after me like myself, who will eagerly peruse the events and transitory acts of this generation in the pages of the chroniclers, so that they may unfold the past fortunes of the changing world for the edification or delight of their contemporaries.[30]

We see narrators bringing the past alive in the present. Peter Damian at the end of the eleventh century describes how deeds done in the distant past are made to seem recent and fresh.[31]

It is especially helpful to be able to demonstrate belief compelled by some wonderful intervention:

> Though it is asserted by many, I have long been in doubt about this matter and deemed it ridiculous to give credit to a circumstance supported by no rational foundation or one of a very mysterious character, yet at length I was so overwhelmed by the weight of so many and such able witnesses that I have been forced to believe and wonder at this matter which I have not been able to comprehend or unravel by any power of the intellect.[32]

These are medieval examples, but the principle has held in every age – that a divine pedagogy continues to work in the process of reception at every level. It has been seen as doing so in the most orderly and comprehensive way in the life of the Church, which we must look at next.

CHAPTER TWO

MATER ET MAGISTRA:
1 MATER

The community

The Church is the 'body' of Christ, made up of 'the faithful'. Membership of that body has usually been marked by baptism, with its public profession of the shared faith which defines 'the faithful'. A 'believing community' is thus created.

The most natural way of understanding it over the centuries has been as a 'society'. But here of course there is the difficulty that models of society change. For example, in the late antique world Greek and Roman ideas of 'citizen' and 'people' interpenetrated in the way the Church was thought of.[1] Christians could see themselves as free citizens of a great city. In the medieval period a different mix produced a different emphasis. The city of the ancient world disappeared. In many parts of Europe society was predominantly feudal and rural. Towns and cities were for trade rather than government. In a town, a medieval gild or 'trade union' saw itself as a *universitas*, by which it meant a group of individuals in solidarity with one another in a common bond. But the dominating idea of the medieval Church tended to match that of feudal society in its emphasis on hierarchy. These are examples of the way contemporary secular social ideas can become inextricable from what is thought at the time to be an indispensable element in the very being of the Church. To put it broadly, on the 'Roman' model reception is marked by the free assent of 'citizens' in the community of the faithful; in the medieval one, both by a solid sense of brotherhood and by a duty of obedience. Other ages and other cultures would see things differently.

The present-day, late twentieth-century, shift is perhaps of another order. The 'society' model is tending to be replaced by a different model of 'Church as communion'. This is not in itself new. It rests upon the *koinonia* ideas of the New Testament.[2] We find the sixth-seventh-century Isidore speaking of *communio* as an intimate union of realities in terms the late twentieth century could certainly engage with. He speaks of the equality of participation of those who 'communicate' in such a community.³

It is not difficult to discover other early examples written in a similar spirit, running alongside talk of the 'society' of the Church. The eleventh-century renegade Berengar, for example, distinguishes between being excommunicated and being excluded from communion (*excommunicatio* and *excommunio*).⁴ We find *communio* spoken of in terms of unity of faith and good Christian living, together with trust in the Scriptures.⁵ But a great deal of active recent work, especially in ecumenical dialogue, has developed the idea of 'Church as communion' a long way from the point adumbrated in these earlier hints.⁶ It is now possible to see the 'faith community' as a sharing in the faith in a much subtler and richly participative way.

For our present purposes an important point is that the 'communion' model takes the focus away from the issue of hierarchy, which so strongly marks the 'obedience' model we shall look at in a moment. But there is nevertheless a need to define the relationship between the ministry of those appointed to pastoral leadership and the remainder of the community. This requirement presents itself inexorably in connection with the teaching office of the Church which is our concern in this chapter. The model consciously proposed until the Second Vatican Council, and not only in the Roman Catholic Church, was still predominantly one of obedience on the part of the faithful to the Church's official decisions and her authorized teachers. It has now in the late twentieth century begun to shift to one in which participation is prominent.⁷ The *Catechism of the Catholic Church* stresses as a defining characteristic of the Church the 'mission of proclaiming the faith and calling people to the Gospel life'. This it sees as something to which 'all the Church's Pastors and the Christian faithful' are called.⁸ But it is apparent throughout the *Catechism* that their roles are not the same. That is the anomaly we must first address in connection with the teaching office of the Church.

The dual community

Who are deemed to comprise the laity? There are two main possibilities. 'The laity' can be defined as that part of the community which is not ordained (or in some other way set apart within the community as a special group for example, professed in a religious order or trained in theology); or simply as the *laos*, the whole people of God.⁹ Much turns on the choice of one or other of these models. I want to suggest that blurring of the distinction is leading us into difficulties.

In Protestant communities in general an understanding of a whole-people *laos* tends to be the norm, in keeping with the concept of an 'all-member ministry' and of the collective[10] 'priesthood of all believers'. The Second Vatican Council takes the second view. It defines the laity as excluding (*praeter*) the ordained and religious.[11] The Anglican position has not always been clear. In a Report commissioned by Archbishop Frederick Temple in 1898, it was argued that 'there is a primitive distinction between clergy and laity', which 'will continue to the end of the age'. This was seen as no 'more than a provision for the purpose of developing the fullness of corporate life in the Church which is Christ's body', for 'the ultimate authority and the right of collective action lie with the whole body, the Church'.[12] Anglicans today commonly consider the ordained to be also members of the *laos*. Yet Anglican practice remains somewhat anomalous here. The Church of England's present General Synod is divided into House of Bishops, Clergy and Laity, so that it is implied by this structure not only that there is a distinct body of the non-ordained, but also that the ordained can be divided into natural classes which are somehow parallel with or even equivalent to that of the 'laity'.[13]

It would be misleading to suggest that the 'dual community' model separates clergy and laity in every respect. No community would wish to diminish the centrality of the common baptism which makes all alike members of the body of Christ. Cardinal Suenens points out from a Roman Catholic viewpoint that 'When a child is brought to baptism, the priest asks the question: "What do you ask of the Church of God?" In responding "Faith" we ask to be admitted into the faith of the Church.'[14] Again:

> Whether they be members of the hierarchy or not, all Christians are first and foremost 'the faithful' in the deepest meaning of this word, that is, 'the believers'. We can never meditate enough on the baptismal foundation of the church, this primal mystery of Christian existence, which unites in one decisive act the acceptance of the Lord, the profession of the gospel, the purification from sin, the active presence of the Spirit, and entrance into the community of the faithful.[15]

It is also important on this view that 'the dominant characteristic of the Christian people is the communal aspect, with all the psychological and pastoral demands that this implies.'[16]

But the 'dual community' view as set out in Vatican II is forced by the acceptance of the duality to give the laity, defined as a separate class, a role of their own, their own 'mode' of being Christians, complementary to that of the clergy but distinct. In the 1950s Yves Congar published *Lay people in the Church* and H. Kraemer *A Theology of the Laity*. These strove to treat the laity as 'mature members of the people of God'.[17] There was a strong emphasis on their equality with the ordained in that respect. But that was not taken to imply that the laity could be regarded as interchangeable with the clergy. Distinction of role must remain. This thinking underlies the formulae of Vatican II which speak of a special vocation of the laity. In the phraseology of Vatican II, the laity are the faithful who 'have been incorporated into Christ by baptism', constitute the people of God, but have been made 'participants in their own way' in the mission of the whole Christian people in the Church and in the world. 'They have their own special character, which is secular.'[18]

Vatican II goes into some detail on the ways lay people can exercise their varied apostolate in the Church and in the world. It stresses that that apostolate forms an indispensable component of the life and work of the Church. 'Within the Christian communities their *actio* is so necessary that without it their pastors cannot fulfil their apostolic task. Thus lay-people with a truly apostolic mind like those who assisted Paul (Acts 18.18, 26; Rom. 16.3) supply what others lack; they build up both pastors and people.'[19] In this way Vatican II gives the laity an active role and a clear responsibility for the maintenance of the faith:

> The laity may expect enlightenment and spiritual help from the clergy. But they should not consider that their pastors always have the expertise needed to provide a concrete and ready answer to every problem which arises, even the most serious ones, or that this is their mission. The laity, as enlightened with Christian wisdom and paying careful attention to the teaching of the *magisterium* have their own part to play.[20]

The laity are themselves 'nourished' by active participation in the liturgical life of their community. 'They bring to the church those who may have wandered far; they cooperate energetically in passing on the word of God, especially by catechetical instruction;' (III.10).[21]

But the twin concept of the 'special lay responsibility for the world' is relatively new, and presents some problems. Statements framed to avoid the implication that as non-ordained the laity are somehow less than those who are members of the ordained ministry can give rise to other implications which may not in themselves be appropriate or desirable. For example, 'Lay people are to be defined not in terms of "non-ordained church members" but in terms of the world, that is, "the whole inhabited earth" which is their proper arena of faith and action.'[22] This might be taken to suggest that the clergy are in some way not directly responsible for the world, or perhaps only through the laity. That would in itself raise ecclesiological difficulties.

So there is an inherent problem in seeking to separate off the non-ordained as a class; it seems to make it necessary to define a role for them which is distinct from that of the ordained; and which has 'special' characteristics in some way the equal of those of the ordained ministry but having in some way to exclude the ordained for the sake of equity.

Soon after the Second Vatican Council, Cardinal Suenens made an attempt to define a difference between the shared priesthood of all Christ's people and the specific responsibilities of ordained ministers, in terms which affirmed the lay tasks in this manner as a high and priestly but still distinct calling:

> These conciliar documents are saying to the laymen: in the Spirit, that is, in the state of grace, live out your daily existence, work and leisure, conjugal life and family existence, prayers and apostolic efforts. All of this is fundamentally your spiritual cult, your common priesthood. All of your activities, whether they be 'profane' or 'religious', if they are lived 'in the Spirit', possess a deep meaning. They are offerings and sacrifices, they are doctrinal witness, they pertain to your royal priesthood.[23]

He also tries to see the lay role as the bringing to bear on everything in ordinary life of a Christian habit of mind. 'We need what we would like to call a "theology of the actual", which is nothing more than a Christian gaze upon what is happening at the moment and its interpretation.'[24]

He points to developments in the actual life of the churches which show this already happening:

> Life is ahead of the law. Since the council, we witness daily the greater part played by the Christian community in the liturgy, we see to what degree pastoral renewal accents and animates the community dimension of the sacraments. Institutions have arisen which actualize the coresponsibility of lay people: there is the parish council, and at the diocesan level the pastoral council, which was established by Vatican II itself.[25]

One more recent commentator suggests from a longer vantage-point that Vatican II

> provided a platform for a challenge to the longstanding view that the Church was a perfect, though unequal society. The search for an alternative was long and tedious, with emphasis eventually favouring those ecclesial charisms – beyond the juridical – by means of which her intimate bond with the Triune God was duly acknowledged, her people were all reckoned to have proper functions within the body, and her close contacts had to include Christians separated from her, other religions and indeed the whole world.[26]

In all these texts there are signs of the strains put upon the construction by the need to find an equal-but-different role for the laity which is not also shared by the ordained. It will be evident that these are problems which are much eased by the adoption of a 'low' doctrine of ministry, in which the ministry is not seen as set apart in a priestly way, and the emphasis is upon the collective priesthood of all believers.

Children in the faith?

At the heart of the problem lies the role of the laity in forming the *consensus fidelium*:

> Pastor, you speak very well. You use fine words and it's obvious you know a lot. But I was wondering, don't *we* have anything to say? Because I feel inside here [said this modern South American complainant] (pointing to his chest) that we all have something to say.[27]

In most centuries we find the assumption that those who are not ordained or professional theologians are in some way children in the faith. The idea of the laity as immature, needing to be taught in pictures, was hard to get away from in the Middle Ages when, even in the later centuries of the period, only a relatively small proportion of lay people seem to have been literate.[28] The undoubted recurring tendency for the Church's leaders to patronize the mass of the faithful has been sharply corrected from time to time in the Church's history, by dissenting or anti-establishment groups such as the late medieval Lollards.

This modern exclamation came from Ramon, from a poor family in Rosario, Argentina. At a local Christian study-group he voiced the paradox of his position. Ramon's expression of the sense of not knowing as much as the professionals and yet *having* a faith and having a view and a right to express it reflects a natural confidence that the *laos*, all Christians together, must be the repository and guardians of tradition. That, then, is the tension and the dilemma. The laity join in forming the *consensus fidelium*, and it cannot exist without them. But they seem not quite on a level footing with clergy and experts in some undeniable respects. We have already met Vatican II's reference to the paying of careful attention to the teaching of the *magisterium*. The fear its *dirigiste* approach reflects is that to let everyone join in freely would be a recipe for chaos and error, that it is simply impracticable to expect everyone to know of, understand and judge for themselves, all the myriad details of the faith as developed in history. Moreover, there is the problem that those with little or no education may go astray in their thinking. And there is the difficulty about what it is 'essential' for everyone to know and assent to.

It has always been easy to see the laity as children in the faith. Scripture seems to offer ready warrant for thinking so in its talk of 'milk' and 'meat'. The Council of Ephesus of 431 warns: 'always . . . be very careful about what you say to the people in matters of teaching and of your thought on the faith. You should bear in mind that to scandalize even one of these little ones that believe in Christ (Matt. 18.6) lays you open to unendurable wrath.'[29]

There is a related dilemma about the competence of the laity. A number of apparently incompatible commonplaces over the centuries touch on this. We have already met them briefly in connection with miracles. Let us bat them back and forth and see their complex oppositions of assumption. On the one hand there is a respect for the instinctive reverence of the simple, who are seen to come running on sure feet when they see real holiness. The type of such an individual is the rude but righteous labourer of Langland's *Piers Plowman*,[30] the 'honest working man' of a later age, decent, honourable, in touch with Christ with a natural directness.[31]

Opposed to this is the tendency to superstition and magic observed among the uneducated in all ages. Charged with preaching against pilgrimages, the Lollard Thorpe differentiates between those who superstitiously visit the sites of reputed miracles and those whose whole lives are a 'travelynge to ward the bliss of hevene'.[32] It is easy enough to find evidences of the continuation of magic well beyond the Middle Ages,[33] together with evidences of the continuation of astrology (in England, for example)[34] and of witchcraft.

This kind of thing must proceed in part from ignorance in ordinary people. Persistent ignorance may be thought culpable. A description survives by the seventeenth-century William Pemble.

> Being demanded what he thought of God, he answers that he was a good old man; and what of Christ, that he was a towardly young man; and of his soul, that it was a great bone in his body; and what should become of his soul after he was dead, that if he had done well he should be put into a pleasant green meadow.

This man had heard two or three thousand sermons in a lifetime.

> But, my brethren, be assured this man was not alone; there be many a hundred in his case who come to church and hear much, haply a hundred and fifty sermons in a year: yet at year's end are as much the better for all, as the pillars of the church against which they lean, or the pews wherein they sit.[35]

> In some parts where I have travelled, where great and spacious wastes, mountains and heaths are . . . many . . . cottages are set up, the people given to little or no kind of labour, living very hardly with oaten bread, sour whey, and goats' milk, dwelling far from any church or chapel, and are as ignorant of God or of any civil course of life as the very savages amongst the infidels.[36]

But descriptions of ignorance and its consequences confront another pattern, seemingly as incompatible with it as the notion of the holiness of the simple. There are accounts of a scepticism, a characteristic arguing some sophistication:

> On Nov 4 1681 as I travel'd towards Wakefield . . . I met with a boy. . . . I begun to ask him some questions about the principles of religion; he could not tell me how many gods there be, nor persons in the godhead, nor who made the world nor anything about Jesus Christ, nor heaven or hell, or eternity after this life, nor for what end he came into the world, nor what condition he was born in . . . yet this was a witty boy and could talk of any worldly things skilfully enough . . . he is 10 yeares of age, cannot read and scarce ever goes to church.[37]

Failure to believe Christian teaching can itself also be linked with bizarre and pagan notions.[38]

In the texts of Vatican II there is a lingering sense that the laity need some protection from undue forcefulness on the part of the professionals. They are not quite deemed to be able to stand up for themselves. Here, for example, the idea of equality looks frail:

Religious communities are entitled to teach and give witness to their faith publicly in speech and writing without hindrance. But in propagating their religious belief they must always abstain from any kind of action that savours of undue pressure or improper enticement, particularly in regard to the poor or uneducated. Any such course of action must be held an abuse of their own rights and an infringement of the rights of others.[39]

But it has also been argued from Scripture that things are revealed to the 'little ones' and the simple which are hidden from the wise. 'It appeareth,' the Anglican John Jewel says, in the sixteenth century,

> by the Councils of Carthage and Hippo Regius that in old times children under 14 years of age were admitted to be readers in the church, and notwithstanding either their age or want of learning, the people was well contented with silence and reverence to give ear to them. . . . These simple unlearned ones, whom you so disdainfully despise, shall rise up in the day of the Lord, and condemn you with all your knowledge. God is able to make the poor ass to speak, to control blind Balaam's wilful purpose.[40]

> In old time, when the Church of God . . . was very well governed, both elders and deacons . . . certain also of the common people, were called thereunto, and made acquainted with ecclesiastical matters. . . . Grant they be the church; let them be heard speak in councils; let them alone have authority to give consent.[41]

> It appeareth that the apostles gave us an example, that in great weighty matters we should call some others to us . . . in the acts, when the Apostles had any great matter to determine, they durst not to discuss it by themselves alone, but called the multitude to sit with them.[42]

This line of argument is, however, perhaps most characteristically found where the clerical hierarchy is being attacked for pride and presumption. And it gains its force from the continuing stress on the simplicity and childlikeness of the ordinary people of God. It does not necessarily turn that assumption on its head. A text which comes closer to doing so is this example which belongs with the thinking of Vatican II.

> Divine truth is preserved in the whole Christian community by the Holy Spirit. Hence within this community you will find truth more easily, if you cultivate closer ties of communion with the entire community of the faithful; if you emulate the humility of

the little ones, to whom our heavenly Father more readily reveals his mysterious nature and his hidden designs.[43]

Alongside the acceptance of lay simplicity has run the assumption that less is actually required of lay people by way of understanding of their faith. The Russian Orthodox tradition, for example, takes it that the faith consists of various articles which Christians must believe and confess:

> of which some are principal, and so necessary to salvation . . . while others, especially for simple people busied with their worldly callings, are less necessary, as being implied in the first, and belonging only to their more exact statement and explanation.[44]

This idea – universal in the West in the Middle Ages – blurs a distinction between the detailed formal theological knowledge, which is of course confined to those who have made a systematic professional study of the subject, and the depth of understanding and perception which all may attain, and which, at certain points, may be as detailed and must be as exact as the understanding arrived at by the route of formal study.

> As regards the means which are ordinarily used by the Christian Church for the conversion of the sophisticated portion of mankind, whether Heathens or Christians, it must, surely, be apparent to every unbiassed judgement, as it is to everyone acquainted with the philosophy of truth, that attempts in that direction have hitherto failed, and must, according to the nature of things fail, on the present system, there being no affinity between the remedy and the disease. For the disease, in the present case, is rational unbelief . . . unless such a ground could be discovered as to show how the God of nature is the God of grace, and that from self-evident principles, the way of the Lord as revealed in the gospel must ever remain a mystery to a large portion of heathen and intelligent minds.[45]

But this is not easily kept in balance. A gulf between 'grass-roots' and 'academic' or 'professional' theology has opened up since the teaching homilies of the patristic period could hold a popular audience as well as educate the theologically sophisticated.

The 'Oxford Movement' in mid-nineteenth century England was fired in part by a sense of the need to bridge this gap. To say that a theological shift or an altered emphasis in the life of the Church has been 'pastorally-led' may imply that popular need has been positively expressed. But it can also be the case that the 'pastoral need' may be unarticulated, not understood even by those who stand in that need. 'Such a deep need, then, has arisen in the case of our youth' comments the nineteenth-century English Anglican Pusey.[46] The surviving draft of instructions written by Newman in the autumn of 1833 for the use of the propagandists of the movement shows the pastoral object to the provision of what is thought to be needed, at a level the generality of the people of God can cope with. To modern ears it can sound patronizing. 'Objects of your journey' include, he says, 'to get together immediately as large a body as we can, in defence of the substance of our spiritual rights . . . but we wish to avoid technicalities and minutenesses as much as possible.'[47] This implies that a key difference between theology at its most sophisticated level, and that theology which will have a direct appeal to everyone, may lie partly in detail. But it clearly also lies in stressing for popular understanding matters which, without instruction, many ordinary people might miss. Pusey wrote to Newman in spring, 1834, on baptism, to stress that people

> need to be taught that it is a Sacrament, and that a Sacrament is not merely the outward badge of a Christian man's profession; and all union, I think, must be hollow which does not involve agreement, on principles at least, as to the Sacraments. Great good also would be done by showing the true doctrine of Baptism in its warmth and life, whereas the Low Church think it essentially cold. Could not this be done, avoiding technical terms?[48]

Walton, another nineteenth-century author, reflects in a very similar way on the educational responsibilities of some for others.

> As the present treatise may perchance fall into the hands of some who have the direction of education in this country [he sets out a programme for study] . . . the pupils might be directed to run through Law's 'Christian Perfection' or some similar stringent casuistical dissertations upon the essential duties and obligations of wisdom and Christianity; or it may be of patriotism and moral virtue. [He asks whether it might be] consistent with the true spirit and genius of Protestantism, as well as the nature and design of pure Christianity, to institute a kind of religious Colleges of retreat, where young persons . . . when their education might be said to be finished, might . . . remain for a period of five or seven years for the simple and avowed purpose of being taught and exercised in the most enlarged practice of the divine virtues of Christianity.[49]

The point need not be laboured. The problem of the existence of a dual community in which some have a less 'expert' role in the forming of the *consensus fidelium* seems inescapable, however confidently we can say with Vatican II that the laity are 'enlightened with Christian wisdom'.

Drawbacks of the dual-community model today

Some of the late twentieth-century entailments of the 'dual community' model seem to underline its drawbacks, in this area particularly.

Attitudes to the laity have proved peculiarly susceptible to tides of change in political theory, in which the concept of a dual community presents itself in a variety of forms. This is as true of ideologies which disapprove of it, as of those which regard it as a necessary and appropriate feature of the Church's life. The two parts of the dual community must seem unequal in privilege if some have authority and knowledge which is not shared by all.

This problem-area exists in every age. But peculiar to the late twentieth century are a number of entailments which sharpen, as perhaps never before, its fundamentally unsatisfactory character. I have already suggested that it is in reaction against the hierarchical view that clergy are senior to laity in the faith that arguments about complementarity (that laity and clergy have different but mutually dependent roles and functions) have arrived at their later twentieth-century forms. Now a theology of complementarity does not necessarily rule out inequality. A key and a lock are complementary but if the task is to prevent entry the lock is more important than the key; if the reverse, the key is more important than the lock. 'Equal but different' is an inherently unstable formula.

Konrad Raiser would argue that at present 'there is a regression to a very much older understanding of the laity as in some sense an inferior status'. That, in his view, means that

> the goal of lay commitment is the rebuilding of viable non-exclusive social forms that will produce a community with a human face in which human dignity is recognized, basic human needs are satisfied and the diversity of cultural identities and human talents are duly recognized.[50]

Others would agree: 'Any educational approach which sets out to be liberating will start from where the people are, from their real, practical needs. . . . It will listen to and make space for the needs they feel.'[51]

One of the features of the recurring need to establish equality of all Christian people is the equally recurrent notion that something *new* is happening, which creates an unprecedented situation requiring novel solutions:

> In recent decades a theology that seeks to translate the voice of the people has flourished in all continents. Brazilian theologian Leonardo Boff has called it 'the theology of the poor peripheral churches of the third world'. Its forms and features vary according to the different historical realities experienced by the communities as they reflect on their faith in God's presence and action, but every version of this theology, this new way of talking about God's saving action, 'has the same aim of creating greater space for freedom and the supreme gift of God's kingdom'.
>
> This new way of doing theology, the discovery that the members of a given community – women and men, old people and children, natives and immigrants, black and white – belong together and are interdependent stirred and mobilized many people, while creating a reaction of fear and resistance among many others.[52]

Within this area of discourse there is talk, characteristically, of freedom as requiring revolt. 'The theology of liberation, as an intellectual product, will have to be corrected and interpreted by each generation in order to make it what it sets out to be: a methodology which tries to create spaces for freedom.' But it seeks the new and the free in fear that they will be denied, and that takes us back to the condemnation and enmity we have already met:

> In the language of longing, a condemnation is actually being made. We are dreaming of a future that is different from the present. God desires this future for us. Together we can achieve it. ... It is in community, through the enriching discussion of our agreements and disagreements that this word [of God] speaks to us and enlightens and guides us. This word gives us the strength, together with others, to resist attempts at domination. It nourishes us spiritually and commits us to solidarity in face of hunger, need, injustice and suffering.[53]

Again and again we meet talk of the need for conflict, resistance, the denial of any call to obedience on the part of the faithful. Here are two or three examples:

> Intercultural living and ecumenical learning do not aim at an intercultural 'melting pot' dissolving cultural differences into *one*

'way of life'. Rather, they start out from the awareness and the acceptance of my own identity, exposing it, as Robert McAfee Brown has said, to 'the eyes of the other'. Intercultural dialogue is always conflictive, since it implies a threat to identity on both sides. Thus it involves both self-respect and humility.

. . . The laity, in ecumenical terms, are the people busy building bridges. While the calling of the clergy is usually to watch and safeguard borderlines, it is the calling of the laity to act as transgressors, tirelessly building bridges, repairing them when destroyed, offering themselves as living bridges if there is no 'material aid'.[54]

Economic injustice and exploitation have led to a degree of victimization of human beings and their environment which many people are no longer willing to bear.[55]

Perhaps the most obvious present-day manifestation of these tendencies is the habit of using the language of victimization and oppression to describe those who are not in positions of authority. We are currently, in the late twentieth century, in a phase of political thought where previous, and for many centuries relatively unquestioning, acceptance of the naturalness of hierarchical order is radically undermined, and ruler and ruled, lord and servant, no longer appear to be so by divinely-appointed universal arrangement. If then some continue to dominate or to enjoy privilege, others will naturally feel resentment.

Resentment polarizes, and that has been leading to further division into special-interest groups. G. Baum notices small groups in Canada working on a variety of justice issues, many short-lived, both 'natural common interest' types (he lists factory workers, native peoples, welfare poor, rural poor, poor immigrants, political refugees); and 'ideological groups' (concerned with industrial exploitation, food production, energy production, northern development, regional disparities, repression of human rights).[56] The existence of such groups is characteristically justified on the grounds that their members have been particularly badly-treated; it is felt that they have been unduly neglected; or that there has hitherto been prejudice against them.[57] This line of argument tends to identify a single issue or set of issues as of such special importance that its claims must be put before considerations which affect the community as a whole. Frequently the needs of unity are relegated to a secondary place in this way, and there can be a concomitant exclusiveness in such groups. Indeed they are bound to be divisive, because it is of their essence that they exclude those who do not share the same concerns in the same measure. (The phenomenon is not dissimilar to that which has been encountered historically in the division of churches, where one or two principles become the focus of the life of a whole community.)[58]

In support of these positions, which are demonstrably coloured by coming to the evidence with an existing political agenda, we find (not as a necessary consequence, but as a matter of fact) some forcing of the case in argumentation. For example, colonialism has had bad, indeed devastating effects. But to couple with colonialism, or to include under the heading of colonialism, matter which may not belong there is to distort the evidence. I give an instance of such historiographical special pleading. It speaks of

> the thread of history which connects the capture of Jesus to colonialism. By 1492 . . . Europe unleashed its vicious 500-year assault on the innocent victims of colonialism. . . . The process of colonialism . . . [with its] consequent dehumanization traumatized the people of God into powerlessness and hopelessness.[59]

The progression of ideas here involves at the very least a number of incompletely examined assumptions.

There are logical inconsistencies, too. Dislike of the formation of power-groups among an élite can cohere with calls to form new ones, hostility to existing structures with the wish to form others, the recognition of a 'communal imperative' with the desire for the return to the old segregated securities.

> If the church has a common witness to bear, it has a common action to undertake and sustain. Pluralism, autonomy, freedom of initiative, cannot take precedence over this communal imperative. . . . It is indispensable for us to establish appropriate organisations. These would not necessarily restore the denominational institutions of former days. . . . Yet they would not affect in any way the legitimacy of the church's undertaking social functions when local communities considered this opportune. . . . The continued professionalization or clericalization of the churches' social involvement has led in some areas to a growing alienation of 'laity' from the church and a reinforcement of the traditional segregation of laity and clergy.[60]

This identification of the laity as a class sometimes becomes the foundation of an ideology:

A broad movement has emerged of groups committed to transformation, expressing the hope for a better world and a will to change what has become intolerable.

Any sort of 'world' faith or 'global catechism' is an irrelevant answer to the particular needs and experiences of 'lay faith' around the globe.[61]

I cite one or two examples of this problem of untidy thinking to make the point that polarization and enmity tend to create characteristic ideologies in which it is natural to bend the evidence to the desired conclusions; for ideological argument is unavoidably a self-justifying exercise.

There is a further danger in ideology: that it will tend to seek universal principles which may be imposed on every situation without due allowance for the real position. G. Baum made an attempt to find such 'theses'. His first two are clearly intended to be general in their application: 'Theology must analyze and critically reflect upon its historical context for reasons that are properly theological.' And: 'Theology affects the choice of the sociological approach of analysing the social context.' His third ('In the Canadian context theology must be based on preferential solidarity') looks to a particular society, with the question whether rules which clearly apply elsewhere will apply there too. 'It is easy to convince people that conflict sociology and the option for the poor apply to certain third world countries such as the Philippines or Latin America. In these countries a fairly small power élite linked to international capitalism stands over against the vast majority of the people.' Baum asks whether this applies to Canada. He answers yes, 'many forms of oppression in Canada, unrelated to one another on the surface, are in fact built around the present economic system'.[62] The thrust of this search to universalize observed political patterns encourages the identification of injustice and oppression everywhere and thus reinforces the negative aspects of 'dual community' thinking.

Implicit in all this is the assumption that the two communities are distinct in their membership. But movement between them is clearly possible. No one is born ordained, or an expert. These states are arrived at. There may be justified resentment about inequality of opportunity to achieve them. But as we shall see, there is in contemporary discussion a rather different resentment of those who, by becoming ordained or expert, in some way cross over to 'another' community.

This brings us to our next area of difficulty. A language of victimization and oppression breeds enmities. The most common symptom of a 'dual community' ecclesiology here is the reappearance, sometimes in new forms, of old patterns of anticlericalism. The Chicago Declaration of Christian Concern (1977) regretted the disappearance of pre-Vatican II large lay organizations and their replacement by smaller, clergy-inspired groups.[63]

Especially notable here is a current hostility to experts, which picks up on some of the enduring difficulties we touched on in connection with the idea that the laity are 'children in the faith'. The phenomenon of anti-intellectualism in grass-roots theology is not new. One author sees the fifteenth century as 'an age characterised by burgeoning anti-intellectualism'.[64] In our own day Konrad Raiser identifies the emergence of a polarization of experts, clergy and church-office-bearers on one side and the laity on the other and this as a development which disempowers the laity. Others have been following a similar line:

> The term 'laity' has been appropriated by an ideology which divides the church into experts and non-experts ... what is needed is a new 'laity-language', grounded in the fact that most of the 'issue-' or 'commitment-groups' who are pressing the advocacy approach in 'laity formation' are not adequately described by a language which is part and parcel of the Babylonian captivity of church structuralism and does not make room for the empowerment of the laity in the sense of 'all God's people'.[65]

Fritz Erich Anhelm distinguishes between 'discursive' and 'conciliar' learning, again so as to show the 'expert' as undesirable because he or she disempowers those who are not experts, and thus diminishes the fullness of the democratic process. The disempowerment of the laity in this way is seen as a concomitant of a growing ecumenical tendency 'for lay people to become the objects of different activities organized by professionalized church agencies (most of them headed by clergy). The crisis of the church – especially in the North – can thus be described as a crisis of participation.'[66]

Two elements seem to be causing disquiet here. The first is the possibility of the treatment of the non-ordained, non-expert community as the object of operations by the other community, in ways which smack of manipulation. Vatican II was aware of this. That would mean a lack of real direct sharing by the whole community in the life and work of the Church. So coupled with the late twentieth-century dislike of experts is a characteristic hostility to existing institutions. (We have already met reference to the

'Babylonian captivity of Church structuralism'.) The same text presses for freedom for the laity, 'intentionally using the opportunities available to the churches and church-groups to promote, organise and structure the discourse'.[67]

> Any theology which takes seriously the real situation of real human beings, which respects the integrity of God's liberating message for the whole human person, will be capable of creating these 'spaces' inside and outside the institutions. This is not the task of a chosen few; it is the task of the whole people of God who are constantly called to launch out into new adventures of faith.[68]

The thrust here is against existing structures but not, it seems, against organization and structures if they are promoted internally by the people of God as a whole.

The second key element is a mistrust of expertise in itself. It seems to be the claim to a special position on the basis of greater knowledge which is being contested. That was not the way it appeared a century ago, and it is instructive to look at the matter for a moment from the earlier vantage-point of the dangers of lack of expertise, not least because it brings out the contrast between the worlds of thought in which assumptions were being made then and those which obtain now. John Henry Newman and his circle had a good deal to say about the danger the theologically half-educated proved to be in, of falling into strong prejudices.[69] T. D. Acland wrote to Newman on 11 May 1834, thanking him for a copy of his book on *The Arians of the Fourth Century*, and describing their mutual acquaintance Bunsen's reactions. 'He was much struck with the beginning, and with the economy. I don't know whether you will succeed in shaking him in his strong Protestantism. He says the Council of Nice was the beginning of Popery.'[70] On 10 August 1834, we find, 'There are multitudes of men who shrink from styling themselves Calvinistic, and yet accuse all doctrine which is short of Calvinism of Pelagianism; again, who call themselves Churchmen, and speak in a sentimental way about the Church . . . yet call any man a Papist who begins to act as if he loved it.'[71] In August 1835 Newman wrote to his aunt Mrs Elizabeth Newman: 'The most religiously-minded men are ready to give up important doctrinal truths because they do not *understand their value*. A cry is raised that the Creeds are unnecessarily minute, and even those who would defend, through ignorance cannot.'[72] These are concrete examples arising at a pastoral level, among the laity as well as the ordinary parish clergy, of the dangers of a lack of expertise, and they were clearly being seen as such.

A particular problem here is the danger which can arise from not understanding, because of lacking expert knowledge, that a given current view is in fact an old heresy. Newman is again useful in noting some striking cases.

> Thus, *e.g.*, Sabellianism has been spreading of late years, chiefly because people have said 'What is the harm of Sabellianism? It is a mere name,' etc. . . . Poor Blanco White has turned Socinian, and written a book glorying in it. Now in the preface to this book he says: 'I have for some time been a Sabellian, but the veil is now removed from my eyes, for I find Sabellianism is but Unitarianism in disguise.' Now what would Mrs. More, or rather her editor, say on hearing this, on seeing that her scoffing at the Creeds of the Church had been a strengthening, so far as it went, of a system of doctrine which ends in Unitarianism? It is most melancholy to think about.[73]

Little seems to be said in the context of today's current discussion about the value of expert knowledge. Yet, as we saw in the case of the present-day awareness of a gulf between 'grass-roots' and 'academic' theology, there is a perennial and significant and natural tension here which goes far beyond present politics.

Conclusion

I have spoken negatively of some of the implications of the 'dual community' model because we need I think to be alert to them. If the 'dual community' model is not satisfactory, what is? It should be stressed that whether we adopt an 'all people' or a 'special class' model does not affect the principle that the laity make up the fullness of the community in a particular relationship with their pastors. This, I suggest, rather than the distinguishing marks, is where we should be looking for definitions of role. This 'united with their pastors' theme is strong in Vatican II. Lay people should be used to working in union with their priests in the parish.[74] But to see the clergy as '*laos* too' creates a different emphasis. It discourages the habit of dividing the Church into a bipolar structure, with all the possibilities of adversariality which that entails, without altering the principle of the existence of a relationship between pastors and people which is constitutive for community in the Church. The 'gathered community' ecclesiology of a number of Protestant churches is capable of bearing a similar emphasis, although such communities would understand the relationship of minister to community in a number of different ways (with such groups as 'experts' deemed to have privileges or powers not directly shared by everyone easily becoming a complicating factor, as we have seen).

We have ample evidence that a 'dual-community' concept must leave room for resentments and polarizations and even adversariality. In the present decade they tend to take the forms we have been sketching. But they are always liable to appear. To see clergy or laity as one people of God in which ministers and experts remain 'laity too' must cohere better with the Lord's intention that all his people should be one. But the theology of ministry which it implies clearly needs more work.

In the light of all this, does the 'motherhood' of the Church have to be questioned? There are certainly difficulties with a model which makes its 'motherhood' chiefly a 'parenting' of a laity who are seen as 'children in the faith'. There is no problem at all with a 'motherhood' understood as a 'matrix' within which reception takes place as the fullest mode of guardianship of the faith.

CHAPTER THREE

MATER ET MAGISTRA: 2 MAGISTRA

In the light of what we have been saying about the problems which arise where the model is one of 'dual community' we need to look carefully next at the ways in which the Church acts as communicator of the faith to the faithful.

'Mother Church' had become 'teacher' too, both *mater et magistra*, in the texts of the Fourth Lateran Council (1215). The Creed of the Council of Trent[1] of Pius IV, published as a summary of the Council's teachings in November 1564, remained operative in the seventeenth and eighteenth centuries. (In 1877 it was extended to include Vatican I's teaching, especially on primacy and infallibility. This continued in force until Vatican II, which decided that there should be a new formula for the profession of faith.)[2] This Trent Creed sets out an unequivocal picture of a 'teaching Church':

> In like manner I accept sacred scripture according to the meaning which has been held by holy Mother Church and which she now holds. It is her prerogative to pass judgement on the true meaning and interpretation of Sacred Scripture. And I will never accept or interpret it in a manner different from the unanimous agreement of the Fathers.[3]

There is, in the documents of Vatican II, a continuing caution about allowing any member of the faithful to teach about the faith without control. That concern for security had long ago led to medieval rules about the licence to teach (*licentia docendi*):

> The task of authentically interpreting the word of God, whether in its written form or in that of tradition, has been entrusted only to those charged with the church's ongoing teaching function (*solo vivo ecclesiae magisterio concreditum est*), whose authority is exercised in the name of Jesus Christ. This teaching function is

not above the word of God, but stands at its service, teaching nothing but what is handed down, according as it devotedly listens, reverently preserves and faithfully transmits the word of God, by divine command and with the help of the holy Spirit. All that is proposed for belief, as being divinely revealed, is drawn from the one deposit of faith.[4]

Tradition

The faith is visibly preserved and handed on within the Church to the new Christian whenever someone becomes a member. That much is relatively uncontroversial. But the machinery of that preservation and 'handing on' (*traditio*), which is Anglicized as 'tradition', is complex and much debated. It is also possible to speak of the faith being preserved *by* tradition.[5] That makes tradition an instrument as well as an act, and a determinative one at that. Again, we say that the faith is handed on from generation to generation 'within' a tradition. So 'tradition' comes to be seen as a body of material as well as an act of transmission. This can make it seem static, in a way which is at odds with the essential dynamism of 'handing on'. In the Orthodox churches especially, tradition tends to be seen as something fixed, indeed as something completed at the time of the first ecumenical councils. So a number of incompletely fused ideas are bound up in 'tradition'.

There is a further difficulty. In the sixteenth century, tradition came to be closely identified with 'authority in the Church'. It was set over against Scripture by the reformers. They were arguing that Scripture must be the only ground of faith. The problem with this is that it creates an artificial separation. Scripture is the product of the early Church and it is itself part of the tradition.[6]

A third problem, again largely a product of the sixteenth century, concerns the concept of 'traditions', a plurality of systems each special to one or a group of churches. This is not a major problem while the variations in the traditions are seen as confined to the rites (*consuetudo*, 'custom'),[7] and do not imply that there is more than one Christian faith. But there can be difficulties with the concept of tradition if it makes a given variation 'traditionally' constitutive for the ecclesial being of a particular church or community.

It seems necessary to press for the opposite view in the interests of unity. In the traditions (plural) thus understood 'Shines forth a [single] tradition which exists through the fathers from the apostles and which constitutes part of the divinely revealed and undivided heritage of the whole Church'.[8] This way of expressing it is helpful in stressing that there can be multiplicity of traditions in the sense that all are parts of a single whole which is tradition. The Orthodox churches themselves have a special place in the documents of Vatican II. It is acknowledged there that the *haereditas tradita*, the inheritance handed on from the apostles, was received (*acceptata est*) with 'differences of form and manner', and 'from the earliest times of the Church it was explained variously in different places, owing to diversities of character and condition of life'.[9] An example of a difference of tradition thus allowed for is clerical celibacy, which is not required 'by the very nature of the priesthood as is clear from the practice of the early Church', and is not in fact required for Orthodox priests.[10] Here, there is an idea of traditions as elements in a greater fullness of tradition: respect for the Orthodox tradition is important 'for the faithful preservation of the fullness of Christian tradition'.[11]

Tradition, then, is not a monolith 'received' once and for all by the Christian community as an entity in the way the canon of the Scriptures came to be. Each community has its own idea of it, and its own understanding of its content and the processes involved. Some would regard their own insights as a contribution to a greater whole; others would prefer to see their own tradition as 'tradition' *tout court*. So the idea of tradition has itself been subject to reception. It is not simply a repository upon which the teaching Church can draw. And in a sense, the whole of this study is concerned with the ramifications of its variformity.

Mission and instruction

Scripture and the tradition in which it is received and which gives it context have in some way to be brought to the attention of those who have never heard about them if there are to be future generations of Christians. This has from the first been part of the conscious missionary task of the Church. It is the beginning from which reception proceeds for each individual. The missionary dimension is just as central in the late twentieth century, but the issues involved have become much more complex. The concept is not now of the bringing of a faith which is already a settled entity, to those who know nothing of it yet; but of converts sharing in the making of their own faith, by 'receiving' the Christian faith into their own existing life and culture. That is the phenomenon now spoken of as 'inculturation'.

In addition, with the spread of ecumenical concerns, especially since the Second Vatican Council, there arises the question of the degree to which churches formed by mission participate as equal partners in the reception process, making their own contributions as much as the older churches of the West. Choan-Seng Song speaks from an Asian perspective of the special perceptions of 'reception' he had in a Christian community brought into being by missionaries from the West when he became ecumenically involved:

> For the great majority of Christians in Asia the ecumenical movement meant church leaders going overseas, particularly to Europe and North America, for meetings and conferences, bringing back ideas and information new and strange to them. In the past missionaries were the presence of the Western churches in Asia, but now on top of that presence 'ecumenical church leaders', both national and international, brought home the Western image of a world Church supposedly united in faith and action. The churches in Asia had been related to the churches in the West as 'receiving churches' through their mission agencies and missionaries. Now some of them also became churches receiving ecumenical 'visions', ideas and practices developed mostly in the West.[12]

THE RECEIVING END

We need to begin with the comparative simplicities of the early processes. Every new Christian has to learn about the faith. So the Church has always made provision for teaching (Luke 1.4; Acts 18.25), catechesis and preaching, their methods modified with change of times and places. These reflect the basic needs which the teaching office of the Church has to meet in every age and provide the necessary foundation of knowledge and understanding on which the judgement and reception of theological ideas and statements by the whole community can proceed: introduction, grounding, continuing education, meeting the challenge posed by those who appear to disagree.

There was from an early date a tradition of catechesis, designed to provide the necessary teaching at a stage between conversion and baptism when the would-be Christian was exploring the faith and preparing to make an irrevocable commitment. When infant baptism became usual in the West from about 400 catechesis had the role of educating the baptized child, and therefore of teaching the faith at a level appropriate to immature minds.

The classic shape of the catechism[13] has given it four 'pillars', the

Creed, sacraments, commandments, Lord's Prayer.[14] This is not invariable, but it has given a common pattern to much preliminary instruction. Catechisms are not necessary brief or elementary. The *Catechism of the Catholic Church* runs to 691 pages in its English translation and is designed to serve the needs of teachers as well as taught.

The crucial decision at the point when an adult or maturing child is given a first systematic introduction to the faith is whether to present it as a body of material to be learned and accepted by the beginner, or whether to enter into active discussion about it with a mind expected to approach it critically.

The *Catechism of the Catholic Church* accepts that at the receiving end of the process there is a living individual and not a blank sheet of paper to be written on, when it speaks of the fundamental role of 'experience' in catechesis.[15] Linked with this is the idea that catechesis should be adapted not only to the individual but to the context. The *Catechism* offers brief summary formulae that could be memorized,[16] to help the individual. There is also recognition of the need 'to provide the adaptation of doctrinal presentations and catechetical methods required by the differences of culture, age, spiritual maturity, and social and ecclesial condition among all those to whom it is addressed'.[17] Roman Catholic Canon Law emphasizes that the task of catechizing is the duty of *singulae ecclesiae* and especially their bishops.[18] It can thus readily and appropriately vary according to local needs, and allow for the special emphases of individual communities (*traditiones propriae Ecclesiae*) which in the case of Eastern (uniate) Catholics are specified as being on the Fathers, on hagiography and on iconography. But within this room for manoeuvre it is said to be the duty of the Church's leaders to ensure that among the varied expressions of the faith in different churches the same understanding of the faith (*idem sensus fidei servetur*) is preserved, so that the 'unity and integrity of the faith' is not damaged.[19]

PRACTICAL CATECHESIS: THE EXAMPLE OF AUGUSTINE OF HIPPO

Augustine of Hippo wrote several books, including *On Catechising the Uninstructed, On Faith in Things not Seen, On the Profit of Believing, On the Creed*, in which we can see what he thought about the general principles and usual processes by which people could be brought to understand and to hold the faith for themselves.[20]

A deacon of Carthage had written to ask Augustine's help. He found that when he was teaching beginners in the faith he did not know how to show them exactly what beliefs make a person a Christian, what are the essentials; nor how far to elaborate them.[21] He wanted practical guidance. He got in response a short course in the skills Augustine had adapted from his own rhetorical training, together with some common-sense suggestions from Augustine the experienced catechist.

The deacon admits that he has often felt disgusted with himself for his inadequate performance. Augustine reassures him that he himself never feels satisfied with what he says; it always falls short of what he had envisaged for it when he planned what he meant to say; but it is his experience that the listener may hear it very differently and may benefit from it a great deal even so.[22] Here he points to a feature of the 'receiving' process very familiar to him as a rhetorician, the need to put oneself in the audience's place sufficiently to be able to shape its reactions. But he writes in a confidence that the former professor of rhetoric could not have, that the teacher is ultimately the Holy Spirit; the catechist only the instrument.

Nevertheless, he was under no illusion about the power of persuasion of a good teacher. A convert who comes for instruction only pretending to the beginnings of faith and perhaps seeking some worldly advantage can, he says, be 'affected by the discourse' so that God really works in him and he becomes sincere in his search for faith. The catechist may not know when this happens, but he can encourage it by praising the good intentions the man expresses so that their beauty becomes apparent to him and he comes to embrace them genuinely for himself.[23] The machinery was apparent to Augustine, and he was a professional in using it. But again he sees its effectiveness as lying in God's hands. The receiving mind is worked on by the Holy Spirit by means of the devices used by a catechist who is a good psychologist. What is at stake is *metanoia*, the changing of mind and heart and direction.

If the convert comes because he is frightened by some warning, the ground is already partly prepared. There is sincere feeling in him already, even if it is negative. The catechist can reassure him that this proves that God is interested in him. He must then discourage him from expecting such special interventions, such help and proof of God's interest, as a matter of course. The way to faith is over solid ground, through the study of the Scriptures.

Augustine recommends the narrative method, by which the truth is unfolded as a sequence of cause and effect and thus shown to follow from something the enquirer can readily accept at the outset.[24] This method, especially helpful for the purpose of winning people to the faith, he suggests, gives an overview of the Christian story, passing quickly over certain details so as to have time to dwell on others and give them prominence.[25] The catechist must tell of the events which were pointers to Christ's coming. In that way, it will be as when Jacob was born with a hand round his twin's ankle, so that he could be seen to follow him out of the womb, if the key episodes are emphasized for him. The convert will be able to see how Christ gave tokens of his coming in the patriarchs and prophets, who were a portion of his body.[26] The convert's mind can be won in these ways by attracting, and so attaching, him to particular points; and then unfolding for him their implications and entailments, which he will thus be led to embrace.

This is all very well, but the prospective convert will not always be a simple man who can be won to faith by being straightforwardly told about it, however skilfully. The young Augustine's mother had no success with him in that way. Sometimes the enquirer will be a professional rhetorician himself – indeed every educated man will know something about the techniques of rhetoric and will be able to identify the machinery in use for himself. He will be less likely to be affected if he sees himself played upon by familiar techniques. Often he will know about the disagreements there are among Christians, and will need to have them explained to him in such a way that he himself will be able to hold the orthodox view and not be seduced into embracing the alternative.

To the first category, Augustine recommends the catechist to stress the importance of humility. He himself understood very well from his own youthful experience[27] the temptation the sophisticated will feel to mock the Scriptures for their apparent simplicity of style, and to despise those of the Church's ministers who speak clumsily. He thinks the critics should be helped to experience the power of the hidden meanings of Scripture. That will be the best cure for their distaste.[28] The underlying process here is in fact the same as for the simple. It is to capture attention by appealing to experience and from there to lead the convert on to 'receive' the consequences of what he already accepts.

For those who have come across divisions between Christians, or have heard Jews or the scientifically minded of the day (the philosophers) scoffingly disagree with Christian beliefs, the technique Augustine recommends (and here it should perhaps be borne in mind that he is considering what it is best to do for *beginners* in the faith) is to avoid trying to deal with these difficulties in detail. Instead, one should stress what must be, for the newcomer to the faith, the key point: that these objections are not surprising. God knew they would be made – they were foretold. Therefore they should shake no one's faith. The purpose of God's allowing them is that they test us and help us to learn patience and endurance.[29]

Augustine is aware that the problems of winning minds and souls are exacerbated by a sense of weariness, either in the catechist or in the listener. That can have several causes. Augustine lists them. The catechist himself has to be able to bring freshness to the telling of the same story over and over again to new catechumens. A sense of newness is not easy to maintain, class after class, as any teacher knows. An unresponsive listener makes the task of exciting him much more difficult. A stupid listener makes it necessary to leave out ideas which may interest the catechist and forces him to keep to simplicities and perhaps the instructor will then feel frustrated and even bored.[30] The teacher may feel unsatisfied because he has not put things as elegantly or exactly as he could. Augustine chastens him for that sort of self-disgust. What matters is that the listener should understand correctly.

If he fails to make his teaching clear the catechist has to learn to accept his failure patiently as God's chastening. If the problem is sheer boredom at having to repeat the same things so often, the trick is to unite oneself in love with the listener so closely that one hears it all newly as he does, and then one will not find it tedious and the jadedness will vanish. Yet another source of weariness is finding the listener unmoved by what we say. The test then is to go on, to try every angle of approach.[31]

Augustine allows for the possibility that the discourse will have to be adapted to suit different kinds of listener. One sort of address is needed when dictating material for a future reader; another when speaking to an actual person who is present. He moves, in thinking about all this, to a point where he begins to consider problems of the winning of minds more than one at a time. It is a different matter to teach a catechumen in private from doing so with a critical audience standing round, some of whom will hold dissenting opinions. The numbers present make a difference, as does their educational level, whether they are city people or country people.[32]

In all this 'rhetorician's talk' and advice by an experienced teacher – for Augustine could never write without that professional sensitivity – while he is subtly and sensitively exploring the interpersonal processes by which the new believer is won, he is dealing with receiving and embracing. He is also, while fully recognizing the inequality between the catechist and the catechumen, describing a process of a mutual sort, in which the faith comes to be embraced by two or more minds communicating together.

This sense of a built-in inequality is at the heart of the *Catechism of the Catholic Church* in the emphasis on the teaching role of the bishop. 'The new catechism was written in the first place for bishops, who have the overall responsibility for the teaching of the faith in their respective local churches.'[33] The *Catechism* itself says as much (para. 12) in its declaration that 'This work is intended primarily for those responsible for catechesis, first of all the bishops . . . it is offered to them as an instrument in fulfilling their responsibility of teaching the People of God.'

The process Augustine describes is almost Socratic; it is informal; it is full of possibilities of gaps being left, as he clearly recognized. It required a teacher of high calibre to make it work at all. Augustine offers (by modern standards non-technical but) detailed and shrewd insights into the psychological complexities of a process in which catechist and catechumen interact and active reception is a reality from the earliest stages of teaching. In later centuries a much more limited and formal style of catechesis was often the best that could be managed. It involved sometimes little more than the learning of set answers to predetermined questions and, at least formally, it allowed little or no scope for the student to raise matters which might be puzzling him. In that framework, not only the interactive character of the teaching, but also the vulnerability of the teacher, the active participation of the student, the appeal to the common 'sense of rightness' are apparent. Nevertheless, the method of instruction is still by dialogue, even if the exchange is now fixed and formal.

CATECHESIS IN ORTHODOXY: THE CASE OF RUSSIA

The standard pattern for catechetics from the Middle Ages has been a dialogue of a different sort from the lively intercourse Augustine describes. The questions and answers are fixed. The catechumen, normally a child (once infant baptism became the regular practice, from about 400 in the West), is intended to learn the answers by heart in a spirit of meekness and obedience. Things are kept simple. Popular catechisms of the Middle Ages often divided material by sevens: seven capital sins, seven petitions of the Lord's Prayer, seven gifts of the Holy Spirit, seven virtues, seven beatitudes, seven sacraments. The essence of the catechesis is that the catechism should seek to answer all questions before they are framed in the learner's mind, indeed should frame them for him. It takes from the shoulders of the catechist the responsibility of making the effort of imagination needed to enter into the catechumen's difficulties. He does not need a high level of theological knowledge himself. Thus it is possible to secure a uniformity of instruction and with it some insurance against error.

To take an instance: in Russian Orthodoxy primers for children and adults have historically been issued by the Synod and therefore given the status of 'official' catechetical material which is, *ipso facto*, deemed to be safe, appropriate and adequate for all needs. The first such *Russian Catechism* of 1720 was the work of Theophanes Procopovich when he was Archbishop of Pleskoff. In 1839 a *Shorter* and *Longer Catechism* were adopted and promulgated by the Most Holy Synod.[34]

The primer begins with daily prayers, for mercy, the Lord's Prayer, the Hail Mary, and prayers for rising from sleep, going to bed, before and after meals. There is the Creed and a series of short moral precepts. All these are intended to become utterly familiar to the child through regular use. There follows a short catechism. The child is asked why he calls himself a Christian. He answers, 'because I believe in our Lord Jesus Christ, and follow his holy law'. He is asked what the Christian faith teaches. 'It teaches all truth and all virtue, as is to be found at length in the books of the Prophets and Apostles.' The whole is summed up in the Creed, which the child is to have by heart. Then the Creed is analysed. The child is encouraged to draw from it the principles that God is one and made the world; that knowing God he must live according to his law; that Christ came to earth to save sinners, which gives the Christian 'the strongest possible motives to the love of God'. The child is asked what benefits he has by baptism and why he receives Holy Communion, why he ought to confess his sins. He accepts that in matters of Christian discipline and order he 'ought to do all things as is commanded or shall be commanded by my holy Mother the Church. And for this cause I will daily pray unto God that I may never fall away from her, but constantly flee all schism, strife and dissension.' By the perfect fulfilment of his Christian duty the child is taught to 'hope to gain from God's mercy all blessing both temporal and eternal'. Faith alone without good works is not deemed enough for salvation. So the Ten Commandments follow. In a similar tone the *Shorter Catechism* consists of a point-by-point analysis of the Creed including under the article on the Church, a detailed consideration of the sacraments. There follows again a similar analysis first of the Lord's Prayer and then of the Ten Commandments. There is clearly nothing at all wrong with the orthodoxy of all this, and it has about it the comforting air of the settled and approved. Yet it is hard to imagine Augustine's argumentative adult pupils all accepting it without raising difficulties. If the Russian children who learned this catechism asked questions, as of course they must have done, they will have been less sophisticated and perhaps easier to settle for young minds.

The contrast of approach, assumptions and even purpose is exemplified in the very shift from the almost 'Socratic' to the fixed 'catechetical' pattern of dialogue. It is helpful here to have an indication of what 'catechism' is thought to be at this late date in Orthodoxy. The *Longer Catechism* of Russian Orthodoxy usefully explores the *idea* of catechism. It takes it to be 'instruction in the orthodox Christian faith, to be taught to every Christian, to enable him to please God, and save his own soul'. It addresses the particular difficulty which Augustine kept encountering with his students, that not everything Christians believe can be straightforwardly demonstrated to the reason. 'Because the chief object of this instruction is God invisible and incomprehensible, and the wisdom of God hidden in a mystery; consequently many parts of this learning cannot be embraced by knowledge, but may be received by faith.'[35] The implicit assumption is that what is happening now is instruction rather than discussion, that some degree of obedience has to be required because not everything can be made satisfactory to reason. In the section on the Creed, a definition of the Creed is given as 'an exposition, in few but precise words, of that doctrine which all Christians are bound to believe'.

In the same *Longer Catechism*, there is an enquiry into the derivation of the doctrine of the orthodox faith from divine revelation. God has given this for all, 'as being necessary for all alike, and capable of bringing salvation to all: but since not all men are capable of receiving a revelation immediately from God, he has employed special persons as heralds of his revelation, to deliver it to all who are desirous of receiving it'. These were first the prophets, 'but it was the incarnate Son of God, our Lord Jesus Christ, who brought it to earth in its fullness and perfection, and spread it all over the world by his disciples and Apostles'. There are illustrative passages from Scripture. It is asked how divine revelation is spread among men and preserved in the true Church. This is done by holy Tradition and holy Scripture. 'By the name holy Tradition is meant the doctrine of the faith, the law of God, the sacraments, and the ritual as handed down by the true believers and worshippers of God by word and example from one to another, and from generation to generation.' Is there any sure repository of holy Tradition, it is asked? 'All true believers united by the holy Tradition of the faith, collectively and successively, by the will of God, compose the Church; and she is the sure repository of holy Tradition.'[36] The catechized are thus taught to think not only in terms of the living community as maintaining the truth of the faith but also of the teaching of a settled body of faith which they guard. Here again the motif is one of compliance rather than debate, at least at the catechetical stage.

What of the catechist himself from this vantage-point? The Russian Orthodox *Duties of Parish Priests* lists preaching, the setting of example, ministry of the sacraments and prayer as the four duties of the office.[37] Teaching is put as the first thing, because without it the people cannot know their faith. And the manual looks beyond the stage of catechism here. Priests must be apt to teach (1 Tim. 3.2). This duty is often neglected today, the text comments. What the priest ought to teach is the Faith and the Law. The Law is taken to mean the rules for doing good. The Faith is seen to consist of various articles which Christians must believe and confess. The Bible is the fundamental text in establishing these:

> The writings of the holy Fathers are of great use: for they contain either the very same articles of the faith explained from the Word of God; or instructions serviceable for holy living; or else canons and rules for the discipline and good order of the Church, and of the whole Christian community, which we call traditions Ecclesiastical. Wherefore we both may, and on occasion ought in our discourses to quote from the writings of the holy Fathers also such passages, as may be suitable for the explanation of any article of the faith.[38]

So the parish priest is to see his duty as teaching a settled body of material, with interpretation and explanation in support taken from Scripture and the Fathers.

That certainly implies that there will be a need to answer questions from the faithful, that learning their catechism will not be enough for them in the long run. So it is stressed that priests ought to teach the faith, root out heretical or superstitious doctrine, correct and bring back sinners, guide the faithful and well-disposed, comfort those in sorrow and despair. Teaching should not be confined to the church building or to Sundays and holy days. Priests ought to visit houses of parishioners and 'duly to examine whether they live godly lives'. 'Such visits, even though they be often repeated, will not offend the people, so long as they feel that their Priest comes to them not for drink or presents, but solely to seek, as he is bound, their salvation.' We can begin to see, here, how the process comes full circle. Adults living out Christian lives will in the end come to need – if not necessarily at such a sophisticated level – the kind of exchange Augustine experienced, a real interaction in the reception process by which the faith is adopted and sustained in the life of the Church.

CATECHESIS AND ELEMENTARY TEACHING: THE SECOND VATICAN COUNCIL

In the texts of the Second Vatican Council this is recognized. Catechesis is given its place within a lively participatory process. The Council sees the teaching office of the Church as beginning in the family in the parish, which is deemed to be the natural and proper first place of Christian nurture. The primary duty of Catholic education lies with parents and those with pastoral care in the Church should help,[39] says the *Catechism of the Catholic Church*. 'Families, alive with the spirit of faith, love and piety are the seed-bed, and they do their work within parishes in whose fruitful life the young people share.'[40] In that way, the whole community is directly involved in the teaching office of the Church. 'Priests ... for imparting ... instruction ... should seek not only the help of religious but also the cooperation of lay people.'[41] This is done not only by means of verbal instruction but by setting examples, giving actual experience of Christian life in its fullness.

On catechism, we find:

> The aim of catechetical instruction is to make people's faith, enlightened by doctrine, a living faith, explicit and active. The formal pattern of question and answer is rendered into a suitable order and method, accommodated not only to the subject-matter but also to the disposition, aptitude, age and environment of the hearers.

The insistence on embedding the teaching in Scripture, tradition and the continuing life of worship in the Church which we met in Russian Orthodoxy is found here in the requirement to 'ensure that this instruction is based on scripture, tradition, liturgy, the teaching authority and life of the Church'.[42] 'None of the creeds from the different stages in the Church's life can be considered superseded or irrelevant,'[43] says the *Catechism*. 'There should be an organic presentation of the Catholic faith in its entirety.'[44]

'But all our Catholic laity need to be well-grounded in their faith ... an educated Christian needs a clear and coherent belief-system.'

'The unity of faith which such a catechism is designed to serve is not insistence upon uniformity, but a statement about the unique oneness of God and about our unity as a human family.'[45]

The element of authoritativeness expressing the Church's duty to teach is present, too.[46] 'This synod proclaims anew the right of the church freely to found and direct schools at every level and grade whatever, a right already declared in many documents[47] of the church's teaching authority.'[48] 'The promulgation of the catechism by Pope John Paul with his Apostolic Constitution *Fidei Depositum* clearly situates this document within the ordinary papal *magisterium*. The apostolic constitution is the most solemn form for official acts of the Pope.'[49] 'The individual doctrines that the *Catechism* affirms have no other authority than that which they already possess. What is important in the *Catechism* is its totality: it reflects the Church's teaching; anyone who rejects it overall separates himself unequivocally from the faith and teaching of the Church.'[50] 'In the Catechism the Church intends to make presentation of all and only that which she regards as the patrimony of Catholic doctrine about faith and morals which the Christian faithful need to believe and practise as Catholics.'[51]

There are, then, historical and pedagogical continuities in the patterns of catechesis and elementary instruction in the history of the Church's teaching of newcomers, with adaptations appropriate to the cultural level and cultural expectations of the communities in which the work was to be done. The early American Lima catechism of St Turibio of Mongrevejo in three languages in parallel columns, Spanish, Aymara and Quechua, became a standard catechetical work throughout much of South America for two centuries. The American Baltimore Catechism is also an 'example of "inculturation" of the faith, a "minor" catechism adapted for use in a particular region'.[52] 'The inculturation of faith in Jesus Christ will always be marked by diversity: the many liturgical and spiritual traditions of the Church are witness to this.'[53] The recognition of the interactive and participatory character of the process was never entirely lost, and sometimes it has been very strongly in evidence.

Preaching

THE HISTORY OF PREACHING

Preaching has been richly human in its variety. Indeed at many periods sermons have been regarded as exciting entertainment; there have been large audiences and a lively audience response. But preaching's interactive and participatory character has necessarily been limited. By its very nature it involves addressing a community whose long-term response to it is largely hidden in their hearts. So it is difficult to assess its effect on the reception process. Nevertheless that effect must have been enormous because this has been the principal vehicle for the continuing instruction of the faithful beyond the stage of catechesis.

There has from the first been a central task of preaching the gospel. Preaching has thus been understood as a vehicle for the communication and unfolding of God's own revelation. The preaching of the gospel was the natural way both of winning converts, and of providing for the continuing teaching which went on regularly in worship week by week. In the early centuries the understanding was that the bishop[54] would teach his people[55] through the exegesis of Scripture; the centrality of this role in the work of the bishop was emphatically stressed by Gregory the Great when he wrote *On pastoral care* (*Regula Pastoralis*), a text which was widely influential for the next thousand years in the West.

For several centuries from the late Roman period there was a tendency for new preaching not to happen very often. There was probably little live preaching to congregations, who could not in any case now understand sermons preached in Latin as they could in Augustine's day. Extracts or serial readings from existing patristic sermons were commonly read aloud in houses of monks or nuns. 'Published' patristic sermons were also studied there by the slow, reflective, digestive[56] processes of 'holy reading' (*lectio divina*).

But from the late eleventh and twelfth centuries a new preaching ministry began to develop. Guibert of Nogent wrote on the 'order' in which a sermon should be put together.[57] This concern with an orderly exposition became a steady preoccupation as manuals on the 'art of preaching' began to be published from the end of the twelfth and into the first half of the thirteenth century.[58] They concentrated on the analysis of a key scriptural text and the development of its implications for faith and life.

The renewed tradition of preaching was first developed in Latin. It was designed to meet the needs of the burgeoning world of scholars in the nascent universities. There was, for example, an emphasis on a crisp division of topics and themes into threes. But there was also a growing awareness of the need for sermons to try to bring the dissenting communities of the twelfth century, especially the Waldensians and Albigensians,[59] back into the fold of the Church.

That required special skills, because they proved to be able opponents who could quote Scripture smartly back at the preacher and cap his quotations. One result was the founding of the Dominican Order early in the thirteenth century. The Dominicans were first and foremost an Order of Preachers, because they were to work for the winning back to orthodoxy of the minds of heretics. They were educated with that mission in mind. A parallel Order of mendicants, begun by St Francis of Assisi, also laid strong – but slightly different – emphasis on preaching from the same period. Its members sought to live the apostolic life by travelling about as Jesus taught his disciples to do, preaching the gospel as they went.

Aids for these preachers were developed by scholars in their own Orders – collections of abbreviated stories and illustrations; 'potted' sermons containing all the necessary elements, ready for expansion, dictionaries of biblical terms, so that a preacher could easily find parallel texts to refer to while he was preaching on a particular passage.[60] The instructive power of a good story was very important here, because it could get a point home to the simplest listener. We saw how that could work when we touched on miracles.

These preaching Orders attracted crowds just as some of the early bishops had done. Once again there was proving to be an audience for sermons. The preaching Orders also however – and inadvertently – encouraged a trend towards the separation of the ministries of Word and Sacrament in the late medieval Church. Itinerant preachers were offering the stimulus of sermons outside the framework of the sacramental life of the Church. In some circumstances[61] the celebration of the Eucharist could take the form of a solitary act by the priest, and although it was understood theologically that this remained the action of the whole Church, it sent 'signals' which made it easy for the faithful to feel left out.[62]

The sixteenth century made its own contribution to the history of preaching, especially in the work of the reformers. Ironically, they were often inclined to separate 'gospel' and 'Church'. This was a reaction to the perception that the late medieval Church was in error in elevating the sacraments and frequently isolating them from the ministry of the Word. The reformers themselves took that ministry seriously, and saw themselves as entrusted above all things in the Christian life with the preaching of the gospel.

There is an issue in all this of controlling tongues; for if preaching can teach it can also mislead. We have already mentioned that there was a consistent policy in the medieval Church of licensing preachers. Dissenters and demagogues could often command bigger crowds than the Church's official preachers, and what they said could not necessarily be controlled. Allowing only the educated to preach with the Church's blessing is a way of regulating what is said, and preventing dissent from having a voice which can be confused with that of orthodoxy.

Conversely, the preacher must have a knowledge of the faith if he is not to mislead through ignorance. But if he has more than a certain amount of education he may begin to ask new questions, get ideas of his own and perhaps to mislead in that way.

There is also the possibility of corruption, as Chaucer's 'Pardoner' illustrates. All this must wait for a more detailed discussion in Part II.

The individual experience

We ought not to go any further without stopping to ask what we know about how all this looked to the individual at the receiving end. We can of course know about this individual experience in any detail only where someone is literate and can tell us about it.

The early ideal was complete agreement of all Christians with their bishops. That implied agreement of all local churches in a common faith. But, like much else in Christian theology, it would not have needed to be so frequently argued for if it was not often under threat. What is to be said of a state of affairs where there is no consensus, nor unanimity in faith? Severus (c. 465–538), the Monophysite Patriarch of Antioch, asked the question, 'On what conditions it is right to form a union with those of the same opinions?' He argued that 'it is right . . . when they are of the same opinions in everything'. But he would make so strict a rule only in the case of the private individual who wants to join a church. He thinks that there has to be a degree of elasticity in the case of churches. 'The complete union of the holy Churches', he thinks, 'needs a lawful concession on certain points.'[63] Because of his own position, he makes allowance here for the distinction between the act of personal commitment to Christ which makes an individual a member of his body the Church, and the corporate act of a local church professing the faith. He thus takes us to the brink of a key question for this study: what is the role of the individual in forming the consensus and how free is he to hold a position not obviously unanimous at every point with the whole? This has been tested again and again in the history of the Church. We have already noted that the long-running stories of the early heresies commonly involve an individual with awkward questions to ask, after whom his view comes to be labelled as an identifiable heresy: Arius, Sabellius, Eutyches, Nestorius.

In early councils of the Church it was usual to stress that decisions were subscribed to by 'each and all'. This is the central problem with which we have to deal if we want to argue that the true faith is that which is received by 'all Christians'. The 'all' is made up of individual minds of infinite variety of viewpoint. They may hold a shared position which is in some way a pooling of their thinking. It does not necessarily follow that 'each' can be said fully to accept what 'all' together hold, unless some further process makes that possible. The individual can have a profound effect on the thinking of others. Pusey argued that 'the decision of the majority of the [First] Vatican Council was owing to the strong will of one man'.[64] Or the effect may be more subtle. Carlyle thinks that such decisions can be made

> only by the instrumentality of those leading minds which as seers and prophets apprehend in clear thought, and reveal in intelligible speech what slumbers unconsciously in the souls of all. Their word brings to consciousness the truth which was previously unperceived, although longed for and dimly surmised, which lay in the depths of the soul, and which is then incorporated in the symbols of religious societies.[65]

The notion of a collective embracing by all does not necessarily allow for each to have his or her own say, and in the culture of the late twentieth-century West that is important. A theology of reception must concern itself with that further stage, by which everyone's contributions can ultimately become the possession of all individually.

From a few exceptional people we hear in great detail about the forming of their own views about the faith. (I stress 'views', for we are concerned here with the content of what is held as faith.) Any selection of examples must be to some degree arbitrary, for every Christian makes this journey. But the common task is fundamentally the same exercise of personal reception: to come for oneself to the position held by other believers. So examples will also in some sense be typical. The most important common lesson of them all, perhaps, is that we are here in the territory beyond 'conversion'. The conversion experience may well be 'instant Christianity'. It may be decisive and not gone back on afterwards. But it leaves a great deal to be learnt.

THE PERSONAL JOURNEY

Augustine of Hippo (354–430) was very interested in his own *interior homo*. He describes how he learned language as a child. He heard sounds made by others and observed how they reacted to those sounds in their movements and gestures. In that way he learned by association.[66] He reflects in the *Confessions* and elsewhere on the mystery of the memory and the ways in which ideas and image get into it and are taken out of it to be used; how when we talk to one another we are able to exchange these ideas and images with one another, and thus recognize within our own minds what was formerly within someone else's mind.

This is mainly about *knowing*, but it is also about 'holding to be true' on some authority which works together with our own innate sense that something is so,[67] or our own capacity for embracing what we are shown is so. That takes place in each mind. But the faith is not only a private thing; it is also a collective believing, and, difficult as it is to know where we are ourselves, it is even harder to explain how and why Christians believe together with a common consent, over so many ages and in so many climates of thought.

The points Augustine makes about all this in his autobiography in the *Confessions* itself have an order governed not necessarily by how they struck him at the time, but because when he looked back this is how they seemed to him to fall into place. He is interested in how others' minds and thoughts acted upon him, as well as in events. It is a familiar story how he read Cicero's philosophical study the *Hortensius*. (That is one of the books we have lost from the library of the ancient world, except for some quotations.) It showed Augustine the real possibilities of philosophy. He was fired with a sense of higher purpose and began to hunger for wisdom. The core of what he had found was a licence to enquire, to stretch for the highest. (It seems to have been the first time that he was impressed by the content rather than the style of a book.)[68] This appears to have been a case of recognition of something he simply needed to be told about for it to call an answering appreciation in his mind. His previous intellectual pursuits seemed trivial and unworthy, so he abandoned them. But when he tried to find the same sort of thing in the Bible the simplicity (indeed to his judgement at that time, the crudity) of Scripture's style got in the way.

Now there was some complex processing going on here. We can see the vantage-points shifting in various ways. In later years Augustine was able to discover more than he could have dreamed of in Scripture, and he came to find the philosophers less satisfactory. So we are certainly not dealing with an innate tendency of his mind to respond to one book rather than another. It was a matter of the right moment, and of the development of the individual mind and soul to a point where it is capable of recognition. Now, reflects Augustine, looking back from his vantage-point as a mature Christian, 'I see something in the Scriptures not revealed to the proud, not apparent to children . . . I was not at the time the sort of person (*talis*) who could see into them.'[69] This element of timing, where maturing is required before recognition can happen, and a belief be grasped and held, proves to be an important element in Augustine's thinking about what it means to 'hold' a truth of faith. That applies equally to the shared believing of the Christian community as a whole.

Augustine was driven by a hunger, which he now sees to have been for the truth. When he was young the very promise of truth could captivate him. That is what he thinks happened in the case of his entrapment by the Manichees. (It is illuminating to make comparison with the successes of seduction by modern sects.) He took in what they taught him ravenously. But some deeper recognition of the presence of truth was missing. He knew he was not satisfied. At the same time, he believed their teaching. So he learned that believing, in the sense of *holding* to be true, can be divorced from that deeper recognition in which he was later to find fulfilment and satisfaction. Indeed, one can believe wrongly (*Conf.* III.vi). We shall come back to this a little later.

One can also assume wrongly that someone speaks authoritatively. Augustine had expected Faustus the famous Manichee leader to be able to answer his questions. In anticipation, he had regarded him as an authority. But Faustus turned out to be a great disappointment. At the time, Augustine's change of heart was undoubtedly largely a result of his discovery of his intellectual and educational superiority to the man. He allows that Faustus himself was not unaware of his shortcomings. In retrospect, Augustine sees it differently. Later he would say that his loss of respect for Faustus's authority stemmed from his perception of the intrinsic unworthiness of what he said, that is, of its inherent lack of authoritativeness.[70] Authority vanishes where it does not compel recognition.

By contrast, Augustine approves, while wondering at it, his mother's submission to the authority of Bishop Ambrose when he told her not to continue in her practice of bringing little gifts to the saints' shrines where she prayed.[71] She had done so out of simple country piety, not considering that the practice was close to that of pagan worship. But she perceived at once the intrinsic rightness and therefore authoritativeness of what this ecclesiastical authority was telling her, and so she submitted to his judgement. Here we have an example of authority which compels recognition and thus demonstrates its authoritativeness.

One of the results of Augustine's having seen through the Manichees was a new willingness to consider the possibility that the Christian Scriptures were not so unworthy of his attention as he had thought. A blockage had been removed. There was a new vantage-point. Things could be glimpsed which could not be seen before. Augustine began to be able to appreciate the modest claims of the Scriptures as more worthy of respect than the grand claims of the Manichees. He could now come to Scripture with the conviction that neither Manichees nor Platonists, nor indeed any of the other sects he had investigated, had all the answers. Then as he read, St Paul no longer seemed to contradict himself, and he began to recognize and consent to the truths he was reading.[72]

He also learnt in this period of personal searching and change of viewpoint that the vivid and easily grasped sensory image can crowd out the spiritual. Only as he learned to reject images of a sensory sort as unworthy did he begin to be able to grasp that God is incorporeal. So being ripe for recognition and reception is also a matter of having a mind whose desk is cleared of distracting objects.

An element of torment of mind seems sometimes to be necessary before acceptance of some truth previously denied becomes possible. It was certainly so for Augustine, both in his wrestling with the problem of evil and in his struggles against what was happening to him before his eventual conversion. A fiery thread in this torment is a burning desire to know the truth, a positive drive which keeps him seeking through the agony.[73] This kind of pain is classically resolved by release and acceptance. It was so for Augustine in the famous episode in the garden when his conversion took place.[74]

This can all be seen as the emotional high ground in this process of shifting about of what had seemed solid underfoot, this changing of viewpoints, which makes things believable which were not so before. So in a prominent position in the catalogue of what Augustine has to say about knowing what to believe comes this very personal story which is also (and Augustine knew it to be so) a paradigm of common human experience. It is, in its way, both a personal and a universal testimony to the complicated experience of coming to know what to believe.

As a second example, we might take John Henry Newman, an individual partly comparable with Augustine in the wide ranging character of his mind, and one highly conscious that for every Christian there is a necessary process of learning what others have believed, of catching up with the *consensus fidelium* in order to share it. The manner in which this tests and enlarges consensus was perhaps clearer still to Newman with the hindsight of a millennium and a half after Augustine. The young Newman and his circle of friends furnish an example, which they themselves documented extraordinarily thoroughly, of what was involved in this catching-up process for them.

Conspicuously lacking was live formal authoritative teaching, at least beyond the stages of childhood. Theirs was largely a self-taught theological journey. 'What is most painful,' says Newman looking back later, 'is that the clergy are so utterly ignorant. . . . We have no *theological* education.'[75] Striking again and again is Newman's sense of making discoveries for himself and often not seeming quite sure whether or not they are known to other people too. In short, he saw that it was far from simple to be sure where the consensus lies. He wrote to Froude in 1834, 'The edition of Dionysius I am engaged on opens a wide field of reading; . . . I hope it may be of use.'[76] But he saw it and explained it as principally an exercise to educate himself.

Newman makes a distinction between those whom he regards as his (informal) *teachers* in the Oxford (and especially Oriel College) society of his formative years; and those he looks on as fellow-travellers on the same journey. ('Not that I had not a good deal to learn from others still, but I influenced them as well as they me, and cooperated rather than merely concurred with them.')[77] Richard Whately, fifteen years Newman's senior, took him up in 1822, and from 1825 to 1826 he was Whately's Vice-Principal at Alban Hall. 'He taught me to see with my own eyes and walk with my own feet,' Newman explains. Of John Keble, ten years older, Newman speaks in his *Apologia* with high admiration. He calls him 'my new master'.[78]

But with these and others, such as Hawkins, the master and pupil relationship was short-lived. Hawkins, who had twelve years' advantage of Newman, was in the 1820s Vicar of the University Church of St Mary's in Oxford. He took Newman in hand as a young cleric and taught him to think and express himself clearly. Newman describes how Hawkins would read his first sermons and point out his failure to limit his subject, to 'distinguish between cognate ideas', how he fell into mistakes by failing to anticipate them. Hawkins had a naturally 'exact mind', which seems to have been irritated by Newman's youthful bravura prose.

The young men who were Newman's contemporaries sought teachers on paper, in the form of the Fathers and also of later authors, at first mainly those which, in one way or another, simply came to hand. Here Newman is illuminating about the difficulties, and especially about how hard it was to judge well and to avoid being led into unexamined prejudices. In his *Apologia pro Vita Sua* he describes how at the age of fifteen he read two works 'each contrary to each, and planting in me the seeds of an intellectual inconsistency which disabled me for a long course of years'.[79] The first was Joseph Milner's recently published but, as it proved, unreliable, *Church History*.[80] Newman was 'nothing short of enamoured of the long extracts from St Augustine, St Ambrose and the other Fathers' which he found there. Their attraction was the sense they gave him of being in the presence of 'the religion of primitive Christians'. Elsewhere Newman sees Bull's works as 'my chief introduction to' the 'principle' that 'Antiquity was the true exponent of the doctrines of Christianity'.[81] The desire to go further into the Fathers drove Newman's researches in his twenties and thirties. 'My early devotion towards the Fathers returned; and in the Long Vacation of 1828 I set about reading them chronologically, beginning with St Ignatius and St Justin.' He says that 'some portions of their teaching ... came like music to my inward ear, as if the response to ideas, which, with little external to encourage them I had cherished so long'.[82] 'It was evident how much there was ... in correspondence with the thoughts which had attracted me when I was young.'[83] Here he can be seen discovering those echoes which his own understanding could respond to in recognition, the beginnings of an expression of the *consensus fidelium*.

The other book was Isaac Newton on the prophecies.[84] Newton convinced him that 'the Pope was the Antichrist predicted by Daniel, St. Paul and St. John'. These two books struck an unformed mind with all the force of his lack of the knowledge with which to qualify what they told him. They left a lasting mark, because it was a question mark. Until 1843 'my imagination was stained by the effects' of the notion that the Pope was Antichrist, admits Newman. 'It had been obliterated from my reason and judgement at an earlier date; but the thought remained upon me as a sort of false conscience.' The conflict between the two was itself a driving force, he found. Some people in his experience made a compromise between the two ideas; others 'beat out the one idea or the other from their minds. In his own case, 'after many years of intellectual unrest' one of them, the notion that the Pope was Antichrist, was gradually extinguished.[85]

The only ways out of puzzlement were by reading more and by consulting with others, again in a process of moving towards consensus. The sixteen-year-old Newman was conscientiously writing to the Revd W. Mayer in January 1817 to ask his view about a passage in Bishop Beveridge,[86] whom he had been reading on Mayer's advice.

I had, before I read it, debated with myself how it could be that baptised infants dying in their infancy could be saved unless the spirit of God was given them: which seems to contradict the opinion that baptism is not accompanied by the Holy Spirit. Dr. Beveridge's opinion seems to be that the seeds of grace are sown in baptism, though they often do not spring up. That baptism is the mean whereby we receive the Holy Spirit, although not the only mean; that infants when baptized receive the inward and spiritual grace, without the requisite repentance and faith.

He wants to know whether this interpretation is right. He ventures to think it is, because 'the sermon Mr. Milman preached on grace last year was exactly consonant with his sentiments'.[87]

Hawkins gave Newman books, Sumner's *Treatise on Apostolical Preaching*,[88] for example. Newman says that led him to 'give up' his 'remaining Calvinism', and to receive the doctrine of Baptismal Regeneration.[89] He put his own sermons into his hands. As an undergraduate, Newman had heard Hawkins preach on tradition. At the time he had found the sermon unendurably long, but he had remembered its theme. 'When I read it and studied it as a gift,' he says, the sermon 'made a most serious impression upon me'.

In both these instances we can see Newman hungrily catching up points which bear on issues he was already thinking about and fitting the new insights into his growing system. That would generate further questions and problems. What struck him when he read Hawkins on tradition was 'a proposition', seeming to him 'self-evident as soon as stated, viz. that the sacred text was never intended to teach doctrine, but only to prove it, and that, if we would learn doctrine, we must have recourse to the formularies of the Church. This view . . . opened upon me a large field of thought.'[90] Like Augustine, he was experiencing the enlargement of ideas which comes from seeing them from fresh vantage-points.

Incidental influences of this sort began to group themselves and to interconnect in Newman's growing mastery of theological topics through personal contact and conversation as well as through reading. Like Augustine, he did not always see their application at the time. Things grew upon him later. William James, then a Fellow of Oriel, taught Newman the doctrine of the apostolical succession, 'in the course of a walk, I think, round Christchurch meadow; I recollect being somewhat impatient of the subject at the time,' he comments.[91] Whately, in the years before 'he made himself dead' to a Newman who could not always agree with him, taught him 'the existence of the Church, as a substantive body or corporation'.[92]

Not all Newman's companions on this theological journey were so easy to pin down in their influence as having fitted a key piece into the puzzle. Richard Hurrell Froude exemplified the subtlety and complexity of the process.[93] He was full of ideas which Newman says 'crowded and jostled against each other in their effort after distinct shape and expression'. And he had 'an intellect as critical and logical as it was speculative and bold'.

> His opinions arrested and influenced me, even when they did not gain my assent. He professed openly his admiration of the Church of Rome, and his hatred of the Reformers. He delighted in the notion of an hierarchical system, of sacerdotal power, and of full ecclesiastical liberty . . . he gloried in accepting Tradition as the main instrument of religious teaching. . . . He embraced the principle of penance and mortification. He had a deep devotion to the Real Presence, in which he had a firm faith. He was powerfully drawn to the Mediaeval Church, but not to the Primitive. . . . He set no sufficient value on the writings of the Fathers, on the detail or development of doctrine, on the definite traditions of the Church viewed in their matter, on the teaching of the Ecumenical Councils, or on the controversies out of which they arose.[94]

It seems to have been partly the anomalies which stimulated Newman here, because they showed him more clearly what he himself needed to account for.

Newman also learned from Froude a valuable lesson in the problems of mutual incomprehension in theological explication. 'On many points he would not believe but that I agreed with him, when I did not. He seemed not to understand my difficulties. His were of a different kind, the contrariety between theory and fact.'[95] This again brings us up against the problems of mismatch, mutual incomprehension and even hostility which seem to make nonsense of talk of a common 'sense of rightness' unless we can give an account of them which harmonizes.

CHAPTER FOUR

EDUCATION OF THE ORDINARY CLERGY

I have been speaking of the processes by which the Church has taught the mass of the faithful about the faith. But teachers must themselves be taught. They must progress to being in some sense 'professionals' in theology.

It is impossible to speak generally on the education of ordained and commissioned ministers as persons able to be responsible for their teaching part in the reception process. It has varied enormously in its quality from place to place and age to age. The Middle Ages furnishes scandalous examples of individuals made bishops in a rush, who had previously not been in orders at all. There have been eras in which clerical education has been badly neglected, when appointment to a benefice depended on patronage, on having the right connections, and the competence of the priest carried very little weight.

At the opposite extreme, there have been circumstances in which a very high level of theological knowledge was attained at least by some, so that even private individuals, working at their books in comparative isolation while serving in their parishes, could make original contributions to scholarship. The lifelong clerical scholar has been typical of the breed. Much here had to do with the availability of resource books and like-minded people with whom to exchange letters. The existence of a university system is a help and a support, but it is not indispensable for such scholarship, which can involve lay people as well as clergy. At the end of the fifteenth century individuals such as Erasmus (c. 1466–1536), who made a start in life on income from tutoring and patronage; and John Colet (1466?–1519), for a time an academic, then Dean of St Paul's; and Thomas More (1478–1535), eventually Lord Chancellor of England but at first a studious young man destined by his father to become a lawyer, were able to engage one another in correspondence and visits and to press forward the great enterprise of shifting biblical scholarship in the West from a Latin base to a return to the Greek and Hebrew. Original work at the highest level was achieved in this way by private 'entrepreneurial' effort, but in an age when the exchange of letters and the dissemination of copies of the new printed books had vastly improved communications.

These are the extremes. There has normatively been a conscientious attempt to provide responsibly for the training of the ministry so as to produce a body of persons in pastoral office capable of discharging their part in the teaching office of the Church. In the education of clergy there has always been the assumption that holiness of life and obedience matter equally with learning. But nevertheless there have been centuries of only piecemeal provision for the instruction of the clergy – much more so than in the case of the laity, for whom there have, as we have seen, at least been catechisms.

A custom of press-ganging promising young men into the priesthood and even the episcopate was common in the early Christian centuries. It happened to Augustine. Nevertheless, in principle, the testing of fitness and character were for a long time key points in the selection of persons for ordination, rather than their learning. The Church could improve their knowledge. Accordingly there was a policy of setting up schools in the period after the fall of the Roman Empire, when it was no longer true that the reasonably well born were educated in the Greco-Roman way which had taught them enough literature and law to enable them to hold their own in public life. The main centres of clerical schooling until the twelfth century were the monastic and cathedral schools. The quality of teaching in these could range from the crude and ineffectual to the shining example who turned out 'seeming-philosophers' among the monks who were his pupils, even the *rustici*.[1] The clerical profession became for a long time almost the only route to literacy, but not necessarily much more than literacy. Yet even after the beginning of the universities in the West in the late twelfth century with their tendency to make theology the queen of studies, there was no real consistency in clerical training. Very few continued to the study of theology. It was a 'higher degree' subject, and in the later Middle Ages could detain the student until his mid-forties if he was to complete the requirements of the set years of courses. William of Wykeham, Bishop of Winchester, founded New College, Oxford (1379) to train men for the secular priesthood. He established a warden, fellows and 70 scholars, of whom 10 were to study civil law, 10 canon law, 50 philosophy or theology.[2] At Lincoln College, Oxford, fellows were intended to graduate eventually in divinity.

EDUCATION OF THE ORDINARY CLERGY

There remained a need for something more modest. John Sawbridge, Bishop of Winchester (1282–1304) founded 'a College for the propagation of piety and literature among his Clergy' (designed for seven chaplains in priest's orders, three deacons, three subdeacons, with six boys, who were to sing in the church and wait on the chaplain).[3]

Good hopes were expressed in the reforming environments of the sixteenth century of improving the level of learning of the clergy. In the Preface to the Church of England's Ordinal, 1550, on intellectual qualifications of a candidate for ordination, we read: 'And the Bishop . . . after examination and trial finding him learned in the Latin tongue, and sufficiently instructed in Holy Scripture, may . . . admit him a deacon. . . .'

The English *Reformatio Legum Ecclesiasticarum* (1551) says that each bishop is required to have around him a body of men who would teach Holy Scripture and instruct others from his household to do the same, plus schools under control of deans and chapters of the cathedral churches 'in order that knowledge of the word of God may be kept in the Church, which can scarcely happen without experience in languages and in order that ignorance may not hold sway amongst our men, and especially amongst ministers of the Church'.[4] Cranmer, according to Bishop Gilbert Burnet (1643–1715):

> had projected that in every cathedral there should be provision made for Readers of Divinity, and of Greek and Hebrew; and a great number of students, to be both exercised in the daily worship of God, and trained up in study and devotion, whom the bishop might transplant out of his nursery into all parts of his diocese. And thus every bishop should have had a college of clergymen under his eye.[5]

But the reality might be less impressive. Questions were asked of the clergy of Gloucester in 1551 by Bishop John Hooper (1550–3) (in Latin):

> How many commandments are there? Where are they written? Recite them. What are the articles of Christian belief? Say them. Give scriptural authority for them. Recite the Lord's Prayer. How is it known to be his prayer? Where can it be found? Of 311 examined in this way 168 could not repeat the ten commandments, and 31 of those could not say where they were in the Bible. 40 could not tell where the Lord's Prayer came from and 31 of

those did not know who was its author. Only 3 or 4 of all of them had ever preached or could do so.

In 1560–1 in the Diocese of Ely, of 68 candidates for ordination, seven were rejected and two respited by the bishop. Several others were respited but admitted afterwards. The 'interrogatories ministered to all such as mindeth to receive Holy Orders' are:

1. What is his name. 2. What age is he of. 3. Where his abiding is. 4. Whether his conversation be good and honest. 5. Whether he can read well or no. 6. Whether he can write. 7. Whether he mindeth to receive Holy Orders of a good zeal that he beareth towards God's word. 8. Whether he mindeth to proceed in the said vocation and holy order of ministry. 9. Whether he be legitimate or no. 10. Whether he understandeth the Latin tongue and can speak the same. 11. Whether he hath studied any thing in the scriptures and what he hath learned therein.[6]

Attempts were made to do something about this limited and sometimes lamentable standard of achievement. The stress on the 'ministry of the Word' in reforming circles from the sixteenth century meant a great deal of emphasis on the principle that the central task is preaching the gospel. The minister therefore needs a level of education sufficient to prepare him for that. The Puritan manifesto of 1572, *An Admonition to Parliament*, seeks the removal of 'ignorant and unable ministers' in favour of bringing 'to every congregation a learned and diligent preacher'. This aim was supported by Thomas Cartwright, who had just been deprived of the Lady Margaret chair of Divinity at Cambridge because of his presbyterian views; it was opposed by John Whitgift, Master of Trinity College, Regius Professor of Divinity and Vice-Chancellor of Cambridge. Whitgift argued strongly that cathedrals were already furnished with 'godly, zealous and learned men' and also 'that they be the chief and principal ornaments of this realm, and, next to the universities, chiefest maintainers of godliness, religion and learning'.[7] By 1573 the regulations for ordination were strengthened. The bishops now required 'competent learning and study at one of the universities, in those that hereafter were to be admitted into the ministry; as well as for their morals'.[8]

A set of Articles or Canons of 1575–6 for the Convocation of the Province of Canterbury endorsed the provisions of the Act of 1571 and allowed that 'where the stipends or livings be very small', it might be necessary to settle for the best-qualified clergy who could be afforded ('there to choose and admit of the best that can be found in such cases of necessity'). Less academically qualified clergy were to be examined in the New Testament by archdeacons and others.[9] Richard Barnes, Bishop of Durham (1577–87) held a visitation of the diocese in October 1577, requiring his chancellor or vicar-general to hold two general chapters each year in every 'warde and deanery', at which he should be assisted by the archdeacon and other officials, when 'examination shall be had of the progress in learning and studying of the scriptures of the parsons, vicars, and curates, ministers and deacons, and exercises and taxes shall be enjoined to them and required of them'. They were to give an account of Matthew's Gospel in Latin or English.[10] The Puritan Sir Walter Mildmay, founder of Emmanuel College, Cambridge, observed that:

> the one object which I set before me in erecting this college was to render as many as possible fit for the administration of the divine Word and sacraments: and that from this seed-ground the English Church might have those that she can summon to instruct the people and undertake the office of pastors, which is a thing necessary above all others.[11]

But there was a real dilemma, There was a shortage of the adequately learned, and pastoral needs had to be met. Robert Sanderson wrote in 1620:

> The severest censurers of non-preaching ministers, if they had lived in the beginning of the Reformation, must have been content, as the times then stood, to have admitted of some thousands of non-preaching ministers, or else have denied any parishes and congregations in England the benefit of so much as bare reading.[12]

One way of filling the gap was for the cathedrals to take responsibility for an educational role which had, after all, traditionally been theirs because of the bishop's duty to teach his flock from the bishop's chair there. Most English cathedrals in Elizabeth's reign ran 'divinity lectures' for the people. Royal Injunctions for Salisbury Cathedral in 1559 require that the chancellor shall appoint a learned man to read a lecture in divinity at 9.00 a.m. at least three times a week.[13] There were also regular sermons and expositions of Scripture. In the

> cathedral churches, upon Sundays and festival days, the canons make ordinarily special sermons, wherunto duly resort the head officers of the cities and the citizens; and upon the workendays

thrice in the week one of the canons doth read and expound some piece of holy scripture.[14]

The ancient concern that ministers should be equipped by goodness of life as well as intellectually, persists. Bacon's *Apologia pro Ecclesia Anglicana* (1562) was translated into English by Lady Anne Bacon in 1564 with an appendix on the Church and the universities. In it it is hoped:

> that the goods of the Church may not be launched out amongst worldlings and idle persons, but may be bestowed upon the godly ministers and pastors which take pain both in preaching and teaching; that there may . . . rise up out of the universities learned and good ministers, and others meet to serve the commonwealth.[15]

But against this traditional patterning have to be set new developments bred by polemic. Matthew Sutcliffe (c. 1550–1629) had a project to train young clergy in polemics so that they could argue against 'papists and pelagianizing Arminians and others that draw towards popery and Babylonian slavery'. Here the aim was not really to train ordinary clergy, but to equip a few prime fighters.

If we look onwards from the sixteenth century we find continuing evidences of care for education for ministry. Thomas Morton, Bishop of Durham (1632–46) examined candidates for holy orders strictly.

> He never ordained any . . . but such as were graduates in the university (or otherwise well qualified in good learning). And for a trial of their parts, he always appointed a set time to examine them in university learning, but chiefly in points of divinity; and in this he was very exact, by making them answer syllogistically, according to their abilities. And he trusted not his own chaplains in this sacred business, though otherwise very able and learned divines.[16]

Much depends on individual bishops' vision and provision. The bishop is again visibly 'maintainer' of the faith here. His own educational level was another matter. There were no schools for bishops. From 1695 Archbishop Thomas Tenison was pressing for care in the examination of ordinands.[17] Gilbert Burnet (1643–1715), Bishop of Salisbury (1689–1715), thought 'the beginning of all the reformations was to be laid down in the education of those who were to serve in the church'. So he decided to choose and train ten, to whom he himself gave an hour's instruction a day on 'matters of learning and piety, and particularly of such things as related to the pastoral care'. He thought universities were doing a very inadequate job. So his plan was to have a nursery at Salisbury of students in divinity who should follow their studies and devotions till he could provide for them. But he found that 'the strictness of my examinations frightens the clergy, so that few come to me'.[18]

That raises the question of how high to aim. William Fleetwood, Bishop of St Asaph (1706–14) and of Ely (1714–23) said that

> the wisdom, prudence, and moderation of the Church of England ... appears conspicuous ... she does not prescribe such qualifications as she can only wish and pray might be the portion of all her priests and ministers, but such as she may reasonably hope they may, and expect they should, bring along with them.... An honest and upright heart, above all things, full of sincere and serious resolutions of serving God.... This, with a competency of learning at the first, hope of proficiency, and promise of endeavouring to increase in all the parts of useful knowledge, as we have opportunity, the Church accounts sufficient, and accepts upon these terms her candidates for holy orders.[19]

The dangers of having not very well-educated clergy are obvious. But there are complications less immediately apparent. It is instructive to take an example which might be expected to test this rule. In dissenting circles in the England of the late eighteenth and early nineteenth centuries, itinerant preachers were important in spreading opinions alternative to those of the Church of England.[20] (These were, indeed, frequently surprisingly ecumenical in the limited sense of including most of the denominations then to be found in England other than the Roman Catholic and Anglican. Interdenominational itinerancies were apparently established in the period after the formation of the London Missionary Society in 1795, but in practice co-operation appears to have been limited.)[21] It became a problem that itinerant preachers, usually of humble origin, had little education, because that meant that they might mislead the faithful. Meeting-houses might send out numerous members on Sunday afternoons to go into several villages and there was recognition that they had to be supervised.[22] It is striking that the ministerial candidates undergoing these courses of study had already served some apprenticeship in practical preaching, as a result of which they had been deemed fit for training, but in the course of which they had inevitably exposed the people to whom they preached to the thoughts of largely untrained minds.

The crucial practical question proved to be not whether these preachers were lay or ordained – it is often hard to say – but whether they had adequate training. Local comment on a member of the Congregational church at Andover in 1817 is illustrative:

> Mr. Canon . . . deliver'd an exhortation with which the members in general appear'd highly satisfied, and were led to hope that by his submitting himself to the advice of the Church and pastor in the exercise of his talent, his services would be render'd useful in the villages.[23]

The question at issue here was put squarely by the *Account of the Constitution of the Bristol Education Society* in 1770:

> Are we to expect miracles, as in the Apostolic age, to qualify us for the work of the ministry; or, are we to use ordinary means? That we are not to expect miracles all will allow, and, if not, then surely we are to use ordinary means. And so far is this from interfering with the work of the Spirit, that it appears to be the only way in which we may reasonably expect His continued influences; and it seems rather to be tempting the Spirit of God to expect that in an extraordinary, which we are authorized to expect only in an ordinary way.[24]

So even for these dissenting communities, the 'ordinary way' came to involve education. That varied a good deal in these experimental ecclesial communities. Tiny and sometimes short-lived institutions were set up, such as one in Manchester, in the vestry of the chapel at Mosley Street, which ran from 1803 to 1808. This produced in its six years seventeen trained individuals. But it lasted only as long as its patron, a local businessman, could sustain it financially.[25] An Independent 'seminary' at Gosport, founded by David Bogue, the local Independent minister, did not survive him long.[26] Others were more durable because they got continuing local support for many years. A few could look to national support and some degree of permanence.

Nowhere was there total agreement on what the courses for these 'dissenting' preachers should contain, what degree of theoretical and what proportion of practical training. In the nature of things, much must have depended on the availability and educational attainments of the instructors themselves. But there was a general acceptance of the need to teach the basics of English grammar and some knowledge of Latin and Greek, to acquaint the students with the heritage of Puritan writing in English since the Reformation and to train them in the preparation of sermons.[27] The thrust here, interestingly, is to maintain tradition, just as we have seen in the case of the Russian Orthodox. Here Scripture is to be studied in the ancient languages and the students are to acquaint themselves thoroughly with the 'Fathers' of the dissenting communities.

The ideals of Vatican II

We must turn to Vatican II again for a late twentieth-century benchmark, for this council's effects have been felt far beyond the Roman Catholic Church. We find, as might be expected, much more orderly provisions within an ecclesiastical organization in which training for the ministry can be highly centralized and closely overseen. The council stresses that 'the study of Scripture . . . ought to be the soul of all theology'.[28] That is taken as fundamental. In building on that foundation the first theme is that of 'formation'. The conception is still the medieval one that the making of a mind and soul go together, the creation of a trained, disciplined Christian, alive in faith, whole, integrated, in whom moral and intellectual being are educated together. This association of the intellectual and rational with the spiritual is also a continuance of medieval priorities.

> Theological disciplines should be taught in the light of faith under the guidance of the church's *Magisterium*. This should be done in such a way that students may accurately receive, making it the food of their own spiritual life, so that they will be able to proclaim, explain and defend it in their own priestly ministry.

Then we move to the systematic character of the teaching of the faith in future pastors.

> Dogmatic theology should be so arranged that the biblical themes are first propounded; then what the Fathers of the Church (East and West) have contributed to the faithful tradition and understanding of the truths of revelation; also the later history of dogma, including its relation to the general history of the church. . . . let the students learn, with the aid of speculative reasons under the guidance of St. Thomas, to penetrate more deeply and to see their mutual connection.[29]

Aquinas himself saw the need to be orderly as a high priority,[30] and again the medieval model remains strong.

I have tried to do no more here than illustrate by these examples the main lines of ministerial training as they appear consistent in all types of ecclesial community. It is supervised, guided. It is linked with an insistence on holiness of life. It seeks to give professional ministers more than the laity normally need by way of formal grounding, knowledge and skills, so that the ministerial office can be a teaching office and the minister answer the questions of those he teaches. This grounding is scriptural, but it also calls on tradition. There is a conscious element of maintaining as well as passing on the faith. So there is preparation for a life spent at the guiding end of the reception process.

At the same time, the 'beginner' in ministry has himself (or recently sometimes 'herself') to receive the faith so as to communicate it to others. 'External' evidences of policy and practice of the sort we have just been looking at will not tell us a great deal about that. But there are clues especially in discussions of the continuing processes of learning by ministers and clergy.

CHAPTER FIVE

CONTINUING EDUCATION

For both ministers and the mass of the faithful, there is a lifelong task of continuing in the faith, through events which will test it and throw up questions which have not occurred before. In eras when preaching has not been widely available, and among the ordinary clergy with modest careers in most centuries, there has been a real gap in provision at the level of what might be called 'continuing education'. Even for those with particularly persistent intelligences, there has not always been any ready means of getting answers to the kinds of detailed, vexing questions which begin to arise as the believer encounters both practical and more speculative theological problems and to progress in the spiritual life. The English Elizabethan clergy were encouraged to go on developing their understanding of the faith. But it was assumed that they would be educating themselves. Robert Sanderson (1587–1663):

> I would not have a clergyman content himself with every mediocrity of gifts; but by his prayers, care and industry improve those he hath, so as he may be able . . . to speak . . . in some good measure of proportion to the quickness and ripeness of these present ties.[1]

The case of Peter of Blois and his clerical correspondents

Needs arising at this relatively advanced stage in the personal reception process could be partly met by such texts as the compilation made from Gregory the Great's sixth-century and still highly popular commentary on the book of Job by the twelfth-century Peter of Waltham (who was Archdeacon of London between about 1190 and 1196). Peter wanted a convenient summary so that he 'might always have at hand a reserve whence my spirit could allay its pangs of hunger'. He had it in mind that those who were not capable of swimming in midstream could at least paddle in the shallows with him.[2]

In the high Middle Ages, monastic communities contained individuals of greatly varying intellectual aspirations and attainments. Much depended on the quality of the available teachers in a monastic school, on exchanges of books for copying, on the rare presence of a quite exceptional thinker such as Anselm at Bec in the late eleventh century. But this was not the norm, and clergy working in pastoral offices often lacked the support of a religious community.

Peter of Waltham's contemporary Peter of Blois[3] was a great letter-writer. He had been a student in the high days of the mid-twelfth-century schools of northern France and seems to have maintained in later years a reputation among the English clergy for knowing about theology. Many of Peter of Blois' correspondents are identifiable persons in the middle rank of the secular and monastic English clergy between 1200 and 1210, and they asked him questions which were troubling them theologically. The collection is thus an important witness to the educational needs of such clergy at this period.

Peter himself was drawing on a theological education gained in the schools of the 1160s. This was a time when a syllabus of theological education was forming which was to shape things for four centuries to come; Peter Lombard composed the *Sentences* which (after a period of condemnation), was to become the staple theological textbook in the West until the end of the Middle Ages. All sorts of tricky little questions with large entailments were beginning to arise out of lectures on the text of Scripture. Peter of Blois draws upon the common pool for support for his answers; there is shared thinking with Peter Lombard and the now increasingly standard gloss on the Bible, the *Glossa Ordinaria*,[4] and with a number of predecessors and contemporaries.

Peter appears to have been acting informally as a place of resort for expert guidance for those not working in the world of professional academic theology. The level of familiarity with current debates in this widespread clerical community which these letters reveal is therefore of great importance in rounding out our picture of the intellectual life of the age of the nascent universities in the West.

Peter's clientele of worried middle-rank clergy with theological questions raise questions about the availability of practical provision for answering them. Only a private scholar such as Peter of Blois seems to have been capable of meeting this need at this date. The anxiety of Peter's correspondents, their hunger for help, is striking.[5]

We may ask how they got to know that he was the person to ask.

Others were evidently turning to him as a person who could bring them up to date with scholarly opinion, with no means of checking whether he was really in a position to do so. He claimed to give a summary of what was said in the schools, but in fact it was some time since he had worked there, and he was certainly out of date. Not all Peter's correspondents by any means can have been so well educated theologically even as he. Indeed, their writing to him for advice would strongly suggest that they were not, or did not consider themselves to be. It is possible to get no more than a hint of the level of their theological sophistication. Peter's forays into theology in the letters are in response to requests from abbots (Coggeshall, letter 29) or bishops (N. in letter 28 may be either) or priors (the Prior of Southwick had asked for an exposition of the antiphons of Advent, letter 16) or archdeacons. (He was not abashed to offer a new bishop advice on his spiritual life.)[6]

It seems that sometimes informal discussion groups were held. These might be said to have met some of the needs addressed by today's 'in-service training'. They were not new. Gilbert Crispin, Abbot of Westminster, describes such a group meeting in London at the turn of the previous century.[7] Peter writes after 1200 to Master Columbus, papal subdeacon. Columbus had been present at a recent discussion which Peter had held with his circle. Columbus remembers that some of what was said pleased him but he cannot now remember the *sententia et ordo*. 'If you remember,' says Peter, 'we asked each other whether it was meritorious to turn from evil, and whether turning from evil was not really the same thing as doing good.'[8] Peter seems to have had remarkably clear recall of the discussion; we can only speculate as to whether notes were kept, or whether he had guided it, as an experienced teacher does, according to a pattern which he had found from long use worked well.

Peter may have been active in instituting such discussions. He certainly felt strongly that ignorance should be turned into knowledge. He thought it culpable to cultivate ignorance, as he tells one of his correspondents. Letter 32, against the cultivation of ignorance, is addressed to Geoffrey, Bishop-elect of Nantes, about 1199–1200. His impending elevation has led to a review of his thinking. Geoffrey is arguing that ignorance is a great good because it makes sin less, excuses from blame and frees from penalty.[9] Ignorance is wrong and culpable when it is willing to ignore what ought to be done. Illiterate priests ought to be silent if they cannot preach. 'Ignorance is sometimes excusable and necessary.' 'When we cannot know everything we are [logically] bound not-to-know something.'[10]

We must ask, but cannot easily answer, whether any of these questions arose from the laity putting them to their priests, and whether the answers travelled back as far as interested lay people. We know that was so in the case of some notorious lay people such as Margery Kemp later in the Middle Ages. And we can certainly point to lay activity in its own right, as we shall see in the next chapter.

The problems persisted of the need for adequate and continuing education of the junior and middle-rank clergy, those in most direct pastoral contact with the faithful, but without the time (or condition perhaps) to keep up with theology at the highest level. In John Jewel's (1522–71) debate with Roman Catholic apologists, he sets side by side the claim that the Church of England's priests are ignorant ('certain of our clergy want the knowledge of rhetoric, logic, philosophy, the Hebrew, the Greek, and the Latin tongues') and the claim that that is also true of Roman Catholic priests (who 'for the most part can neither speak Latin nor read English, nor understand the articles of their faith, nor any portion of the scriptures', and who are 'lanterns without light').[11]

So the kinds of issue with which Peter of Blois sought to deal have their parallels in the questions raised by those involved professionally in theology as ordained or ordinands in other ages. It has not always been easy to get the level right. The *Heidelberg Catechism*[12] of 1562, the work of Ursinus (a student of Melanchthon who was later influenced by Peter Martyr and Bullinger) and Olevianus, was recommended for undergraduates to read by an Oxford University Statute of 1579.[13] Ursinus gave lectures on it, which sold remarkably well. In its unresolved contradictions, it exemplifies the kind of problem which arises where no solution to a theological problem is generally agreed and reception has thus not yet done its work. Ursinus could argue both that God makes a covenant with man with conditions attached to it; and that election is absolute and outright.[14] But this was a teaching text for students, and it shows how difficult it can be to prevent awkward questions arising.

The case of John Henry Newman and his circle

Let us come back to the story Newman and his friends in the first half of the nineteenth century tell of their own individual processes of learning theology. It reflects their sense that, for reasons I shall come to in a moment, they had to make a fresh start; they saw what they had to attempt with eyes better attuned to a sense of the *movement of* theological history than was possible for Peter of Blois and his friends, or even for Jewel's generation.

This circle of young men responded to the educational needs they had themselves felt. They tried to address the problems which had been created for them by the lack of systematic provision for theological study when they themselves had needed it. The training of Church of England clergy in the early nineteenth century had become a comparatively superficial business. Little was formally required for ordination. That had the result that there was a lack of syllabuses and textbooks. Hugh James Rose[15] wrote to Newman on 8 August 1835, about the problem of setting on foot the work which was needed to make good the deficit. *'Let something be done,* for the want is a crying one. What do our students, what do our clergy, read? What is there to recommend to them but Mosheim and Milner, and Milner and Mosheim?'[16]

So here, in the first half of the nineteenth century in England, were young men who felt themselves theologically uneducated and had to design methods of bringing themselves and their contemporaries into possession of an existing world of theological thought. They had a strong awareness of doing theology 'after the event', of catching up with the literature and explorations of the past in order to equip themselves. In their intellectual pilgrimage we see the coming to consciousness of a number of principles of the reception process within the teaching office of the Church.

Yet Newman and his circle were in an uncommonly advantageous position for anyone who wanted to find his way through the story of the Christian faith. They were mostly working in Oxford or Cambridge, where copies of almost everything they sought were to be had in libraries or bookshops or on the bookshelves of friends, although they lacked the materials which would have given them the Middle Ages. They had a good deal of time for study. They had Greek and Latin and the possibility of Hebrew. They had like-minded friends with whom to discuss the progress of their theological pilgrimage.

The body of young English scholars of which Newman became the central figure consciously set about two tasks. The first was a practical scheme for editing texts and writing books to fill the gaps. As early as 1830 a proposal had been made by Hugh Rose that a history of the principal councils should be written. To attempt this, Newman discovered, 'was to launch myself on an ocean with currents innumerable'.[17] It very quickly taught him the first of the lessons he was repeatedly to learn, the interconnectedness of theological topics and the complexity of the ebb and flow of theological opinion.

Newman's friend and contemporary Pusey encouraged him in this project, especially to treat the history of Christian thought with reference to its contemporary 'circumstances'.

> With regard to the Councils, though, as generally treated, they are the driest portion of Ecclesiastical History, I should think an account of them might be made both interesting and improving, by exhibiting them in reference to, and as characteristic of, the ages in which they occurred.

The work did indeed bring the faith of the past before Newman in a vivid present. In 1839 he is saying,

> I wish to make a volume or two of the mere *Acta Conciliorum* for the 'Library of the Fathers'. Those of the Council of Chalcedon are most exceedingly graphic and lively, though the exclamations of the Bishops have less dignity in them than R. H. F.[18] would have approved.[19]

It was thus demonstrably in the groups' minds early on that theology has a character and preoccupations special to each period, and that that character is an expression of the Church's distinctive and intense life at that time and in that place.

Pusey made a further point. 'You may also be of much service, I hope, in stemming heterodoxy, one of whose strongest holds is, perhaps, the so-called history of doctrines.'[20] Pusey is here underlining for Newman a principle we find him placing at the heart of his work, that a faithful history of Christian thought will cohere; it will not support unorthodox teachings because these will be shown to fall outside the *consensus fidelium*. The peculiar vitality of each age is its own; but it is part of a single great whole.

The making of books to fill the gaps became a steady course of work for Newman and others for many years, but in these ways it also formed their thinking about the nature and purpose of the theological endeavour in which they were engaged.

If we compare all this with the level of sophistication at which Augustine expected to catechize his educated adults, we can see likenesses. Above all we must recognize how modest a portion of the full needs of reception is met within the formal catechetial process when that is reduced to a fixed sequence of question and answer, and even by the education of the clergy, when that is limited and no adequate provision is made for its lifetime continuance.

The most important point I have sought to begin to make here concerns the huge range of the Church's teaching office and the participatory character it must unavoidably have as it creates partially informed and therefore questioning minds and seeks to meet ever-growing complexities of the demands for answers. This is the bedrock of the reception process.

II
OBEDIENCE

CHAPTER SIX

BEING OFFICIAL

It is possible to bring about 'reception' of a sort by requiring the faithful to believe what they are told. Belief compelled must be in important ways different from belief freely given. Yet for belief compelled, the documentation is a good deal more easily visible. 'Official' pronouncements seem on the face of it designed to require obedience. I use 'official' here to refer to decisions made and promulgated within the Church's formal structures, and carrying the sanction of the authority claimed for those structures.[1] Their authoritativeness is itself a vexed question, and what it consists in is one of the questions this book tries to answer. But let us take it for now as 'given', and as a context for the 'official'.

There have always been teachers in the Church, and their teaching has normally been associated with leadership. Gregory the Great certainly saw the two roles as profoundly interconnected in the *rectores* of the Church. There are always also the taught, and those who are sheep to these shepherds. So there has been a tradition of obedience, compliance with teaching about the faith coming from above (*ob-audire* is 'to listen to', stresses the *Catechism of the Catholic Church*.[2] Leaders of the churches, usually acting together (for example, in synods and councils), have decreed canons of discipline and frameworks of order and (less often) made credal statements. (Of these the most important example is probably the Niceno-Constantinopolitan Creed framed by two councils of the fourth century.) These formulations have frequently been laid down with the intention of guiding, even directing the faithful.[3] This 'from the top down' story of the development of life and doctrine is relatively familiar because there is no shortage of formal and official documents. I want to look here at its underlying principles, the long and relatively consistent tradition of the coupling of 'official' teaching with the requirements of obedience to it.

The good intentions of 'official' decision-making

The 'official' process has had high ideals of unanimity, consistency, continuity, faithfulness, of witness to what has been held by all Christians always and everywhere. These ideals, with their greatness of vision and intention of rigour, have been consciously striven for and sustained in the formal processes.

The conciliar decision-making of the early Church consistently tried to ensure that what was being decided was in conformity with the faith of the gospel, with the decisions of previous councils, with the teachings of those who had been leaders and authorities in the community or who were the authors of texts the Church had come to respect.

Cyril, Patriarch of Alexandria wrote to Nestorius at the Council of Ephesus of 431:

> The most effective way . . . will be zealously to occupy ourselves with the words of the holy Fathers, to esteem their words, to examine our words to see if we are holding to their faith, as it is written (II Cor. 13.5), to conform our thoughts to their correct and irreproachable teaching.[4]

He claims that

> We have driven off erroneous doctrines by our collective resolution, and we have renewed the unerring creed of the Fathers. We have proclaimed to all the creed of the 318 [Fathers of Nicaea]; and we have made our own those fathers who accepted this agreed statement of religion – the 150 who later met in great Constantinople and themselves set their seal to the same creed.[5]

There is a consistent wish to show that 'The holy Fathers, who have gathered at intervals in the four holy councils, have followed the examples of antiquity.'[6]

The Second Council of Nicaea in 787 says in the same spirit:

> So it is that the teaching of our holy fathers is strengthened, namely, the tradition of the catholic Church which has received the gospel from one end of the earth to the other. So it is that we really follow Paul, who spoke in Christ, and the entire divine apostolic group and the holiness of the fathers, clinging fast to the traditions which we have received.[7]

In the primitive councils all this carried within it a great purpose of unity. At Constantinople in 381:

> With the account of the faith agreed between us and with Christian love established among us, we shall cease to declare what was condemned by the apostles, 'I belong to Paul, I to Apollo, I to Cephas,' but we shall be seen to belong to Christ, who has not been divided up among us; and with God's good favour, we shall keep the body of the church undivided, and shall come before the judgement-seat of the Lord with confidence.[8]

Here the original thrust of 'ecumenical' is clear and vigorous.

It is important to be conscious of the scale of the shift which took place with the divisions of the Church which arose from 1054, and increasingly from the sixteenth century. These made it plain that a claim to faithfulness in continuity can also be made in separation. After the Reformation, we find claims of this sort: 'The Church of Ireland [Anglican] doth, as heretofore, accept and unfeignedly believe all the Canonical[9] Scriptures [and] doth continue to profess the faith of Christ as professed by the Primitive Church.'[10] It would be easy to multiply examples, especially of Western Churches speaking since the sixteenth century, who would deem themselves to be sustaining this faithfulness in continuity with the primitive Church but while divided from other contemporary churches to the point where they could not share the sacraments with them and perhaps even denied that they were churches at all.[11]

Yet in the early undivided Church not all councils were intended to be ecumenical in the sense of being universal. In fact, such councils were rare. Much more usual were meetings of bishops in a local region, designed to deal with a problem (often disciplinary), which had arisen locally and whose solution was of only local application. There was a well-established rule from an early date that a council had authority only over the local churches whose representatives had participated in it.[12] But it was accepted that there could be no legitimate 'local points of faith'. In matters of faith only the universal would do. Any attempt to settle a dispute about the faith must therefore involve a universal or 'ecumenical' council, and be made with the intention that the decision would apply everywhere. It was in keeping with the rule of thinking on the largest possible scale of responsibility that independent creed-making was forbidden at the Council of Ephesus:

> It is not permitted to produce or write or compose any other creed except the one which was defined by the holy fathers who were gathered together in the Holy Spirit at Nicaea. Any who dare to compose or bring forth or produce another creed for the benefit of

those who wish to turn from Hellenism or Judaism or some other heresy to the knowledge of the truth, if they are bishops or clerics they should be deprived of their respective charges and if they are laymen they are to be anathematized.[13]

But the circumstances in which a decision has been made formally and officially with the intention that it should settle a disputed point of faith once and for all have arisen relatively infrequently. Less than two dozen councils have been held which have called themselves 'ecumenical',[14] or been summoned at the instigation of the Western patriarchate as 'Lateran' or 'Vatican'[15] Councils intended to be ecumenical (as far as was possible in circumstances of schism), or else been held (as Lyons 1274 and Ferrara–Florence in the early fifteenth century), with the purpose of making it possible for the schism of 1054 between East and West to be mended. Not all these councils have dealt with disputed points of faith. For example, the first three Lateran Councils are almost entirely concerned with other matters, and the Fourth Lateran Council gives only a small (though crucially important) proportion of its texts to the subject.

By comparison, in the divided churches of the post-Reformation period we find talk of decisions made 'officially' by 'this Church'[16] or that, on points touching the faith. The Evangelical-Lutheran Church of Finland, for example, can say that it 'holds as the highest law of the confession' and mean the highest law of the faith as set out in its own Confession.[17] It is possible for another church to speak of, 'The faith, confession and doctrine of the Church of Sweden'. That is not to imply that these are thought to be matters of faith exclusive to the churches in question. It is rather that they are seen as 'the true faith' held secure in a given community. There is, then, a purpose of unanimity with the primitive faith, and of universal intention, but coupled with a mistrust of the faithfulness of some or all other communities.

When a disputed point of faith has been discussed by a conciliar body there has almost always been a foregoing debate which has made it seem necessary, or the asking of questions on a significant point of faith, often by a persistent individual who seems likely to mislead the faithful and indeed begins to form a group around himself. Arius is an obvious case in point.[18] (We shall be looking in detail at dissenters later.) Declarations made in the divided churches too, have often been prompted by an existing debate, but the perception of the nature of the prompter is different. A whole ecclesial community is deemed to have gone astray in its belief and practice in some way, or even all others but the one making the declaration; so that it becomes necessary for a remnant to preserve the integrity of the faith. That can seem to require that something 'official' be said to make it firm and to compel obedience.

The intention of permanence and faithfulness in continuity goes with the intentions of universality. 'The profession of faith of the holy fathers who gathered in Nicaea in Bithynia (325) is not to be abrogated, but it is to remain in force.'[19] It is a principle to be found everywhere in 'official' decision-making on points of faith that the decision is intended to stand indefinitely; this is as true of decisions in the divided churches as of earlier 'ecumenical' decision-making. It is also intended from at least the Council of Nicaea of 325, that a credal formulation shall be complete. The Third Council of Constantinople in 680–1 reflects that the Nicene Creed ought to have 'been enough for a complete knowledge of the orthodox faith and a complete assurance therein', and so settled things, but Satan does not rest and new problems arise.[20] Completeness remained an ideal; repetition and revision the reality.[21]

It was not in question in the early Church that there should be unanimity. The Letter of the Synod of Constantinople (381) to the Emperor Theodosius describes how 'first of all', the bishops had 'renewed unity of heart each with the other'. The same council's Synodical Letter to the bishops assembled at Rome declares that its 'disposition is all for peace with unity as its sole object' and that it writes 'with common consent'. The Synodical Letter of the Council of Antioch in 431 had spoken of 'joining together in unity of mind and concord and the spirit of peace'. At Chalcedon in 451 it is intended 'that all ambiguity be taken away, by the agreement and consent of all the holy fathers, and by their united exposition and doctrine'. When he composed his letter on the paschal controversy, Cummianus, Abbot of Iona (d. ?669) was able to assemble a great many patristic authorities in support of unanimity. The episcopal role was essentially collective, though it was also true that individual bishops carried a special authority in their writings. A high proportion of the Fathers were bishops.

It was understood from an early date that this unanimity of those with responsibility for guardianship of the faith keeps the faith unblemished. It is the means of 'cutting off every heresy', as the Synodical Letter of Nicaea in 325 puts it. At Ephesus in 431 the synod received a letter from Pope Celestine stressing the bishops' duty to keep incorrupt 'in common the faith which has come down to us today, through the apostolic succession'; 'let us be unanimous, thinking the same thing, for this is expedient ... let us be in all things of one mind, or one heart, when the faith, which is one, is attacked'.[22] This twofold conception of the function of unanimity thus created a habit of thinking in terms of acceptance and rejection, and with it the fundamental adversial pattern which has been persistent and destructive in the history of reception processes. The motif becomes one of obedience or refusal of obedience to what is laid down.

Structural features of official decision-making

We must move now from the good intentions to the devising of structures. This is most markedly where elements of compulsion can enter into the process, with the accompanying sanctions. That which is formally enacted by due process in a properly constituted authoritative body with the stamp of authority is normally deemed to have lawfulness. (Though legislative force may need to be ratified by the secular government in some times and places, as with the Church of England.) This is often seen as tied both to proper constitution and procedure and to a known date and place of enactment:

> And this Church [of Ireland] will continue to use the same, subject to such alterations only as may be made therein from time to time by the lawful authority of the Church.[23]

> The Church of Norway has as its confessional basis by a law of 1687 the Apostles' Creed, the Niceno-Constantinopolitan Creed, the Athanasian Creed, the Augsburg Confession of 1530, Luther's Small Catechism is as 'explicated and elucidated in The Book of Concord and other documents approved by the Church of Sweden'.[24]

This 'lawfulness' will make the enactment binding to a degree dependent on the way it is 'set up' to be binding. Of these by far the most usual in the history of the Church has been exclusion from the community, either by excommunication, so that the breaker of the law is shut out from the sacraments, or by some other form of banning, such as refusal to speak to or eat with him or her. In the Roman Catholic *Veritatis Splendor* of 1993 we find simply but imperatively: 'The Church's *magisterium* ... teaches the faithful specific particular precepts and requires that they consider them in conscience as morally binding.'[25]

It is not, however, always clear in texts stressing authoritativeness in this way where 'lawfulness' of this sort ends and divine sanction begins:

> This synod, legitimately assembled in the Holy Spirit, constituting a general council, representing the catholic church militant, has power immediately from Christ, and that everyone of whatever state or dignity, even papal, is bound to obey it in those matters which pertain to the faith and the eradication of the said schism.[26]

The urge to claim that proper procedures and due process have been followed seems to reflect the need to be able to point incontrovertibly to 'where' and 'when'; the sanction of the Holy Spirit and the gift of Christ's authority arguably cannot, by their very nature, be used in this way because they are gifts of grace and therefore actively at God's disposal.[27]

There is a tension here between the finished, and the open-ended; the human and limited, and the divine with its infinite possibilities of surprise. This is an aspect of the paradox of 'official' decision-making, that the 'official' cannot easily be matched with the tidal ebb and flow of the wholeness of the reception process as it involves everyone.

What, then, with these provisos, have been the patterns of structures? The letter of the Synod of Nicaea 325 to the Egyptians stresses that the council has been called together from different provinces and cities to 'constitute' the great and holy synod.[28] A principle which scarcely needs to be underlined here is that decisions about the faith ought properly to be made by the whole Church ('whole' in quantity or extendedness) in the Holy Spirit (who assures its sanctity), and that means that representatives of as much of it as possible have to be brought together to form the council, so as to make the meeting as comprehensive a test-bed of the Spirit's intention as possible. (Doubts about the rightfulness of the outcome of the deliberations of the First Vatican Council increased when the number of absentee bishops became known.)[29]

So official decision-making has classically involved a conciliar process, defined as one in which the leaders of the local churches in particular[30] have met to take counsel together and agree on a decision. Their positions of local leadership, and especially their episcopal relationship to their communities as ministers of oversight, are seen as giving weightiness to their deliberations. For many centuries, throughout most of the Christian world, the persons who have a special responsibility in the Church for teaching and the maintenance of the faith were taken to be 'bishops', especially when they made a pronouncement together in this way in a synod or council. That has continued in the divided churches where an episcopal structure has been maintained. Thus, 'received and approved by the archbishops and bishops and the rest of the clergy of Ireland in the synod holden in Dublin, AD 1634'[31] is a way of giving official status to a declaration of the Church of Ireland. The principle holds strongly in modern Roman Catholic documents.

Once they had evolved, the assumptions we are exploring as to what constituted 'official' decision-making remained relatively constant for the first fifteen hundred years of the Church's life. Bishops met, representing their local churches.[32] Thus the whole Church could be held to meet in unity. If a smaller geographical area than the whole Church was represented, the decisions of the resulting council applied only to the area in question. No part of the Church could bind another without the other being present and consenting.[33]

But with the Reformation of the sixteenth century and its consequent divisions, something new began to happen. The structure of local churches with leaders who are all bishops, and bishops in the same way, with the same understanding of the nature and whole of the episcopate, broke down. New polities were set up, some led by ministers who refused to consider themselves in any sense episcopal. The old patterns of succession in the ministry were disrupted.

Leaders of local churches in the alternative polities devised from the sixteenth century did not stand in the same relationship of focus and representation as bishops to their people. Changes of structure (and, perhaps more importantly, of ideology about the structure) in many of the reforming communities, were calling into question the viability of such conciliar patterns. It became much more difficult to say what 'conciliarity' meant in the polities of the churches which did not have bishops. The conciliar pattern in which bishops act as guardians of the faith and spokesmen for their communities, depended on the continuance of the traditional episcopate. This disappeared in the Radical Reformation, in the Reformed tradition, and partly in Lutheranism and Methodism, in favour of conceptions of all-member ministry, of gathered churches appointing their own local ministers to hold an office (not an order) for a limited period. That destroyed or altered various understandings of the way in which, when bishops met in council, the whole Church could be said to be meeting in its representatives.

At first in the sixteenth-century crisis a council was called for, as a means of common and official decision-making about the need for reform. It was long and painfully delayed, and by the time the

Council of Trent met it was no longer possible for the whole community to come together, but only for the reformers and dissidents to be, as it were, summoned before the council to give account of themselves. It has never since yet been possible to hold a council which would, even in principle, be a council of the whole Church.

Within some of those churches which retained an episcopal structure and which could still hold councils in the traditional way (except that they could no longer be deemed ecumenical), a fresh series of developments has been at work, especially in the last century or so. These have, again, begun to alter the understanding on which the whole Church can be deemed to make a decision in and with its bishops, and therefore by a process within which the leadership instructs the faithful in the faith, and can require their obedience to what they are taught.

The most notable changes within the episcopal system have been in the role of the laity in the 'official process'. A House of Clergy had sat with the House of Bishops in the Church of England since the Middle Ages. It was always the junior House and dependent upon the House of Bishops to allow it to make its contribution to the decision-making process. From the nineteenth century there were calls to allow the laity to have a part in consultation. In the early nineteenth century John Henry Newman wrote to his friend Hurrell Froude, 'I want your view of the extent of power which may be given to the laity in the Church system, e.g. the maintenance of the Faith is their clear prerogative. Qu. What power may they have in synods? Judicially? In legislation? etc.'[34] There were already questions about procedure and enfranchisement here which are only gradually being resolved even in the twentieth century.

In England Henry Hoare and the Society for the Revival of Convocation did not think the laity ought to be included in the synodical process but took a lead in encouraging their participation at parish level and in rural deaneries. The result was a growing pattern of co-operation between clergy and laity in the running of the Church. In 1884 there was a proposal to set up 'Houses' of laymen (not yet of women, of course), to meet simultaneously with clerical Houses in their Convocation and to be consulted about 'the definition or interpretation of the faith and doctrine of the Church'.[35] The first session of the Canterbury House of Laymen was opened in January 1886, York's House not until 1892. There were proposals for a national Synod of Laymen, with the result that in 1898 the two provincial Houses of Laymen met together in London.

In conception these 'Houses' of laymen were advisory. They were therefore not attractive to the lay membership because they had no authority and could not participate in legislation.[36] Attendance was poor. The Report of the 1898 Joint Committee to consider the position of the laity recommended the setting up of a National Council to represent the clergy and laity. A Representative Church Council emerged from this in 1903, but it was still deliberative, and without legislative functions. A new Commission was set up in 1913, under the presidency of Lord Selborne. This proposed, when it reported in 1916, that a Church Council should be brought into being, consisting of the two Houses of the Convocations and a House of Laity.[37] This was the origin of the Church Assembly, the ancestor of the present General Synod.[38] But that involved a shift of principle. The bishops of the early local churches meeting in council are deemed to 'bring their churches with them'.[39] The new 'representatives by election' could not do so in the same way, and indeed the two modes of 'representation' must inevitably coexist somewhat uneasily. There is the further danger that the use of the same word for two different relationships of 'representation' can be confusing and 'send out the wrong signals'.

So in a House system the local churches are no longer the natural focus, as the primary ecclesial entities entering into discussion with one another, and trying to reach decisions together. The old rules of unanimity and so on can easily be lost sight of in a system of majority voting. Interest groups and 'parties' can arise which put 'universal intention' out of focus. Decisions can be made for short-term reasons or out of 'party interest', and so the intentions of permanence and completeness are weakened. The continuance of a 'conciliar' system of official decision-making, even in a church which has preserved an episcopal polity, can thus become uncertain in its continuity of purpose. And, more importantly, with lay participation in such decision-making on the basis of a different kind of representation, the boundary between 'official' decision-making by leaders in the Church and a process of reception in which all the faithful actively share, becomes blurred.

Consultation in official decision-making

The conciliar process has not always involved actual problem-solving. Nevertheless, 'official' decisions were in principle and intention arrived at by the pooling of opinions, the real forming of a common mind. At the Second Council of Constantinople (553):

They dealt with heresies and current problems by debate in common, since it was established as certain that when the disputed question is set out by each side in communal discussions, the light of truth drives out the shadows of lying. The truth cannot be made clear in any other way when there are debates about questions of faith, since everyone requires the assistance of his neighbour.[40]

At the Council of Constance, session 1, November 1414, the Pope called for the active assistance of everyone:

> Considering, moreover, that a council should specially treat of those matters which concern the catholic faith, according to the praiseworthy practices of the early councils, and aware that such things demand diligence, sufficient time and study, on account of their difficulty, we therefore exhort all those who are well versed in the sacred scriptures to ponder and to treat, both within themselves and with others, about those things which seem to them useful. . . . Let them bring such things to our notice and to that of this sacred synod, as soon as they conveniently can, so that at a suitable time there may be decided what things, it seems, should be held and what repudiated for the profit and increase of the same catholic faith. . . . We exhort, moreover, all catholics assembled here and others who will come to this sacred synod that they should seek to think on, to follow up and to bring to us, and to this same sacred synod, those matters by which the body of catholics may be led, if God is willing, to a proper reformation and to the desired peace. For it is our intention and will that all who are assembled for this purpose may say, consult about and do, with complete freedom, each and all of the things that they think pertain to the above.[41]

Consultation could be unwieldy, however. The Constitutions of the Second Council of Lyons, 1274, express gratitude that so many 'patriarchs, primates, archbishops, bishops, abbots, priors, provosts, deans, archdeacons and other prelates of churches, both personally and by suitable procurators, and the procurators of chapters, colleges and convents, have assembled at our call'. But they ask for understanding that, 'although for the happy pursuit of so great an enterprise their advice would be useful, and their presence as beloved sons is so delightful', that presence presents problems. They are a jostling crowd. 'Their absence may be harmful to themselves and their churches.' So it is decided that those who have been specifically invited shall stay on. There is a list of 'patriarchs, primates, archbishops, bishops, abbots and priors'.[42] Some of the calls for active consultation were undoubtedly window-dressing, or had political purpose. But the intention is clear, that there should be sharing of thoughts and an attempt to win one another's minds in unanimity.

Similarly, the sharing of thoughts is extended to the announcement of the council's decisions. From Nicaea 325, the letter of the synod to the Egyptians further explains that the council needs to send a letter 'so that you may know what was proposed and discussed and what was held to be true (*quae vera placita*)'. There is concern to make the local application plain. 'These are the chief and most important decrees as far as concerns Egypt. . . . Alexander will tell you more when he comes' for he was himself a leader as well as a participant in the events.[43] This rule of openness has remained important, and when there has been suspicion that it has been broken, that has sometimes been thought to invalidate the synodical process.

Frequency or regularity of meeting was not a noticeable characteristic of early councils. On the contrary, they tended to be extraordinary events. The Council of Basle (December, 1431), claims the warrant of Constance (1415) for 'the frequent holding of general councils'.[44] But that was principally because its own meeting came so soon after, and is a testimony to the unusualness rather than the customariness of the practice. It has become commonplace in the modern world as a response perhaps mainly to the call for democracy to be seen to operate. This is a kind of ecclesiastical 'no taxation without representation'.

The interplay of obedience and participation

A culture of obedience to official teaching has reached perhaps its furthest development within the Roman Catholic community.[45] At the Fourth Council of Constantinople in the ninth century we find an assertion that the Pope-in-council-with-his-bishops can make a definitive ruling, which no individual bishop or lowlier member of the clergy is authorized to challenge:

> We declare and order that everything which has been expounded and promulgated by [Popes Nicholas and Hadrian] in a synod at various times, both for the defence and well-being of the church of Constantinople and of its chief priest . . . as well as for the expulsion and condemnation of Photius the upstart and usurper,

should be maintained and observed together with the canons there set forth, unchanged and unaltered, and no bishop, priest or deacon or anyone from the ranks of the clergy should dare to overturn or reject any of these things.[46]

At the Council of Vienne (1311–12) there is an assertion that primatial[47] authority, when it is acting collegially and is in harmony with earlier authoritative teaching, is definitive.

> we, therefore, directing our apostolic attention, to which alone it belongs to define these things, to such splendid testimony and to the common opinion of the holy fathers and doctors, declare with the approval of the sacred council that the said apostle and evangelist, John, observed the right order of events in saying that when Christ was already dead one of the soldiers opened his side with a spear.[48]

The particularly Roman assertion of a personal primacy which could 'make pronouncements official' developed in the later Middle Ages and reached its apogee at the First Vatican Council.[49] It is important to what was claimed there that the special primatial responsibility of the see of Peter was not seen as anything new. Nor was it seen as a claim accepted only within the Western patriarchate. It was itself, it could be argued, collegially based:

> The apostolic primacy . . . includes the supreme power of teaching. This holy see has always maintained this, the constant custom of the church demonstrates it, and the ecumenical councils, particularly those in which East and West met in the union of faith and charity, have declared it.

In this text the whole Church is deemed to be 'in' its primate, so that he does not speak for himself but for the whole people of God. But this has been a highly controversial claim.[50] It holds precariously in tension the participatory and the obediential, and the text reflects that. The reason put forward by the First Vatican Council to explain the necessity for a model in which obedience is paramount is the argument for *safety*.

> In the apostolic see the catholic religion has always been preserved unblemished, and sacred doctrine been held in honour . . . to satisfy this pastoral office, our predecessors strove unvaryingly that the saving teaching of Christ should be spread among all the peoples of the world; and with equal care they made sure that it should be kept pure and uncontaminated wherever it was received.

> It was for this reason that the bishops of the whole world ... referred to this apostolic see those dangers especially which arose in matters concerning the faith. This was to ensure that any damage suffered by the faith should be repaired in that place above all where the faith can know no failure.[51] [Sometimes the Pope has taken an initiative in similar circumstances] by summoning ecumenical councils or consulting the opinion of the churches scattered throughout the world.

This safety, it is stressed, derives not from human effort but from divine promise.

> The Holy Spirit was promised to the successors of Peter not so that they might, by his revelation, make known some new doctrine, but that, by his assistance, they might religiously guard and faithfully expound the revelation or deposit of faith transmitted by the apostles ... this gift of truth and never-failing faith was therefore conferred on Peter and his successors ... so that the whole flock might be kept away by them from the poisonous food of error and be nourished with the sustenance of heavenly doctrine. ... Thus the tendency to schism is removed and the whole church is preserved in unity, and, resting on its foundations, can stand firm against the gates of hell ... since in this very age ... not a few are to be found who disparage its authority ... we teach and define as a divinely-revealed dogma that when as shepherd and teacher of all Christians, in virtue of his supreme apostolic authority, he defines a doctrine concerning faith or morals to be held by the whole church, he possesses, by the divine assistance promised to him in blessed Peter, that infallibility which the divine Redeemer willed his church to enjoy in defining doctrine concerning faith or morals.[52]

The key point here is the use of arguments from danger. But together with the 'warfare' motif, the 'defence' motif, the 'poisoned food' motif is to argue from emergency and from the exceptional to special needs of the moment. That is not the same thing as describing a normative pattern in which obedience is simply the proper response of the faithful to what they are taught.

The Second Vatican Council spelled out more fully the character of safeguards against these 'emergency provisions' overriding the 'whole Church' and 'participatory' character of reception.

The Pope speaks *with* the bishops and so not alone.

> The order of bishops, which succeeds the college of apostles in teaching authority and pastoral government, and indeed in which

the apostolic body continues to exist without interruption, is also the subject of supreme and full power over the universal church, provided it remains united with its head, the Roman pontiff, and never without its head, and this power can be exercised only with the consent of the Roman pontiff.[53]

The Pope speaks in accordance with revelation and so not according to his private opinion.

But when the Roman pontiff or the body of bishops together with him define a decision, they do so in accordance with revelation itself, by which all are obliged to abide and with which all must conform. This revelation, as written or as handed down in the tradition, is transmitted in its entirety through the lawful succession of the bishops and in the first place through the care of the Roman pontiff himself; and in the light of the Spirit of truth, this revelation is sacredly preserved in the church and faithfully expounded. The Roman pontiff and the bishops, in virtue of their office and the seriousness of the matter, work sedulously through the appropriate means duly to investigate this revelation and give it suitable expression. However, they do not accept any new public revelation as belonging to the divine deposit of faith.[54]

In order that the gospel should be preserved in the church for ever living and integral, the apostles left as their successors the bishops, handing on their own teaching function to them. By this link, the sacred tradition and the sacred scripture of the two testaments are like a mirror in which the church, during its pilgrimage on earth, contemplates God, the source of all it had received, until it is brought home to see him face to face.[55]

The Pope speaks under the guidance of the Holy Spirit and so not as a human authority.

The infallibility promised to the Church exists also in the body of bishops when, along with the successor of Peter, it exercises the supreme teaching office. The assent of the church, however, can never fail to be given to these definitions on account of the activity of the same Holy Spirit, by which the whole flock of Christ is preserved in the unity of faith and makes progress.[56]

So alongside the emphasis on leadership and magisterium,[57] it is understood in the Vatican II accounts that the maintenance of the faith is a task of the whole Church, in which all participate:

Tradition and Scripture together form a single sacred deposit of the Word of God, entrusted to the Church. Holding fast to this, the entire holy people, united with its pastors, perseveres always faithful to the apostles' teaching and shared life, to the breaking of bread and prayer. Thus, as they hold, practise and witness to the heritage of the faith, bishops and faithful display a unique harmony.[58]

The recent *Catechism* is a useful statement of the *status quaestionis* in the Roman Catholic community at present. The *Catechism* is officially described as 'the result of very extensive collaboration', in 'a spirit of complete openness and fervent zeal'.[59] There was a participatory character to its making. 'The observations of numerous theologians, exegetes and catechists, and, above all, of the Bishops of the whole world' were considered. 'The project was the object of extensive consultation among all Catholic Bishops, their Episcopal Conferences or Synods, and theological and catechetical institutes. ... It can be said that this *Catechism* is the result of the collaboration of the whole Episcopate of the Catholic Church.' This active sharing in the actual framing of the *Catechism* was not able to include the whole people of God directly in its structures, except insofar as they are represented by their bishops. On the other hand, it is intended that the resulting *Catechism* should be a presentation of 'living tradition in the Church', and 'suited to the present life of the Church'. It has grown out of the 'doctrinal statements and norms' of Vatican II 'which were presented to the whole Church'. And the text is intended to be an 'instrument for ecclesial communion'.[60] Moreover, it is a 'reference text' only, and thus allows scope for interpretation and application.

The *Catechism* explores its own making at some length in its opening chapter on 'The Profession of the Faith' which is itself a document about reception. At one end of the scale, it speaks in terms of the great classic issues of the human hunger for God, and of the way God meets it by revealing himself; of the problems of the limitations of human language when it seeks to speak of that which is too great for it to say. At the other, it looks at *minutiae* such as the mechanics of its own use of summaries to make the content of each section easier to grasp. The 'authorities' which support the arguments in the text quietly take their place in the footnotes.

Between the two lie the solid bodies of material in Scripture and tradition which, it says, form 'one common source' with 'two distinct modes of transmission'.[61] Here the concept of the 'heritage of faith' is central.[62] This heritage is described as something to which 'the entire holy people, united to its pastors, remains always faithful'. But only the 'living teaching office' is entrusted with 'the task of giving an authentic interpretation'.[63]

It is clear in these attempts to get the balance right that the tug or tension between the 'participatory' and the 'obedience' models is strongly felt in this community which has made a large investment in obedience.

The overall picture as it looks to the Orthodox, a community very keen on tradition and unaffected by Western divisions of the sixteenth century, can usefully be seen from a vantage-point near our own century, in Russian Orthodoxy. Here the emphasis is upon weightiness and maintenance in the truth, on compelling obedience by the sheer authoritativeness of what has always been accepted as so by the whole Church and expressed decisively in the early councils; and anathematizing the disobedient because they threaten to diverge from it. It is asked:

What is an oecumenical Council?

The answer is:

> An assembly of the Pastors and Doctors of the Catholic Church of Christ, as far as possible, from the whole world, for the confirmation of true doctrine and holy discipline among Christians.

It is asked:

Whence is the rule for assembling Councils?

The answer is:

> From the example of the Apostles, who held a Council in Jerusalem. This is grounded also upon the words of Jesus Christ himself, which give to the decisions of the Church such weight, that whosoever disobeys them is left deprived of grace as a heathen. But the mean, by which the Oecumenical Church utters her decisions, is an Oecumenical Council.[64]

Despite the apparent stress on the participation of the whole Church, the 'obedience' model is if anything stronger here, and with less evidence of a sense of the counter-tug of the demand for participation by the whole community.

It is instructive to compare recent Old Catholic–Orthodox thinking, in bilateral ecumenical conversations between the two.

Here are two communities for whom a 'conciliar' model works not really because it is participatory but because it enables the Church to speak as one body through its representatives. The resulting declaration is regarded as binding on the faithful, partly at least because the faithful are deemed always to have been bound by the same truth.

> The Church is only infallible as a whole but not its individual members themselves, be they bishops, patriarchs, or popes, or be they clergy, people, or individual local Churches themselves. Because the Church is the fellowship of believers who are all taught by God, infallibility uniquely applies to the whole Church. . . . For that reason the highest organ of the Church in declaring belief infallibly is an ecumenical council. . . . The continuity of belief maintained in the Church based on this includes the necessity to hold firm to the fullness of the witness of the Church at all times.[65]

This is an important qualification of the natural tension I have been describing between the 'obedience' and 'participatory' models.

The modern scene

A unanimous vote was achieved at the Faith and Order Conference held in Edinburgh in 1937 by 414 delegates. The largeness and geographical spread of this number was emphasized in much the way it might have been in one of the early ecumenical councils.

> The Second World Conference on Faith and Order, held at Edinburgh in August 1937, brought together four hundred and fourteen delegates from one hundred and twenty-two Christian communions in forty-three different countries. The delegates assembled to discuss together the causes that keep Christian communions apart, and the things that unite them in Christian fellowship. The Conference approved the following statement *nemine contradicente*.[66]

But the Edinburgh Conference, although it found itself of one mind on certain points, was not a council, and did not aspire to be. That is to say, it did not purport to be a meeting of all the churches in their representatives with the intention of arriving at conclusions binding on them all. It had limited if any powers and could not make decisions which it could oblige participants to obey.

A very recent Roman Catholic document is confident that such a meeting can, despite these limitations, do other things of value in advancing the reception process, such as bear 'witness' and 'give the stamp of authenticity'.

> Meetings of authorised representatives of Churches and ecclesial Communities can help greatly to promote ecumenical cooperation. As well as being an important witness to the commitment of those who participate in the promotion of Christian unity, they can give the stamp of authenticity to the cooperative efforts of members of the Churches and ecclesial Communities they represent. They may also provide the occasion for examining what specific questions and tasks of ecumenical cooperation need to be addressed and for taking necessary decisions about the setting up of working groups or programmes to deal with them.[67]

Nevertheless, there is still a substantial difference between the aspirations of an early ecumenical council to speak for the whole Church, and what such a modern meeting of the divided churches can do.

Early 'official' decisions were often made with the intention that they should be accepted as a matter of obedience by the faithful who were not present and directly involved. The Council of Ephesus of 431 in its synodical letter to the Eastern bishops says that even if any bishop was not able to be at the synod he should still know what it decided and obey.[68]

There is, therefore, a difficulty. If the intention of official declarations is that they should at a given point determine on behalf of the community what the community must then accept, that would appear to be incompatible with a participatory and gradual process. Now these are not incompatible processes if the 'official' decision always gets it right. It can then be argued that the free process of arriving at consensus will, under the guidance of the Holy Spirit, in the end come up with the same view of the one faith as the official machinery, if that is also under the guidance of the Holy Spirit.

But if there is any possibility of even short-term error, or incompleteness in the working of the 'official' system, we must postulate that the forming of a participatory consensus is not merely a correlative to the framing of official decisions, but sometimes a shaper of it, sometimes a corrective to it, sometimes a completion of it:

> Revelation is already complete [yet] it has not been made completely explicit; it remains for Christian faith gradually to grasp its full significance over the course of the centuries.[69]

CHAPTER SEVEN

DEFENDING THE FAITH

No one sets out to be a heretic. An individual (usually it is an individual)[1] expresses a view which strikes a chord with others. This is not something Christians have said before, or it is at odds with the usual position. (The accusation of 'novelty' – *nova dogmata* – is common in connection with heresy.)

Others begin to say the same thing. If the idea did not prove attractive in this way there would be no problem because the individual would merely appear idiosyncratic, or misguided, and his opinion would not put orthodoxy in question. It is when a group forms and begins to grow and to teach the new view that the crucial problem arises, not least because this makes for schism. Augustine, in his battles against the Donatists, came to the conclusion that schism is the worst heresy. We find the Third Lateral Council (1179) stressing the danger of the forming of bodies of opinion, and especially a 'going public' which will attract still more people to error:

> In Gascony and the regions of Albi and Toulouse and in other places, the loathsome heresy of those whom some call the Cathars, others the Patarenes, others the Publicani, and others by different names, has grown so strong that they no longer practise their wickedness in secret as others do, but proclaim their error publicly and draw the simple and weak to join them. We declare that they and their defenders and those who receive them are under anathema, and we forbid under pain of anathema that anyone should keep or support them in their houses or lands or should trade with them.[2]

The contagiousness of heresy and schism was a frightening idea.[3] Moreover, heresy was thought to be at root a single offence, so that it gained forcefulness from its common ground and common cause with other heresies. Gilbert of Poitiers in the mid-twelfth century links

Arians and Sabellians in this way, and stresses the hiddenness and deceitfulness they have in common.[4] At the Fourth Lateran Council of 1215 we have:

> We excommunicate and anathematize every heresy raising itself up against this holy, orthodox and catholic faith which we have expounded above. We condemn all heretics, whatever names they may go under. They have different faces indeed but their tails[5] are tied together inasmuch as they are alike in their pride.[6]

So it was necessary to be extremely vigorous in attacking it. The Council of Trent speaks of the 'uprooting of heresies'.[7]

Thus we see the Church's authorities taking a position on the new teaching to welcome it or condemn it, or to find a way to make a statement about it officially. Heresy must be recognizable, and so it needs to be identified officially: 'We define "heretics" as those who have previously been banned from the Church and also those later anathematised by ourselves.'[8]

The sanction which it is natural to impose against heretics is exclusion:

> Those who are only found suspect of heresy are to be struck with the sword of anathema, unless they prove their innocence by an appropriate purgation, having regard to the reasons for suspicion and the character of the person. Let such persons be avoided by all until they have made adequate satisfaction.[9]

In the Middle Ages a lord who 'required and instructed by the Church, neglects to cleanse his territory of this heretical filth . . . shall be bound with the bond of excommunication by the metropolitan and other bishops of the province'.[10] 'We render void the ordinances enacted by Peter Leoni and other schismatics and heretics, and deem them null.'[11]

The aim of the Church's condemnations is to get the defectors back, and especially those who have been led astray by the heresiarchs. The following rules are laid down by the First Council of Constantinople (381): 'Those who embrace orthodoxy and join the number of those who are being saved from the heretics, we receive in the following regular and customary manner . . .' There is a distinction between classes of heretics, depending on the degree and basis of their separation from the Church and failure to receive the Church's faith:

> Arians, Macedonians, Sabbatians, Novatians, those who call themselves Cathars and Aristeri, Quartodecimans or Tetradites,

Apollinarians – these we receive when they hand in statements and anathematise every heresy which is not of the same mind as the holy, catholic and apostolic Church of God. They are first sealed or anointed with holy chrism on the forehead, eyes, nostrils, mouth and ears. As we seal them we say, 'Seal the gift of the Holy Spirit'. But Eunomians, who are baptised in a single immersion, Montanists (called Phrygians here), Sabellians, who teach the identity of Father and Son and make certain other difficulties, and all other sects . . . we receive all who wish to leave them and embrace orthodoxy as we do Greeks. On the first day we make Christians of them; on the second catechumens; on the third we exorcise them by breathing three times into their faces and their ears; and then we catechise them and make them spend time in the church and listen to the scriptures; and then we baptise them.[12]

It goes without saying that official pronouncements seek to defend the integrity of the faith.[13] This will allow the light of the truth to shine: 'With the banishment of the darkness of all heresies from the bounds of the Christian people, the light of catholic truth . . . may be resplendent.'[14] But they are also actively concerned with the defence of those who hold the faith from being misled to the peril of their souls:

> Always . . . be very careful about what you say to the people in matters of teaching and of your thought on the faith. You should bear in mind that to scandalise even one of these little ones that believe in Christ (Matt. 18.6) lays you open to unendurable wrath. If the number of those who are distressed is very large, then surely we should use every skill and care to remove scandals and to expound the healthy word of faith to those who seek the truth. The most effective way to achieve this end will be zealously to occupy ourselves with the words of the holy fathers, to esteem their words, to examine our words to see if we are holding to their faith, as it is written (II Cor. 13.5), to conform our thoughts to their correct and irreproachable teaching.[15]

So writes Cyril to Nestorius, in connection with the Council of Ephesus of 431. He got a reply from Nestorius arguing various points, but recognizing that the thrust about the stumbling-block or 'scandal' has gone home:

> The care you take in labouring for those who have been scandalized is well taken and we are grateful to you both for the thought you devote to things divine and for the concern you have

even for those who live here. But you should realise that you have been misled.... This is our advice from a brother to a brother. 'If anyone is disposed to be contentious' Paul will cry out through us to such a one.[16]

The theme of the importance of protecting the faithful from damage to the faith is thus a widespread concern in giving reasons why 'official' and 'binding' rulings have been necessary. The same council orders that 'those who have been condemned [Messalians] are not to be permitted to govern monasteries, lest tares be sown and increase'.[17]

Such personal mis-leading is one aspect of the problem, misreporting another:

> We have learned that even the letter of our glorious father Athanasius to the blessed Epictetus, which is completely orthodox, has been corrupted and circulated by some, with the result that many have been injured, therefore ... we have despatched to your holiness accurate copies of the original unadulterated writings which we have.[18]

Orthodoxy is unitary, misrepresentation manifold, the tendencies of heresies infinitely multiplicatory:

> Every heresy is to be anathematised, and especially that of the Eunomians or Anomoeans, that of the Arians or Eudoxians, that of the semi-Arians or Pneumatomachi, that of the Sabellians, that of the Marcellians, that of the Photinans and that of the Apollinarians.[19]

Defending the true faith in 'regulatory' and 'official' ways requires that the official bodies get it right. A danger of the official process against heretics is the room it gives to those entrusted with the extirpation of heresy to become oppressive:

> The apostolic see has received many complaints that some inquisitors, appointed by it to suppress heresy, have overstepped the limits of the power given to them. They occasionally so enlarge their authority that what has been wisely provided by the apostolic see for the growth of the faith, oppresses the innocent ... and results in harm to the faithful.[20] While it is a grave offence not to work for the extermination of heresy when this monstrous infection requires action, it is also a grave offence and deserving of severe punishment to impute maliciously such wickedness to the innocent.[21]

> No prelate should excommunicate anyone unless he first knows that the person has been excommunicated by God; he who does so thereby becomes a heretic and an excommunicated person.[22]

So the most straightforward way to defend both the faith and those who hold it from attack, it seemed to the early councils, was to determine what was orthodox and then condemn what did not conform to it and try to prevent anything further being heard of that false view. On the matter of Arius, 'it was unanimously agreed that anathemas should be pronounced against his impious opinion and his blasphemous terms and expressions'. The expressed aim was to silence him, so that these opinions and words will not 'even be heard'.[23]

The point about silence is important, because not only the ideas but the personalities of heretics were disruptive, and they tended not merely to upset the faithful, but to draw them away from the Church:

> We define 'heretics' as those who have been previously banned from the church and also those later anathematised by ourselves: and also those who claim to confess a faith that is sound, but who have seceded and hold assemblies in rivalry with the bishops who are in communion with us.[24]

(The context here is the problem of those who accuse orthodox bishops falsely, of for example injustice, so as to destroy their reputations.)

In the early centuries the maintenance of the faith against what could thus be seen as its enemies clearly went with the maintenance of unity. That changed with the later division of the Church. And the theology outlined in the history of Roman Catholic and Orthodox practice takes it that mistakes cannot happen, when the conditions are fulfilled for proper official decision-making. That was not a view to which all could subscribe at the Reformation.[25] It has demonstrably been the case that the Roman Catholic Church itself has altered its position on some matters where it once asserted that it could not – the use of the vernacular in the liturgy and for rendering Scripture, for example, and the giving of communion in both kinds to the laity.

Once separated communities began to question whether others were any longer the true Church, the condemnation has a different thrust:

> The Church of Ireland, as a Reformed and Protestant Church, doth hereby reaffirm its constant witness against all those innovations in doctrine and worship, whereby the Primitive Faith hath been from time to time defaced or overlaid, and which at the Reformation this Church did disown and reject.[26]

There are other options than seeking to compel obedience. Instead of condemning the Church can tolerate dissident opinions. Or it can refuse to tolerate, but refrain from condemnation, seeking to win back the dissenter to the orthodox view. It was certainly possible even in the early centuries to glimpse reconciliation as the desired end in view, and to exercise some degree of toleration. In the case of Meletius (where the problem was to deal with the people ordained by him in schism), the principle adopted was to let the individuals he had ordained work their way naturally out of the system. They were to be allowed to exercise their ministry in a way not challenging to other ministries, but not to ordain anyone themselves.[27] But we have to wait many centuries before toleration is discussed as a good in itself.

The issue arose in England in the seventeenth century in the context of the need to ensure loyalty of ministers to the Established Church. From the Reformation this had involved the requirement that they should make a public profession or declaration beyond the baptismal one, identifying their ecclesial position by showing that they accepted the provisions of the Thirty-Nine Articles.[28] On the Restoration of Charles II in 1660 the situation was complicated by conscientious objection and the presence of many who had adhered wholly or partly to the Puritan cause in the years of Cromwell's rule and the exile of Charles. Some felt unable to take the oath of canonical obedience, some unable to subscribe to the Articles.[29] A concession was devised:

> And because some men, otherwise pious and learned, say they cannot conform unto the subscription required by the canon, nor take the oath of canonical obedience; we are content . . . (so they take the oaths of allegiance and supremacy) that they shall receive ordination, institution, and induction, and shall be permitted to exercise their function, and to enjoy the profits of their livings, without the said subscription or oath of canonical obedience. . . . In a word, we do again renew what we have formerly said in our declaration from Breda, for the liberty of tender consciences, that no man shall be disquieted or called in question for differences of opinion in matters of religion, which do not disturb the peace of the kingdom.[30]

The governing consideration here was political. Peace must be achieved and held, even at the cost of allowing internal dissent. So the internal dissent was contained.

But the problem recurred. In the nineteenth century the Revd W. Sewell of Exeter College writing to Newman referred to 'profess' as a word useful for getting round difficulties on the Thirty-Nine Articles: 'I think the word "profess" very happy, and if the practice of subscription is retained, might not such a form obviate all objection?'[31] Other terms have been found helpful as a means of avoiding a direct confrontation with 'tender consciences': 'Will you affirm your loyalty to this inheritance of faith as your inspiration and guidance under God in bringing the grace and truth of Christ to this generation and making him known to those in your care?'

The Declaration of Assent says:

> I do so affirm, and accordingly declare my belief in the faith which is revealed in the Holy Scriptures and set forth in the catholic creeds and to which the historic formularies of the Church of England bear witness; and in public prayer and the administration of the sacraments I will use only the forms of service which are authorised or allowed by Canon.

Less quarter might be allowed to the laity, although it was never the practice to require a formal declaration of assent from lay people in the Church of England:

> That none may be admitted to the Lord's Supper, till they competently understand the principles of Christian religion, and do personally and publicly own their baptismal covenant, by a credible profession of faith and obedience, not contradicting the same by a contrary profession, or by a scandalous life: and that unto such only confirmation (if continued in the church) may be administered: and that the approbation of the pastors to whom the catechising and instructing of those under their charge do appertain, may be produced before any person receive confirmation; which course we humbly conceive, will much conduce to the quieting of those sad disputes and divisions which have greatly troubled the church of God among us, touching church-members and communicants.[32]

This exemplifies very well the complexity of the relationship between toleration and reconciliation, in which the 'official' policy is designed to hold within the Church as many as possible while not conceding to dissident opinion its claim to be right where the orthodox position is wrong:

> We are asked to affirm today, not that the Articles are all agreeable to the Word of God, but that the doctrine of the Church of England as set forth in the Articles is agreeable to the Word of

God. That is, we are not called to assent to every phrase or detail of the Articles but only to their general sense.³³

So to move away from the 'obedience' model within official structures is not easy when dealing with the threat of heresy or schism. Nor is it easy in such contexts to think naturally in terms of a 'participation' of 'heretics' and 'orthodox' alike in the process of reception, though that may very well in the long term prove to have been what was happening.

We ought not to leave this area without saying something about the problem of those who become structurally anomalous.

CHAPTER EIGHT

THE ANOMALOUS

> I am a sort of modern chimaera, neither clerk nor lay-man. I have kept the habit of a monk, but I have long ago abandoned the life, I do not wish to tell you what I dare say you have heard from others: what I am doing, what are my purposes, through what dangers I pass in the world, or rather down what precipices I am hurled.[1]

Bernard of Clairvaux means by this heartfelt cry only that he feels himself torn in two by incompatible tasks, dragged from the monastic life to public duties which distract him from God. He was in fact still Abbot of Clairvaux, with a clearly-defined place in the system. But at the same time he could be drawn into tasks which took him outside the round of tasks usual to his position. He was quite respectable in doing this, and consequently respected. The ecclesiastical authority called upon him in the 1140s, when there were 'trials' of individuals whose teaching was found to be dangerously misleading, Peter Abelard and Gilbert of Poitiers. He was asked to confront their teaching and test its orthodoxy in public debate.

From time to time certain individuals and communities have moved out of the structures within which official decision-making has gone on or, for various reasons, have not fitted into them. Not all of them, by any means, were heretics or schismatics or created pools of dissent, but they were always liable to be a source of anxiety to the ecclesiastical authorities. Or even where, as in Bernard's case, those authorities used the individual concerned, there was a consciousness of anomaly.

The problem lay with the underlying assumptions of the 'official' decision-making process. The most common pattern throughout the history of the Church until the sixteenth century was to see guardianship of the faith as entrusted to bishops, working together in council to make a pronouncement 'official'. Even after the sixteenth century that continued, broadly speaking, in Orthodox, Roman Catholic, Anglican and Old Catholic communities. In non-episcopal churches some form of appointing or 'making official' is usual. It is not usual, nor considered proper, for individuals to take it upon themselves to speak. That is what the 'anomalous' have been feared and resented for doing.

One category of those we are loosely calling 'the anomalous', containing theologians who were not clerics, produced from time to time some first-rate work as well as material of dubious acceptability. Justin Martyr, Lactantius, Didymus the Blind, Aristides of Athens are examples of such lay theologians in the very early Church, whose work was in due course accepted as a valuable contribution to the formulation of the faith. One might point to others much later. The layman poet John Milton, for example, arrived in *Paradise Lost* at fresh insights into the character of a hell of the mind's own making; but he also agitated politically in directions which in many quarters had him classified as dissident. Now of course this later example is different in that when Milton wrote politics or theology, he knew that he was acting as an anomalous agent in the system. It was part of his purpose to question that existing system. So the first need is to distinguish between those who are anomalous by chance, and those who consciously make themselves misfits in the system, in order to speak to more startling effect.

From the twelfth century there came into being within the evolving universities in the West a third, and new class, the cleric who was a theologically relatively highly educated individual who taught the next generation and published theological opinions partly within the protection of an institutional framework, while not himself holding episcopal office (though he might do so later).[2] With the rise of this 'professional academic theologian',[3] there came into being increasing dispute over what was authoritative. The figures of Peter Abelard and Gilbert of Poitiers among these early academics seemed to present such a challenge to the Church that – as we have seen – it was thought appropriate to bring them to trial, Abelard twice and Gilbert of Poitiers once.[4] As the Middle Ages wore on, academics began to act as recognizable communities. Attempts by ecclesiastical authorities in the thirteenth century to suppress dangerous academic opinion addressed whole Faculties. The 'theologians of Paris' spoke together in their Articles of 1544.

The problem of the relationship of the long-term professional academic, to the episcopally structured authority of what from the nineteenth century we should call the magisterium in the maintenance of the faith, has been something of a running battle since the beginnings of the universities. It continues. To take an instance, modern Roman Catholic canon law for the Eastern Churches stresses that theologians must not 'rock the boat'. They are to be obedient to the magisterium. They are to co-operate with the bishops in their teaching office.[5] There is a stress on the principle that teaching in universities should be seen to be in conformity with the faith of the Church.[6] There is supervision of the publishing of books.[7]

But from the beginning the academic world was not wholly separate from that of the Church's official machinery. The universities served as a recruiting-ground for the ecclesiastical civil-service and also for the highest offices in the Church, such as the episcopate. Innocent III made use of them in that way, seeking out, for example, the scholar Stephen Langton in the University of Paris as a candidate for the Archbishopric of Canterbury.[8] Sometimes, too, these 'experts', while remaining in an academic position, came to have a place in the Church's conciliar process when they were called in to serve as advisers. This was an important factor at the Council of Trent, for example.

Yet even when the Church's authorities worked 'with' and not 'against' the academics, in the Middle Ages there was a directness of popular interest in the debates within the universities which could be a source of unrest. The *Quodlibets*, for example, involved a *disputatio* which was a public occasion, to which came people who did not belong to the university; the audience decided the subject-matter of the disputation by asking the questions, and entertainment was to be had as at the first session a bachelor tried to arrive at an answer, while at the second a master 'determined' it.[9]

A lively illustration of the complexity of this phenomenon is the story of the academic row (with political interference) which brewed about the person of Wyclif in the late fourteenth century. The English King Richard wrote to instruct the Chancellor of Oxford and the Proctors that they are to make an *inquisitio generalis* throughout the University with the help of all the recent theologians, to root out heresies of a Wycliffite sort or the books which contain them.[10] At the end of the process against the priest, William Swynderby, by the Bishop of Lincoln, intended to 'extirpate the perfidy' which was dividing the Church by usurping the preacher's office and spreading errors, Swynderby was commanded to read a set recantation in eight churches of the diocese.[11] That implies that it was held to be important for the laity to hear him repent of what he had said. More *Acta*, this time against Master Henry Crompe the monk at the King's

Great Council at Stanford in the Carmelite House (May 1392), reveal he has been saying that confession to the friars breeds discord and division, and that the friars who insist that those who confess to them need not confess to their own parish priests are heretics.[12]

The fact is that scholars are always to some degree anomalous within the Church's structures, and remain so. Numerous examples might be cited from the late twentieth century of the theologian whom his church attempts to silence because his teaching seems to be disturbing the faithful. The Church's relationship with the academic community remains a little uneasy because academic independence makes it impossible to pin it down tidily. To quote Pope Paul VI:

> Sacred theology has a twofold relationship with the Church's *magisterium* and with the worldwide community of Christians. It earnestly seeks to discover how the Christian community might translate its faith into practice, and it tries to grasp the truths, opinions, questions, and tendencies, which the Holy Spirit stirs up in the people of God: 'what the spirit says to the Churches' (Apoc. 2.7).
>
> Using the methods and principles proper to its field, sacred theology must evaluate the faith of God's people as actually lived ... in order to bring them into harmony with the word of God and the doctrinal heritage faithfully handed down by the church. . . .[13]

The old assumptions themselves have now had to be called in question more radically. It cannot be overemphasized in the context of reception that to speak of 'error' is to be adversarial. It is to take it that the task is to compare right and wrong views and fight for the right against proponents of the wrong. As we shall see, the more recent 'reception' model is different. It can accommodate – indeed sees as normal – an interim stage where the Church does not yet see its way, where the right answer simply is not known. It allows for the possibility of the persistence for some time of the complementarity of views which are only later reconciled.

III
PARTICIPATION

CHAPTER NINE

SHARING A COMMON MIND

Reception is the story of the living 'mind of the Church'. The Christian faith has been held by millions of individual minds, and it is they who have, understanding themselves to act under the guidance of the Holy Spirit, by infinitely complex processes, both taken in the new, and kept faith with the old. That is our context, because it is the context in which 'reception' has to work.

If reception is a collective, shared process the multitude of individual minds must in some ways work together. Believing is certainly a matter of each individual's personal assent and commitment in response to the grace of God.[1] This faith which each believer receives from God and returns to him is of its essence an act of communion between God and believer. But it is also an act of communion which takes place in the community of the Church. Every Christian is told to be ready to 'give a reason for the hope that is in him' (1 Pet. 3.15). That giving account of one's faith has always happened publicly in baptism. The individual then makes a formal declaration of faith personally (or if an infant, through parents and godparents), in front of the community of other believers. This declaration is a short statement and it is not made up by the person who is going to be baptized but is provided by the community as an agreed statement for him or her to say. So it is the community's faith he or she expresses. It has always been clear liturgically, for example in the use of the Creeds in worship in the Eucharist and in daily community prayer, and thus in the very life and worship of the Church, that faith has a 'both individual and collective' character.

So we can define 'reception' as the process by which Christians come to be able to say '*we*[2] believe' about a given point of faith.[3] Indeed we must if consensus is to be seen as its hallmark. But that is clearly a far from simple statement. The ideal of a single shared faith has been consistently fallen short of in dispute and disagreement. Yet if it cannot be shown to be a reality the faith itself is in vain, for it is axiomatic that it is 'one faith' (Eph. 4.5). That is the practical problem about 'reception' in which lie embedded the multitude of theological problems we shall be looking at. What I believe and what we all believe, the particular and the universal, are often in tension.

Consensus and truth status

The reconciliation of individuality of view in a shared unity of faith has to do not only with persons and their minds, but also with the content of what is believed. Faith is not only *in* God, but *about* something. When the worshipping community says *credimus*, 'we believe', it goes on to make a short statement of what Christians believe.[4] The text is usually described as a 'creed' (from the Latin *credo*, 'I believe'). It can be very short and simple. In *The Alternative Service Book of the Church of England (1980)* this is all that is asked:

> Do you believe and trust in God the Father, who made the world?
>
> *I believe and trust in him.*
>
> Do you believe and trust in his Son Jesus Christ, who redeemed mankind?
>
> *I believe and trust in him.*
>
> Do you believe and trust in his Holy Spirit, who gives life to the people of God?
>
> *I believe and trust in him.*

But behind the few words lies a vast area of possible discussion about their meaning. Here, for example, the 'trinitarian' character of the Christian faith is emphasized. It was from an early stage seen as a distinctive and decisive feature of Christian baptism that it should be 'in the name of the Trinity'. But each person of the Trinity is given a special role here in this declaration. It was controversial at various stages in the Church's history whether all these attributes were in fact 'proper' to one Person only. (Did the Father alone make the world? Does the Spirit alone give life?) Even without the theological training and a knowledge of the history of the tradition which would make such an underlying 'agenda' noticeable, each individual believer will have his or her own thoughts about the meaning of even the most apparently straightforward statement of faith; and there are bound to be more and more questions in his or her mind about the details of the faith as experience tests them and new problems arise. So the 'collective' and the 'intellectually demanding' character of faith are inseparable.

But just as faith is not solely an act of the intellect, but includes spiritual and emotional elements, so in discussing its content we are not dealing only with points of doctrine. The aspects of the maintenance of the faith which have often been most in evidence in discussion for the majority have been those to do with right behaviour and those to do with spirituality. In the first Book of Langland's *Piers Plowman* in the fourteenth century the 'teaching of holy Church' is mainly on these subjects. In 1648 Lewis Bayly's book *The Practice of Piety* begins with this stricture, 'Whoever thou art that lookest into this Booke, never undertake to reade it; unless thou first resolvest to become from thy heart, an unfained Practitioner of Piety.'[5]

This broader, richer and deeper context needs to be borne in mind as we go along. There is a long tradition of distinguishing among degrees of certainty in knowledge in terms of a graduation of growing certainty; one may have an opinion, or believe or actually know. 'To believe' is both less certain than knowing and more certain because of the degree of commitment it carries with it.[6] 'Faith is the perception of the truth of something with assent, but without there being a cause for knowledge.'[7] So faith somehow stands between opinion and knowledge and in this way it seems less certain than knowledge.[8] What then is the relationship between everyone agreeing about something and its being accepted as true?

To assent to something is to agree with it, to adopt it as one's own belief. To *consent* is to do something more, to agree about something *with* others, to share a belief. It can be argued that this 'sharing' of belief alters its status, at least in that it makes it more credible because believers can look to other believers for support. That is not the same thing as showing that it is likely to be true. Nevertheless, Aristotle seems to have seen consent as a proof that something is true;[9] and for the pagan geometer Euclid and the (probably) Christian Boethius in the sixth century alike, the conception of the common mind, the *communis animi conceptio*, is a truth attested by universal acceptance,[10] as something which is apparent to all reasonable minds.

But the category of such 'self-evident' truths (of the 2 + 2 = 4 type, which compel all rational intellects) is small. Truths of faith are manifestly not like that. As Aquinas pointed out in the thirteenth century[11] it is not even a universally self-evident truth that God exists, let alone all the other things Christians believe about him.[12]

Others have been more optimistic. One nineteenth-century Quaker author thinks:

> This divine revelation and inward illumination is that which is evident and clear of itself, forcing, by its own evidence and clearness, the well-disposed understanding to assent, irresistibly moving the same thereunto; even as the common principles of natural truths move and incline the mind to a natural assent.[13]

But experience shows that that is not the case for all minds. So we cannot set up a model in which shared belief interacts reliably with the truth-status of what is 'believed in the sense that all reasonable people will accept it'. If that could be done, obedience to leadership and submission to instruction would not be the issue we shall see them to be in the next section; for there would be no need for a model involving 'binding' or 'compelling'. On the other hand – and this is very important – a very solid and comprehensive core of Christian beliefs has persisted century by century. We have to look, in order to account for this, not only to 'divine revelation', but also to the notion of mutual support, the confidence that the sharing of belief helps the believer. This is to argue that the 'cloud of witnesses' creates a persistence of the beliefs to which it bears witness.[14]

But to say that collective witness encourages belief is not the same as saying that this operation of consent alters anything; it still has to be seen as not a creating of truth but a witness to what is already true, a process of recognition of a truth which already exists.[15] Augustine of Hippo (354–430) thinks that consensus constitutes a form of proof of this particular sort, weighty by virtue of the common witness. 'Had you read the Gospel with care,' he argues,

> and investigated the places where you found opposition, instead of rashly condemning them, you would have seen that the recognition of the authority of the evangelists by so many learned men all over the world, in spite of this most obvious discrepancy, proves that there is more in it than appears at first sight.[16]

Thomas More in the sixteenth century speaks of the authority of consent, and Erasmus thinks there is a binding force in the belief and consent of the Church.[17] Charles Wesley often uses 'prove' in the sense of a collective testing, in lines such as 'We prove thine utmost power to save'.[18] To describe the laity as witnesses, says John Henry Newman, does not mean that they are required to *judge* orthodoxy. Instead 'their belief, is sought for, as a testimony to that apostolical tradition, on which alone any doctrine whatsoever can be defined . . . and because their consensus through Christendom is the voice of the Infallible Church'.[19]

A collective, whole-community conception of witness of this kind appears in modern ecumenism too. Here it is in Orthodox–Old Catholic conversations:

> The common consciousness of the faith shows itself in diverse ways. It finds its expression with the confessors and martyrs, the desert fathers and the mystics, the holy monastic fathers, the believers gifted with a charisma and generally with all who have received the gift of the Holy Spirit in Baptism and Confirmation and who are also called to bear witness to the Gospel in the world, in worship and in other expressions of the life of the Church.[20]

A very recent testimony to the principle occurs in the *Catechism of the Catholic Church*: 'The apostles entrusted the "Sacred deposit" of the faith (*depositum fidei*), contained in Sacred Scripture and Tradition, to the whole of the Church.'[21]

So if we sample century by century we find the view expressed again and again that there is a reassurance in the fact that others have thought it right to trust the belief in question.

For everyone to agree is surprising. It is central to this argument that 'consenting witness' encourages belief that consensus is a *phenomenon*. That is to say that it is itself a piece of evidence. This 'authority of consent' has been regarded as a gift of God to the Church, just as personal faith is a gift to the individual. The truth can thus be deemed to rest ultimately upon a divine author, with the human consensus reaching for a sense of rightness which is actually a consonance with that inalienable truth. On that hypothesis rests the only logical possibility of absolute certainty in matters of faith.[22]

THE EXAMPLE OF AUGUSTINE

We might take a 'worked example' at this point, to see how some of these principles were tested in practice from an early stage. Augustine of Hippo considers the ways in which the Church as a whole comes to know what to believe. One of his starting-points is the premiss that this involves a sharing of experience, a knowing as one knows friends. If someone asks, 'Why should we believe what we cannot see?' we believe in the affection of friends, although we cannot see it, Augustine points out (*De fide rerum quae non videntur* 1). Those who dispute this will say that there are proofs of such friendship. Can Augustine offer proofs of the things he wishes to be believed as matters of faith? Indeed he can, he rejoins. Here he addresses the way in which not one single catechist but the whole Church wins minds by evidences in her own life and confession. Prophecies concerning Christ have been fulfilled (5). He chooses at this point to allow the Church to speak, to make her case for herself. 'The Church speaks to you with a mother's love,' he says. She explains that she is the Queen of the Psalm (Ps. 45.6–17), in golden robes of wisdom, who confesses everywhere that Christ is Lord (5–6). Her witness is the witness given by things seen, to things not seen, both past and future (8). This is to rest faith on the testimony of trusted witness rather than upon rational proof, and above all (for our purposes), it is to ground it upon the Church's collective witness as a community of faith, interpenetrated with scriptural influences.

On the Profit of Believing (*De Utilitate Credendi*) was written for a friend who had been misled by the teachings of the influential contemporary 'dualist' sect of the Manichees. Augustine identifies it in his *Retractationes* (i.14) as an early work, written while he was still a priest at Hippo. He is highly conscious in writing it that he himself had been a Manichee for nine (in fact ten) years and knows only too well the seductiveness of the sect. In writing the *De Utilitate Credendi*, Augustine explores further the kinds of evidential process involved in the Church's own witness. Let us put the case, says Augustine, that someone has not as yet heard a teacher of any religion. The first thing to do is to find believers each of whom can teach us about his or her own faith. Suppose there are people who profess a number of different religions. Should we not try first the one which holds most adherents? Would it not also be plausible that though only a few would attain to a full understanding and the highest practice of that religion, multitudes of simple people would agree that they were right?[23] Their agreement would be a sign of the truth of the faith in question. Now there are (in the Christian Roman Empire of Augustine's time), more Christians than Jews and pagans put together, and that ought to tell us something, Augustine thinks, because their collective witness is larger. This optimism about the correctness of the majority view may not look so compelling with twentieth-century hindsight, but the thrust of Augustine's argument is that the observation of existing agreement ought to reassure us and compel our own agreement.

Augustine also explores further in this work the links between witness and receptivity. All laws divine and human *allow* us to seek the Catholic faith. Nothing *hinders* the enquirer from looking into it. Augustine describes his own experience of the positive face of this permission, how he himself felt *driven* to search, how he heard

Ambrose of Milan preach on the Old Testament (which the Manichees consider accursed), and was led to want to know more of Ambrose's solutions. Under the influence of this witnessing, Augustine was at a certain stage willing to become a catechumen, and knows that he would then have been highly receptive to a teacher and could have been won to faith by having things explained to him.

The line of argument which stresses the importance of faith in, and response to, living witnesses is strongly continued in the *De utilitate credendi*. Augustine asks his Manichee correspondent whether people ought to believe in religion at all. It is clearly one thing to believe, another to be credulous. If the first is as blameworthy as the second it would be base to believe even one's friends, and common sense says that that is not so. Therefore there is a proper place for belief. But even if that is the case, is it not unworthy to believe before one knows? Augustine asks the Manichee to consider the position of the instructor. If he casts pearls before swine by revealing truths of faith to someone who is only pretending to a serious interest, he himself does something unworthy. So there is a two-way act of faith. The teacher has to believe the would-be catechumen to be in earnest just as the hearer has to believe his instructor.[24]

But surely, the Manichee objects, it would be better if you were to give me a reason. Augustine points out that not everyone will be capable of understanding the reasoning. It cannot be God's intention that only the most intelligent should be allowed to know him. More: even such a man must first believe that he will come to understanding, and must give himself up to the enquiry and submit to the rigours of a life which will purify him and render his intellect capable of grasping the truth. It will certainly be no hindrance to such a one to come as do those who simply believe, and who humbly give themselves to God in that way.[25]

The 'sense of rightness' and the principle of harmony

I have already touched on the problem that it is hard to believe in a communal Christian 'sense' of right faith in the face of wars of religion and centuries of dissent and division. Nevertheless, calling oneself 'Christian' does not cure the 'Babel' phenomenon of the raising of many discordant and mutually unintelligible voices.

It is certainly possible to speak of a 'common mind'. *Phronêma* is biblical (Phil. 2.5; Gal. 5.10).[26] But there are difficulties with that. Human minds are demonstrably diverse, at the very least in that some have different capacities from others. And experience shows that sharing one faith does not mean all thinking identical thoughts – a point to which I shall return in later chapters. If 'to be of one mind' were to involve loss of that diversity which makes the common mind more capacious than any single mind, it would arguably be an impoverishment. But to bring the diversity into a relationship of harmony and unity of intention is something else entirely. The evidence with which we shall be concerned in this study suggests that that, the very 'symphony of the faith',[27] is the essence of Christian consensus.

The existence of a 'sense of rightness' may be easier to defend in terms of a common reference to some authoritative touchstone, rather than of shared opinion. But if that is right we have to identify that touchstone, and candidates which have been proposed over the centuries prove to be capable of many interpretations, and thus of supporting different conclusions, so that they fail in practice to provide a consistent focus of a sense of rightness.

Central is the role of the Holy Spirit as guide and inspiration, the understanding that we need to look to an altogether higher authority for the 'sense of rightness' than human reason. This must be inseparable from the notion of 'the mind of Christ' to which the New Testament refers (I Cor. 2.16), for the faith taught by Christ and the faith taught by the Holy Spirit cannot logically be two different or discrepant things.

For most Christians, 'Scripture' must be the ultimate point of reference, the supreme test of rightness of faith. It is, however, as we shall see later, very far from being the case that Christians have always agreed about its meaning. A considerable agenda of items to do with 'exegesis' stands in the way of any straightforward statement about using the Bible as the test of the rightness of faith. Similarly, we shall be looking as we go on at a lengthy agenda of problems to do with regarding the authority of the Church as a simple touchstone.

Augustine was naturally introspective, and he tells us a great deal about his personal discoveries and difficulties; but he was also, as the mature Christian who wrote the account in the *Confessions*, always conscious that he ought to be 'thinking with' the whole community of Christ's people in forming his judgements about the faith. For him, the private and the collective exercise of judgement in the community were intimately interrelated, indeed inseparable. That had ceased to be so obviously the case by the sixteenth century in the West. Indeed it was the reformers' contention that the late medieval Church had been imposing beliefs on the minds of the faithful and requiring their compliance on pain of the loss of hope of heaven. If it is possible to frame a sentence in that way, so that 'the Church' is seen as conceptually separable from 'the faithful', that looks like identifying 'the Church' with 'the clerical hierarchy'. There were many in the later Middle Ages who would argue that that was right. But it made some of the more articulate among the ordinary faithful see themselves as disenfranchised. That is very evident among the Lollards, as we shall see. The effect for them was to thrust the emphasis back upon the intercourse of the individual soul with God and away from consciousness of the shared and ecclesial character of believing. By the sixteenth century the reformers' characteristic response was to encourage not only resort to 'Scripture alone' to settle disputed questions, but also to insist that the individual, reading for himself, may trust the Holy Spirit to guide him into right faith. His 'private judgement' is to be taken to be the proper and normal place of reception. This is a very important shift because of the way it partly obscured the interaction and interrelationship of personal and shared reception, and with it the 'participatory' character of the understanding of reception we have been exploring.

It should be stressed that it was not envisaged by sixteenth-century reformers that the result of the private journey of the individual soul ought to be anything but conformity with the true and apostolic faith. This was not seen as a recipe for diversity, let alone for divergence. The English Puritan divine William Whitaker (1548–95) stressed that the individual should not follow the interpretation dictated by his own private spirit, but the Holy Spirit's teaching in Scripture.[28] If the judgement of individuals is formed by the Holy Spirit through the biblical text it is not to be censured as mere private judgement, he argued.[29] Indeed, it should presumably prove to be the same as the judgement formed by others if they too are under the guidance of the Spirit.

By the nineteenth century the area of concern and of preoccupation had shifted again. It was possible for John Henry Newman to envisage the role of the individual without these tensions between the private and the collective conditioning his thinking to quite the same degree. For him, private judgement does not stand 'over against' the teaching of an ecclesiastical hierarchy whose claim to an absolute and enforceable authority is being rejected. His own emphasis (and personal concern) lies with the growth of certainty, as something integral to the moral, intellectual and spiritual formation of the person. He takes the strong example of a saint to point up sharply what ought to happen in all faithful people as they grow more secure in their grasp of apostolic faith. Newman's emphasis is also upon the nuances and subtle shifts of the process of reception of an idea as an article of faith. In his account this is scarcely a conscious, and certainly not wholly an intellectual growth. Here he stands perhaps closer to Augustine in his intellectual temper.

> The gifted individual whom we have imagined, will of all men be least able (as such) to defend his own views, inasmuch as he takes no external survey of himself. . . . The longer any one has persevered in the practice of virtue, the less likely is he to recollect how he began it.
>
> Concerning the body of opinions formed under these circumstances [they will be] not accidental and superficial, the mere reflection of what goes on in the world, but the natural and almost spontaneous result of the formed and finished character within.[30]

This is what we must aspire to, even we who are not saints and therefore not exceptional:

> Doubtless beings, disobedient as most of us, from our youth up, cannot comprehend even the early attainments of one who thus grows in wisdom as truly as he grows in stature; who has no antagonist principles unsettling each other – or errors to unlearn; though something is suggested to our imagination by that passage in the history of our Blessed Lord, when at twelve years old He went up with His parents to the Temple. . . .

With an awareness that the individual's conviction must, if it is right, form a consensus with those of others, Newman turns next to the question of the standing of such growing certainties as truths of faith. He asks how far consensus can be self-correcting in and through these private individuals and their minds. Here he makes two points of importance for our purposes. The first is that not everyone follows this course through to its end.

> Some hearers of it had their consciences stirred for a while, and many were affected by the awful simplicity of the Great Teacher; but the proud and sensual were irritated into opposition; the philosophic considered His doctrines strange and chimerical; the multitude followed for a time in senseless wonder, and then suddenly abandoned an apparently failing cause.[31]

So he would say that the consensus is not overwhelming. Those who enter it must want to enter it, and must come in humility and must persevere. This argues for an actively-embraced consensus, an element of willing as well as judging.

Secondly, the faith in itself forms a system. Newman suggests 'that every part of what may be called this moral creed will be equally true and necessary'. He even goes so far as to propose that 'every part of the Truth ... seen detached from the whole, becomes an objection'.[32] Thus the web or network exists as the matrix of 'ideas about which there is consensus', as well as the minds which participate in that consensus. This is a notion of importance, and much stressed in the recent Roman Catholic *Catechism*.

Both these notions in Newman's thinking make room for complementarity, as well as for give and take; the confidence is that some have one insight, some another, and all angles of view will in the end fit together. This makes it possible to see how the 'sense of rightness' can operate piecemeal without losing its integrity.

This picture of individual and varied contribution to an ultimately (if not in the short term) harmonious whole began to make sense to Newman. He saw that the contribution would be unequal, with some leading, others following, or even challenging for the leadership. Newman defended the *Tracts for the Times* which profoundly stirred up the Church of England in the 1830s by noting that:

> They were ... intended as ... the expression of *individual* minds, and individuals feeling strongly; while on the one hand, they are incidentally faulty in mode or language, on the other they are still peculiarly effective. No great work was ever done by a system, whereas systems rise out of individual exertions. Luther was an individual. The very fault of an individual excites attention; he loses, but his cause, if good, and he powerful-minded, gains.[33]

He is seeking here a way of expressing the relationship between the manner in which individuals come to understanding, and the organically complex living processes of the *consensus fidelium* in which all those individuals participate, where the individual contribution may be pioneering, even rough-hewn, even faulty, but sometimes attractive in its vigour. Here is no merely inward journey of the private judgement, but a process of forming an individual position in which stages *before* completion are exposed and shared with others and can influence those others, so that there is a testing and a trying out, in advance of the arrival at a relatively finished position.

CHAPTER TEN

THE EBB AND FLOW OF INFLUENCE IN THE COMMUNITY

The interaction of ministers and people

We must now tackle the historical muddle in which the viewpoint of the mass of the faithful has, piecemeal and by various routes, made itself felt, the ebb and flow of mutual teaching and learning in which reception takes place. The theory can intrude on the practice, conditioning it by observing and commenting on it. When in a recent article Konrad Raiser writes, 'ecumenical learning understood as a process of finding a new language is also a form of fighting back against the disempowerment of ordinary people and their pragmatic knowledge and experience by the domination of experts',[1] there is a sense of the presence of an activist agenda, a politically-coloured determination to 'raise consciousness' in ordinary people and to encourage them to see the theorist as perhaps an enemy. But it is equally arguable that the practice can intrude upon the theory, shaping it in its turn, as was particularly clear in the evolution of the system of penance and indulgences in the Middle Ages. A high proportion of the illustrative material in this chapter comes from the medieval West. That is deliberate. At no other period perhaps are the tugs and tensions so apparent. We have more evidence for them in this period than for earlier centuries; and these centuries set the terms of what happened at the Reformation and after.

Those who serve the community as its ministers also wield power. This is especially noticeable in the implementation of patterns of Church government through the ages.[2] That power has sometimes been abused, and more importantly for our purposes it has been *felt* to be abused by those the ministers shepherd. An individual is placed by his (or recently, her) ordination in a relationship of 'representative-ness' and 'focus' to the community (so that the minister is 'with and among' his people, as Augustine puts it). There is one inevitable tension here. There is another further obvious one. Once a community sees itself as 'dual' it tends to break itself up further in pursuit of special interests and leading ideas, each of which is held by those to whom it is important to be the key to the whole situation. But *consensus fidelium* speaks of *agreement*, of *harmony* among the faithful about their common faith.

Out of these tensions the great body of the faithful somehow speaks for itself. It responds to the formal pronouncements of the Church's hierarchy and the published writings of theologians. It spontaneously expresses thoughts formed within the body of the faithful itself, especially that part of it which is commonly called 'the laity'. The complex and hard-to-retrieve processes we are about to dip into show the laity taking an active role in the framing of the consensus, not always affirming but sometimes querying what they are told, pointing out gaps and imbalances, actually altering the position.

The assumptions in force in this medieval period are conspicuously hierarchical. There is really little or no evidence of a sense that the laity are 'equal but different'. Cleric, expert, professional offer a 'top-down' pattern of reception, with lay people accepting or rejecting what they are told. Yet even in this unlikely area history does seem to show 'the people of God' as a whole to be a real presence in the forming of the Church's mind over time. This activity seems to be led or driven not only from 'above', but from below, too, by needs felt by lay people. Some of these they identify for us; some can be inferred from the pastoral pressures they exert.[3] Something crucial to our wider enquiry is detectable in the pressures within the life of the later medieval Church from those who were not in positions of leadership or themselves professional theologians, but who had a voice in this indirect way in forming and sustaining the *consensus fidelium* during a thousand years in the West in which the bones of sacramental theology and ecclesiology underwent the great 'growth spurt' which largely determined their modern patterns. It is also the period in which the distinction between minister and people is sharpest, the minister holding almost all the cards educationally and the people vigorously taught obedience.

In a hierarchically dominated structure the first question must be whether it is really possible to show the non-ordained (for that is the group we are chiefly concerned with at this point) to be an active force. Lay thinking in the late medieval scene in the West was undoubtedly encouraged, directed and even manipulated by the Church's hierarchy, so that we are seeing some conscious or unconscious collusion in the forming of lay pastoral pressures.[4] In the literature there is a strong current of indications that the clerical and 'professional' theologians' response to the exertion of pastoral pressure by the faithful commonly went even further. In fact we hear almost more about that than anything else, when the reformers move to the attack in the sixteenth century with the accusation that this had been done for corrupt ends, in search of power and wealth. It is worth pausing for a moment over this accusation, for it shows us the negativity which is perhaps to be expected in expressions of opinion by a laity who cannot join in the positive reception processes by the same routes as the hierarchy, and can therefore make their voices heard only in protest or complaint.

The accusation of clerical corruption is a commonplace in the later Middle Ages, from at least the twelfth century, with the triple focus of unworthiness for the office held, abuse of power and misappropriation of wealth. William Langland's fourteenth-century *Piers Plowman* is graphic in its descriptions:

> Bishops and novices, Doctors of Divinity and other great divines – to whom Christ has given the charge of men's souls, and whose heads are tonsured to show that they must absolve, teach and pray for their parishioners, and feed the poor – I saw them all living in London, even in Lent.[5]

He saw, too:

> Troops of hermits . . . with their wenches following after. These great, long lubbers, who hated work, were got up in clerical gowns to distinguish them from laymen, and paraded as hermits for the sake of an easy life.

Tellingly, he argues that this hypocrisy making its leaders unworthy infected the whole community:

> I saw pilgrims and palmers banding together to visit the shrines at Rome and Compostela. They went on their way full of clever talk, and took leave to tell fibs about it for the rest of their lives.

Greed for money and abuse of power were linked in what Langland observed:

> I saw the Friars there too – all four orders of them – preaching to the people for what they could get. In their greed for fine clothes, they interpreted the Scriptures to suit themselves and their patrons. Many of these Doctors of Divinity can dress as handsomely as they please, for as their trade advances, so their profits increase. . . . There was also a pardoner, preaching like a priest. He produced a document covered with Bishops' seals, and claimed to have power to absolve all the people from broken fasts

and vows of every kind. The ignorant folk believed him and were delighted. They came up and knelt to kiss his documents, while he ... raked in their rings and jewellery with his roll of parchment.[6]

Distrust and resentment of the clerics on these and like counts is widespread among the Lollard dissidents of the late fourteenth and early fifteenth centuries. Criticism of clerical misuse of power[7] is frequent, with talk of betrayal and oppression.[8] It is argued that those who are morally unfitted for their high positions have no claim to the privileges or powers they enjoy. 'It says in the Law,' argues one Lollard,

> that the people may not accept the ministry of priests who are fornicators. That is why I have said that I should prefer to receive bread from the hand of a good-living layman who is pleasing to God, which that layman has himself blessed, than from the hand of such a priest.[9]

Elsewhere we find: 'No one is a civil lord; no one is a bishop; no one is a prelate, while he is in mortal sin.'[10] If a bishop or priest is in mortal sin he may not ordain ... or baptize. (There is an important issue of 'order' here. Augustine had stressed that the unworthiness of the minister does not invalidate the sacraments because they are ultimately the work of God himself, and grace can operate even through imperfect channels.)

The mention of civil lords underlines the fact that this resentment about power is to be met with against the nobility too. They kill in warfare, say Lollard texts, and get indulgences for those who help them murder Christian people in distant lands for worldly gain.[11] It is also impossible to separate altogether accusations of abuse of power from accusations of misuse of money. Indignation runs high that those who conspicuously do not deserve it should have so much power over the lives of others and should indeed even profit by it financially. There are strong, repeatedly expressed preoccupations with clerical misuse of money. It is argued by some to be against Holy Scripture for the clergy to have temporal possessions.[12] It is contended that they ought not to exact a fee for performing such duties as baptizing or the purification of women.[13] A connecting thread in all this would seem to be one (not of course confined to the medieval period) of resentment at others' privilege and the use of that privilege to make the underprivileged still more so.

Within this general framework, we find a multitude of detailed expressions of resentment of the exercise of particular claims to power. If auricular confession is said to be so necessary to the salvation of mankind, with the pretended power of absolution, that merely exalts the pride of priests, and gives them opportunity to know other people's secrets, which they do not want to be forced to tell. For both lords and ladies bear witness that they do not dare to tell the truth for fear of their confessors, says one comment.[14] Special prayers applied to one person by prelates or religious do not benefit individuals more than general prayers, other things being equal, says another.[15]

Here we see something of the tendency to preoccupation with relatively small grievances which resentment creates. But there is also an outraged sense of that proper order on a much grander scale is being disrupted, and that betokens something significant about the 'sense of rightness' as a key feature of the reception process. It is important that this sense of rightness does not always locate itself in the same things. In the fourteenth and fifteenth centuries, nuns, for example are accused of breaking such rules when they take it upon themselves to exercise leadership in the Church, which is not permitted to women, as well as receiving tithes which ought to be applied to the needy, and keeping them for themselves.[16] In another age, in other churches, the first stricture would not apply, although the second would.

The 'power' problem had an aspect which makes the conflict not strictly one of 'clergy' and 'laity' but rather of 'higher clergy' and everyone else. If a cleric questions the rules publicly that is seen as dangerous because it can affect the faith of ordinary people. In medieval dissenting communities 'middle rank' clergy frequently sided with, or even led, the disaffected, where they regarded themselves as unenfranchised or, to use modern terminology, 'disempowered'. They could feel as left out, not only of the councils but also of the counsels of the Church, as the laity. In the twelfth century, Henry the renegade monk and other demagogues were of this sort. In the condemnation of Wyclif,[17] the offence is deemed to be partly that Wyclif and others, inside the university and outside it, dogmatize publicly, so that the Catholic faith is put at risk and popular devoutness diminishes.[18] Wyclif, unrepentant, replies with a confession in which he reasserts his position, and overtly calls on the faithful to judge.[19] But the same Wyclif would himself acknowledge the people are easily led. In his response to accusations in the first year of Richard II's reign Wyclif speaks of the blindness of the faithful. So the assumption that the laity are 'children in the faith' proved hard to shift even among those sympathetic to their claims.

Various issues arise in connection with this dual phenomenon that the laity can be led astray; and that they are, paradoxically, entitled to their view; and that view is a constitutive part of the *consensus fidelium*.

Most striking in this connection is concern with loss of control through unlicensed preaching. William, Archbishop of Canterbury comments (on the condemnation of Wyclif), that the people were getting stirred up. Some are preaching without licences, and there is thereby engendered a threat against the stability of the whole Church and in subversion of the peace of the realm, when propositions and conclusions full of errors, and already condemned by the Church, are put forward.[20] As to the content of the preaching, that is condemned and prohibited from being taught within the University of Oxford. The letter of the Oxford religious orders and John of Lancaster against Nicholas of Hereford and other 'disturbers of the peace' sees this stirring up of the laity as the undesirable result.[21]

This disquiet is partly about sedition, with its secular aspects. More profoundly, it is about the division of the Church, though the two prove hard to separate.[22] It is seen as uncontroversial theologically that it would be better for a person not to be born than to sow weeds among the faithful.[23] That has to be read here in the context of the fact that it is axiomatic in our late medieval commentators that division is not the formation of disagreeing groups with a claim to an equal hearing; but the setting up of those who should be obedient against those they should obey. Thus it can be argued that Satan, the 'first sower of discord', separated the servant from his lord by disobedience. That is one of the reasons why in late medieval minds division of the Church and sedition in the State go together.

The complexity of the apportioning of blame for the misuse of power, the misuse of money, the sowing of division and incitement to breaches of due order, is evident in many late medieval comments. The religious complain that

> this creates resentment against our religious orders and makes us blamed for causing the late rebellion, partly on the grounds that we have impoverished the people by expecting them to support us with alms, and set an example of idle mendicancy, but also because since we were the general confessors we could have prevented the uprising. Since we did not, we must in fact have incited the people against their lords.[24]

We have merely dipped a toe here into a mass of material making these and related points. But perhaps enough has been said to show that it is far from satisfactory to say simply that the hierarchy, or the theologians, were corrupt manipulators of popular opinion. It is true that sometimes they were. But clearly popular opinion could and did see that, and protest.

We must not leave out of account the possibility of a more indolent form of corruption. One source speaks of

> the carelessness and evil conscience of ... parish-priests, who caring not for the flock committed to them, but only for their wool and their milk, do not instruct them through preaching and the confessional, or by private admonitions, but walk in the same errors as their flocks, following their corrupt ways and not correcting them for their faults.[25]

This is an important corrective to the 'conspiracy theory' that all clerical imperfections err on the side of efficient manipulation; there was incompetence and laxity too.

Between the deliberate exploitation of the faithful and culpable neglect by the clergy fall a myriad infinitely subtle variations, where the priest may indeed be acting conscientiously and in goodwill, but with understandable human limitations which lead him to make mistakes. In a short passage on what to do with intractable cases, the thirteenth-century Thomas of Chobham gives us some earthy insights into the kinds of problem the confessor will encounter at parish level. A well-born married woman falls in love with a young man and tells her confessor that she would rather go to hell than give him up. All persuasion fails. Thomas suggests a policy of direct intervention. The confessor should go to the young man and ask for some trinket the woman has given him. He should then make sure that it is seen in the possession of another woman. The confessor can then cautiously awaken resentment in the noble lady that the young man has shown that he feels contempt for her by giving her gift to someone else. 'And so the lady is freed,' he ends triumphantly.[26] Now this is crude and could certainly be criticized on the grounds that it deliberately replaces love with hatred. But it is also realistic and practical, and it must have innumerable medieval parallels about which we do not hear.

This brings us naturally to the wealth of theological lessons to be found in the ordinary sins and excesses of ordinary people. The concrete can be used to illustrate the abstract. It is easy, for example, to show from common experience that vices are the mirrors of virtues. Peter of Blois in the twelfth century distinguishes between *avaritia* and *largitas*, greed and generosity. He gives the theory context by entering into the current debate over one Thomas, who tries to argue that beer should be Britain's national drink.[27] Such lessons could be correctly or incorrectly drawn, depending on the adequacy of the teaching the laity received.

There is evidence of the theological muddle in which many, perhaps most, ordinary lay people – and many of their pastors, to judge from our earlier example – must be presumed to have lived. People could be very casual about churchgoing, either because they did not care for it, or, arguably, because it had a familiarity which made it an ordinary and routine part of their lives, so that the Church was somehow 'there' for them, even if not attended, or attended to only with part of the mind. The text *The rich man and the poor man (Dives et pauper)*, of Chaucer's period, mentions people coming in and out of services casually and chattering.[28] We find the comment, 'Poor folk come seldom to church, seldom to sermons.'[29] Either way, the comfortable but irresponsible manner in which people treated churchgoing was inseparable from a certain theological confusion.[30] Of fifteenth-century Tuscan peasants we read:

> Very many of them do not confess once a year, and far fewer are those who take the Communion, under the false belief that they need not communicate except when they grow old or are sick unto death. They do little to instruct their families in the manner of faithful folk. They use enchantments for themselves and for their beasts. Of God, or their own soul's health, they think not at all. And being commonly ignorant . . . this it is which helps to bring them along the broad way leading to destruction, to wit, their ignorance of their own vices.
> Often women give a sum of money for baptism, thinking to pay for it; [there were attempts to pay for communion, too,] and here they sin gravely in that they think they can buy the body of Christ, or other sacraments.[31]

Then there are the 'quickeners', those who stimulate the faith of others in striking ways. It is to state the obvious to say that personal and individual influence is detectable in the lives of the laity, as well as in that of clerical authors, but it is worth noting that contemporaries recognized the fact in the medieval period. This involves a rather different principle from pointing to the examples set by the saints, whose virtues as identified tend to be relatively standard ones, and do not necessarily carry the immediate conviction of having the stamp of real personalities. These are individuals of personal grace, even spiritual charm. They are attractive. A great span of differences of tone and expectation of such exemplary figures could be set in different contexts. The example set by the pious at home was recognized to be a factor in making for shaping of pastoral context. St Margaret of Scotland led an exemplary life which, for a time, seems to have transformed the style of the royal court there. As a direct result of her influence King Malcolm's son Edgar became *dulcis et amabilis*, says a historian who knew him.[32] Clergy could be seen to be notable examples in the same way, working a direct influence on the lives and attitudes of the laity. Much later Erasmus wrote to the Bishop of Basle:

> Do we not see, as soon as one arises who is commended by any opinion of sanctity, and who shows any appearance of a Gospel-preacher, with what enthusiasm the people hang from his lips, and what heartfelt favour they grant him? . . . If the people sees a man to be a true priest and bishop, his exhortation will not be without fruit. But if his publicly irreligious (*impia*) life, his impure morals, his gross ignorance, his insatiable greed, and his barbarous savageness, have utterly alienated people's minds, how shall they profit by his precepts?[33]

So we need to be alert to a number of distinguishable things in the interaction of ministers and people. They will include: spontaneous popular demand; popular demand fed by the leaders of the Church with a sound pastoral intention; popular demand directed by some of the hierarchy for their own ends; lack of direction as a result of clerical inadequacies, allowing popular exploration and even error to go unchecked, lowlier clergy acting as 'middlemen'.

Finding expression

It is a phenomenon of common experience that it is difficult to remember things when merely told them, and especially to do it accurately. For much of the Church's history, the majority of the faithful have learned about the faith orally. Charlemagne made laws which priests were to read aloud to their flocks, who are supposed to remember, and recite them by heart when their priest asks them to.[34] The ordinary faithful have also had their say about the faith orally. But the evidences as to what ordinary people felt they needed are difficult to assess because they were not always articulated in words, or at any rate, in words which have survived.

An exception is the accounts of debates with those who were classified as dissenters or heretics, for example, the investigations of Lollardy in late fourteenth- and fifteenth-century England. These distort the picture to some degree precisely because in their time (though not necessarily in the long-term reception of their ideas), they were apparently going against the consensus. But they give what is often the most visible evidence we have of the quality of popular lay theology at its most ambitious.

When dissent spreads it does so because a given set of ideas proves attractive and gains a following. For example, among the Lollards, Margery Backster and her friends were applying their own minds to the Church's teaching and practice and disagreeing with certain elements in it. She was a carpenter's wife in Martham in Norfolk in England. It was alleged that Margery had said, for example, that since images were made by common carpenters, it was wrong to kneel or pray to them. These were reservations many could share.

There is a question how such ideas come together as a set with such regularity. That they do so is indisputable. To read the *Fasciculi Zizaniorum* is to read about the same opinions again and again. Some of these characteristic ideas are to be found among Waldensians, Lollards and later Protestants alike, for example, the call for Scripture in the vernacular. Others appear only in the sixteenth century (the controversy over eucharistic sacrifice, for instance). These groups were not necessarily teaching unorthodoxy about the fundamentals of faith. Mostly they were concerned with principles of order, although this certainly overflowed into the area of overlap between faith and order in disputes about the nature of and need for the sacraments. Their doctrine of ministry was equally dangerous to the Church's established position. They attacked clerical corruption and went so far as to argue that the individual might (at a pinch) find his way to God without clerical assistance. It is perhaps significant that such challenges tended to cluster round ideas of an identifiably 'Waldensian' or 'Lollard' and later of what would in the sixteenth century be thought of as a 'Protestant' character.[35] These clearly have a certain coherence or interconnectedness in practice because in some way they touch a nerve of discontent among the laity.

There is a problem here, of a sort encountered with any inquisition process, that the accusers are likely to be looking for certain indicators that the accused are dissidents; accordingly their questions will be somewhat standard. This can be found in the trial of Peter Abelard, in the Cathar inquisition[36] and elsewhere. Nevertheless there do really seem to be common preoccupations. These are typically reducible to concerns with the abuse of power; they have their negative, resentful side, as well as their constructive aspects. The inquisition-type process which makes a list of erroneous opinions and then looks for them in the suspect dissident is very visible in the *Fasciculi Zizaniorum*. Thus *The sixteen points* discusses the questions bishops put to suspected Lollards: 'True Christian men should answer here advisedly, truly and meekly to the points and articles which are put against them: advisedly that they speak not thoughtlessly; truly that they speak not falsely; and meekly that they speak not proudly in their answer.'[37]

That of course raises the possibility that the inquisition listing of questions is in fact creating or helping to create the dissent-pattern; or conversely that it may misrepresent it. Whatever is to be said about that – and a good deal is to be said – there is clearly a kind of 'power of travel' in certain sets of related reforming ideas which keeps them going and makes them attractive in broadly similar terms generation after generation.

The people and the text

In the last few centuries, the interpretation of Scripture has increasingly been done by the ordinary faithful for themselves. That is the inevitable result of the provision of a text in people's own language and a population more of whose members can read. The interpretation of Scripture has therefore become a part of the reception process which actively involves the whole body of the faithful.

Because there was a (sometimes justified) fear that if people read the Bible without expert guidance they would fall into error, there was resistance by the hierarchy to the first stirrings of this popular recourse to Scripture in the late Middle Ages. There had been a gap of some centuries since the late antique period when translation from the Greek and Hebrew into the then vernacular of Latin had been a natural step, and at least the educated among the laity expected to be able to read Scripture for themselves and discuss it with the Church's leaders. Jerome had rendered the Vulgate text in the late fourth century precisely to provide such a resource in a reliable form to replace the 'Old Latin' translations previously in circulation. The Latin Bible would thus have been readable by any literate person when Latin was itself the common language of the late Roman world, at least in the West. So the notion that the Latin text should be a resource kept safe by being restricted to scholars was a development of medieval centuries when Latin was a learned language and the learned were normally clerics. But once entrenched it proved hard to shift, because the issue became one of principle: that the laity must be saved from themselves by being denied independent access to Scripture in their own present-day vernaculars, in case in their ignorance they failed to understand it correctly and drifted into error.

That became a self-fulfilling prophecy. We have already seen that it was among such dissenting communities as the Waldensians that protest claiming a biblical base began. But at the same time it was their independence of approach, their taking matters of interpretation into their own hands, which got them classified as dissenters. For the Lollard dissenters of the fourteenth and fifteenth centuries, too, the chief focus of independent theological enquiry was the Bible. In 1428 the Bishop of Norwich sat in judgement on Margery Backster. She and her husband had been reading the Bible and encouraging others to join them in a 'Bible-study group' at home. Such self-help groups have commonly discussed the Bible together in this way in most centuries. She and others like her joined in a process of more or less independent evaluation of the teaching of Scripture.

Wyclif thought this likely to be hard work. He argued, as one recent scholar has expressed it, that the Bible offered infinite wisdom, but its offer was extended only to those willing to do battle with its intentional difficulties.[38]

The Bible is not the only possibility for the ordinary reader to learn theology through a text in the Middle Ages. There can be buried theology in a popular text, such as the *Jeu d'Adam*, the first surviving wholly vernacular play (mid-twelfth century). When Adam is introduced to Eve he is told: *Tu la governe par raison* ('In reason hold dominion over her'). She is taught to see Adam thus: *Lui a paraille e a forzor* ('him as my equal and my master'). This traces a fine line on the question of the proper relationship between the sexes, and implies a particular position in the debate. In the play the Devil comes to Adam first, but Adam sends him away. Then Satan comes to Eve and succeeds in seducing her. His winning argument is that Eve and Adam are unequally coupled because she is more tender and more wise than he (*Mal cuple em fist li criator*). He tempts Eve with the promise that she shall be Queen. Adam is conquered at last not by unworthy motives but by trust in his wife: *Jo t'en crerra: tu es ma per* ('You are my wife: I will trust you'). Whereas Eve's eating of the apple leaves her triumphant, and erroneously believing herself to see absolutely clearly, when he has eaten the apple Adam immediately recognizes what he has done.[39] Thus again a theological understanding is portrayed in the text.

But the Bible was always the most important text, *scriptura sacra*, because it alone was God's own Word. The fear that the ordinary faithful would go astray if left to themselves with the Bible proved not altogether well-founded, except at points where a challenge had been in lay minds from the start. Reading it for themselves, coming fresh to it in their own language, ordinary people of the late fourteenth and fifteenth centuries found that 'no preacher in the pulpit speaks better than that book',[40] and that they themselves could attempt criticism and exegesis. There is evidence that a surprisingly sophisticated critical technique was developed. In a poem of 1415 Thomas Hoccleve asks what are obviously intended to be recognized as typical Lollard questions: 'Why is this word here and that word there? Why does God say this here and something else in another place? Why did God do this when he might have done that?'[41] These are the commonsense but crucial questions which underlie the more sophisticated ones of scholarly exegesis through the ages, as it discusses the Bible's choice and use of language, the problems of apparent contradiction between one passage and another, and the need to account for seemingly uncharacteristic acts of God. So there was potential for profound and serious work in the methods developed and used by at least these dissidents.

The condemnation of such practice of lay Bible study helped indirectly to set the authority of the Bible against that of the Church in many late medieval dissenters' minds in the West, and thus to strengthen the predisposition to challenge the authority of the Church. It came about naturally in the course of such study that Scripture's authority was weighed against that of a Church which appeared to be trying to prevent the study of the Bible as though it had something to hide; as though, critics suggested, what it had been teaching contradicted Scripture. Here, as in the battle over vernacular access, the reception process was inadvertently but decisively distorted. To make an *issue* of allowing the laity to judge for themselves was implicitly to exclude them from the decision-making process, and even to open it to debate who actually constituted the Church, for some argued at this date, and in the context of this debate, that only the clergy counted.

It is but a step from there to asking whether the Church can give warrant to what Scripture does not explicitly endorse. Small stirrings of this important Reformation issue are noticeable in the twelfth and early thirteenth centuries. In a discussion touched on by Peter of Blois as to whether forgiven sins are counted against the sinner again if he commits a mortal sin, some say that happens only if we commit apostasy or hatred of a brother, for these are the only two of which we have examples in the gospel.[42] (This is an interesting early occurrence of a Reformation theme, that only what Scripture warrants should be found in the life of the Church.) A little later, Henry of Ghent shows a similar sensitivity to what was evidently a debated point. He sees that 'indulgences' are not in Scripture, but thinks 'we must firmly believe that Christ conferred general powers on this head, even though [prelates] have not received them in so many words' but he says of the effectiveness of indulgences 'whether that be so, God knows; I do not'.[43] Lollards often stuck to Scripture as their test. In Richard Wyche's 'Response' on a list of articles recently imputed to him, he says that he will gladly recant and revoke anything he says which is not founded on Scripture.

At the Reformation Western Christianity was tugged sharply back to the questions which arise about the place of Scripture at the heart of the reception process. *Sola scriptura*, 'Scripture alone', is a call away in another direction from the conception of a corporate enterprise of faith in which the whole community is involved, this time often to a reliance upon the ways in which the Word speaks privately to the individual soul. Again, this is too large an issue to go into here, and much has been written about it to which the reader is referred. But it is important not to leave it out of account as a stage in the historical process by which the divinely-given material of Scripture has itself been received in the Christian community as definitive of the faith.

Active self-education

Among the Lollards, as among other communities containing lay people seeking to take the theological reins into their own hands, there were real rebels. That led to patterns of opposition between dissidents and officials in which warfare is the motif.[44] There is adversariality: 'So weren the archebiscop and his three clerkis alwei contrerie to me and I to hem.' The Lollards were eager for combat. They were not merely passive victims of repression of dissidence. They needed an enemy. They used the friars as well as the Church's hierarchy.

We can see these dissenters learning about the faith under pressure of challenge. Standard questions will arise, so advice was needed on how to answer your accuser. It pays to be circumspect in your answers, says one source.[45] But circumspection is sophistication as well as self-control. The trial of William Thorpe is presented as an instructive drama, like the 'tyrant' play and other contemporary Church drama. The examination takes place in a room off the great chamber of the archbishop. Thorpe, Arundel, a parson of St Dunstan's and two clerks of the canon law are present. What then takes place is a 'trial of truth'. 'Thorpe plays Christ, Arundel plays Caiaphas, and his clerks play the tyrant's minions.'[46] Thorpe is self-possessed. 'Arundel's initial calm soon collapses into the frantic behaviour of the tyrants of the mystery cycles. Cursing and threatening, he apes the high priest's barely restrained impulse to trade forensics for fisticuffs.' This seems an artful reconstruction, where other heresy trial records are tightly formal and official. He suggests that it illustrates in a lively way the principle that 'the nonconformist first learns what he is by recognizing what he is not'. He also learns to think and to sort out his priorities in this challenging situation.[47] Similarly it can be argued that 'the identity and doctrine emerged from the delineation of reversed, falsified images of themselves'.[48] The accused will find his mind being cleared and instructed by grace. 'Than schall be grace in the speiking or answering, be [= by] the helpe of Crist.'[49]

There seems no doubt that some of the medieval dissenters and 'heretics' actively sought education so that they could explore their faith for themselves. Waldensians had been suspected since the twelfth century of meeting in *illicita conventicula*, in which the laity discussed Scripture in their own languages and listened to preaching.[50] The English Parliament was nervous in 1382 of the congregating of people in market-places and fairs to hear preaching. Any such preachers were to be arrested.[51] The dissemination of books was also a cause for concern and there were provisions for confiscating them if they were found in heretic hands.[52] In a letter sent to the mayor and sheriffs of London in January 1393, Richard II warns of the problem. Lay people and artificers are mentioned and it is suggested that 'not a few' of these meet secretly and hold heretical discussions of the content of Holy Scripture and the settled articles of the faith. In this way they exchange nefarious opinions and stir up the people to open revolt.[53] Henry Knighton's Chronicle for 1382 refers to a *gignasium malignorum dogmatum et opinionum* in which again it is feared that heretical opinions are communicated and heretics are intellectually formed.[54] *De haeretico comburendo* of 1401 specifically sets out to suppress the efforts of the heretics to set up schools.[55] Records of the diocese of Norwich between 1428 and 1431 have a good many individuals accused of Lollardy over a considerable period, admitting they had been at such schools, or run them in their own houses.[56]

There are also indications of the style of the work, in terms of the acceptance of an accountability of teacher to taught. In one English Wycliffite text the author leaves behind the words of a sermon, with the intention that those who have heard it shall reread it and study it, and with the promise that if it can be shown from Scripture that he is anywhere in error, the preacher, on his return, will do his best to answer the objections, or else amend the text.[57]

Some individuals can be identified as significant leaders of the

Lollard movement. William White, for example, with five followers from Kent, was clearly a major disseminating influence. But equally clearly, Lollard ideas cropped up in places where no known leader had yet been. One Richard Belward was convicted of running Lollard schools before White arrived in Ditchingham in Norfolk.[58] Convictions for running schools continue through the fifteenth century. A group of laymen from Devizes and Marlborough admitted in 1437 that they had been listening to the Bible in English in private houses. Five heretics were charged with holding schools in Coventry in 1485. In the period 1518–21, it is possible to point to a number of examples of men and women who were running local schools.[59]

It is striking how strong a contrast there is between the Church's consistent emphasis on the education of the clergy and its resistance to education of the ordinary faithful beyond the level of the safe territory of catechetical instruction, and particularly when the faithful set about systematically educating themselves. The position about schools changes of course. Robert Raikes (1735–1814), an English philanthropist, perceived the way in which children in Gloucester were educationally neglected, and set up parish schools for them to attend on Sundays, and later during the week. There they were taught reading and studied the Bible. At first there was resistance from those who thought educating the poor would lead to sedition. But the system gained supporters, Hannah More and others followed his example, and Sunday schools became a common feature of parish life in the Church of England throughout the nineteenth and twentieth centuries. As universal elementary education was introduced their purpose became more strictly one of providing religious education.[60]

There came into being 'small communities of confessing Christians in the midst of the church of the majority at Strasbourg' in the mid-sixteenth century.[61] The *Christlichen Gemeinschaften* were 'small communities of confessing Christians', created by Martin Bucer in his last years there (1547–9).[62] Bucer's idea was to 'restore to the Strasbourg church the small community forms of the New Testament churches'.[63] He encouraged the formation of small groups which would put themselves under discipline and work together to live a life of special dedication and holiness. The local pastor preached the urgency of living as a true Christian community, and those who felt the call to respond were visited at home by their minister. Then they met 'in a suitable place at an advertised time'. Then they chose one or two of their number to form a disciplinary 'board' with the pastor and perhaps others, to undertake the pastoral and disciplinary supervision of the group.[64] The fundamental idea is of a 'core-church'.[65] They were not liked in Strasbourg. Luther's idea of a *Sondergemeinde*, discussed in his Preface to the Mass in German, had been similar. Luther had the idea of a nucleus of really serious Christians, forming themselves into a group voluntarily, willingly putting themselves under discipline and meeting together for a purpose.[66] (There is some irony in the encouragement of the notion that some are holier than others, in view of the round attacks made by reformers since Wyclif on the religious orders for pretending to higher holiness.) These groups can be seen as an example of a phenomenon to be encountered elsewhere: 'the local Church at its most concentrated form' (in Methodism at the level of the class meeting).[67] These phenomena in Methodism had direct precursors in the devotional religious societies which were developing by the end of the seventeenth century, spread from London to the provinces, and survived into the 1730s as recruiting-grounds for the Revival.[68]

The common theme is of 'cells of fellowship at the local level', seen

> as essential for the effective life of the individual Christian and Christian congregations. Benjamin Gregory and J. H. Rigg do not unchurch bodies that lack such structures . . . but they do argue that institutions analogous to the class meetings are of the *bene esse* of the Church (though they do not use that particular expression).[69]

> It is to the same institution that the brotherly feeling which makes the Methodist people one people the world over, is owing.[70]

It is possible to find examples of similar patterns in other kinds of 'voluntary religious societies'.[71] The 'House Church' movement of recent times is perhaps a little different in its underlying ecclesiological conception. Voluntary Societies are unofficial. 'Groups of like-minded people associate with one another, but they alone are responsible for their joint action. No one delegated power to them. They took it upon themselves.'[72] Such *ecclesiolae* are *in ecclesia*. They do not as a rule develop into new sects or new churches.[73] The object of religious societies is to be leaven *in* the lump.

We do not need to labour the point, which is apparent from all this, that participation in the reception process cannot be seen as an equal 'mucking-in' of all concerned. It is an infinitely complex affair of tugs and checks and balances; leading and following; resistance as well as consent. There is a 'necessary interconnectedness of the Church', which makes itself felt in the process whether or not it has explicit recognition as a phenomenon in the thinking of a given time.[74]

IV
NARRATIVE

CHAPTER ELEVEN

IDEAS IN THEIR CONTEXT: HISTORIES OF RECEPTION

Reception has to go on and on. New generations are born and the mind of every Christian has to be 'formed', and join the others in believing. This creates two kinds of need.

The first is for a sense of the continuity of the faith, so that new Christians join a community which is recognizably the same as that which Jesus founded. That 'recognizably' is the nub of the matter, for 'recognition' is itself part of reception. It goes with consciousness of tradition, the need for the keeping of records, a 'history' of faith.

The second need is for a means of picking up the story again where there has been a breakdown in continuity, when in other words, division has created a situation where the new Christian becomes a 'Baptist', a 'Methodist', an 'Anglican'. Here, too, there is a historical or rather a historiographical task. David Thompson speaks in this connection of 'the need for critical examination of self-justifying explanations for particular events'. He is pointing to the tendency for separated communities to create and sustain an account of how they became separated, in which the history is unavoidably portrayed so as to show that it was right and necessary that the division should happen. Yet, he stresses, 'the claim that something happened demands interpretation'.[1] And the interpretation of other communities will be different, less inclined to accept the justification in the same terms. The telling of a story is a sophisticated business when it carries on its back theological and ecclesiological implications.

Reception is a process, and therefore it takes place over time. This is conspicuous in the fact that the problems requiring 'official' solutions are not the same in every age. The Nicene Creed was framed to settle a number of earlier disputes and debates then in progress, and almost all its clauses reflect that fact. For example 'maker of all things both seen and unseen' is directed against the Gnostic dualists who had been arguing that there was a second power in the universe who created matter. The extended creed of the Fourth Lateran Council shows the same signs of the influence of controversies then current as does the Nicene and its successors, but the controversies are now different. Here one preoccupation is with the contemporary dualism of the Albigensians in the south of France and northern Spain. So, in much more detail than the Nicene formula 'maker of all things both seen and unseen', Lateran IV has:

> creator of all things ... spiritual and corporeal, who by his almighty power at the beginning of time created from nothing both spiritual and corporeal creatures, that is to say, angelic and earthly, and then created human beings composed as it were of both spirit and body in common. The devil and other demons were created by God naturally good, but they became evil by their own doing.[2]

There is also a concern at Lateran IV with the debates which had been running since the second half of the eleventh century about transubstantiation and the eucharistic role of the priesthood:

> There is indeed one universal church of the faithful, outside which nobody at all is saved, in which Jesus Christ is both priest and sacrifice.... Nobody can effect this sacrament except a priest who has been properly ordained according to the church's keys which Jesus Christ himself gave to the apostles and their successors.[3]

There is a comment on the penitential system, again something much in the twelfth-century news. 'If someone falls into sin after baptism he or she can always be restored through true penitence.'

The changing anxieties of the second Council of Lyons (1274) reflect the attempt to mend fences with the Greeks, estranged from the Western Church since 1054, partly on differences over the Procession of the Holy Spirit and partly on the issue of the Primacy of the Patriarch of the West in Rome over the Eastern Patriarchs:

> We profess faithfully and devotedly that the Holy Spirit proceeds eternally from the Father and the Son, not as from two principles, but as from one principle.... This is the holy Roman Church, mother and mistress (*magistra*) of all the faithful; this is the unchangeable and true belief of the orthodox fathers and doctors, Latin and Greek alike.[4]

The essence of formulations like these is that they seek to spell out what did not need to be spelt out before, because no one had asked the particular questions which now needed to be answered for the reassurance of the faithful.

From the vantage-point of a much later age, one Lutheran church sees clearly the partially linear character of this process.

> In explaining the Holy Scripture [we keep] to the Apostolic, Nicene and Athanasian Creeds, the unchanged Augsburg Confession, the Catechisms of Martin Luther and other writings gathered in the Book of Concord, as they came into being in the flow of the history of Christianity.[5]

But although such shifts of emphasis and concern are obvious now, when we can easily turn to collections of documents and see them at once, the fundamental understanding that there would be changing concerns was slow to come. The writing of Christian history had for many centuries gone on the assumptions that there was simply a providential unfolding of God's plan for the world. That is the foundation-principle of Augustine's *City of God* in the fourth century as much as it is of Joachim of Fiore's prophecies in the late twelfth century. No one had been looking at the vicissitudes in search of changing emphases. It was not until the nineteenth century that 'ecclesiastical history' began to develop seriously as an academic discipline with chairs in the subject at universities. Even then, the discipline largely failed to work systematically on the history of Christian thought and kept more to the story of the development of institutions.

There have been, nevertheless, spokesmen for the need to look at theology historically. John Henry Newman came to see the need to frame what was in effect a new discipline of the history of theology. The theme keeps cropping up in the discussions of the circle of Newman and his friends, and gradually Newman in particular began to formulate his ideas about it, as his own perspectives shifted with his reading. He wanted it to have rules and subject-matter which would make it a practical working instrument, and a flexibility which would allow for insights about the interconnectedness and coherence of a living body of knowledge sustained in a vital community.

For our present purposes perhaps the most important realization of all by Newman and his friends in this area of the framing of the 'new discipline' was that the past teaches about the present, that conscious continuity in the faith requires the study of earlier events and thinking as something interacting with present trends. Froude wrote to Newman on 31 July 1835, 'I forget whether I told you how much my father was taken with the historical part of your "Arians", and particularly its bearing on the present times.'[6] That would not be striking if it meant only the recognition that the present stands on the shoulders of the past. But the way in which the point is here put acknowledges that, for those who live in any given present, that present has powerful claims.

Respect for the present in its own right was a relatively new departure of the nineteenth century and it set up new tensions of continuity and change. In short, there is precedent in every age for looking back to what earlier, and especially the earliest, Christian authorities have said as a reference-point for what has been argued since. (Vincent of Lérins, who died before 450, was already able to state the principle that the test of truth is whether all in all ages everywhere teach the same faith, the *semper, ubique et ab omnibus* which was to alter the course of Newman's life when he perceived its implications). But Froude was stressing that the needs of the present are themselves a reference-point against which the teaching of the past can be measured.

There was something new afoot here, in this recognition that the present will have its own insistences, that it is not merely the servant of the past. Newman and others made an attempt to look back over periods of division and controversy, when it would seem that there has not been concurrence, and when God's intention can be hard to perceive, with the purpose of finding these patterns of common faith and life.

Newman also discovered on his own account that one thing led to another in sometimes unexpected and disturbing ways in the complex interactive historiographical process. Newman wrote to Froude on 23 August 1835, 'The more I read of Athanasius, Theodoret, etc., the more I see.'[7] On this intellectual pilgrimage foreseen conclusions were overthrown and prejudices had to be revised. What Newman saw in the previous comment was 'that the ancients *did* make the Scriptures *the basis* of their belief, as he had not realised before'. Newman wrote to Rogers on 22 September 1839:

> RW., who has been passing through, directed my attention to Dr. Wiseman's article in the new 'Dublin'. I must confess it has given me a stomach-ache. You see the whole history of the Monophysites has been a sort of alterative. And now comes this dose at the end of it. It does certainly come upon one that we are not at the bottom of things. At this moment we have sprung a leak.[8]

A conversation with Newman is reported by H. W. Wilberforce, October 1839, on a walk in the New Forest. Two things have made him think: 'the position of St. Leo in the Monophysite controversy, and the principle *securus judicat orbis terrarum* in that of the Donatists'.

> He added that he felt fully confident that when he returned to his rooms, and was able fully and calmly to consider the whole matter, he should see his way completely out of the difficulty. But he said, 'I cannot conceal from myself that, for the first time since I began the study of theology, a vista has opened before me, to the end of which I do not see.'[9]

Newman and others were beginning to perceive the existence of the repeating patterns in theology which the study of the coherence of the history of ideas could reveal. Pusey observed that schism tends to go with disproportionate emphasis on one or a few points:

> I have made some observations . . . on the Inspiration of the Church; and, as if justifying Irenaeus, have said that there was nothing harsh in supposing that those who wilfully, etc., separated from the Church, excluded themselves from some of the benefits intended by God for us . . . and I have said proof might be brought from the partial manner in which Christianity has generally been embraced by separatist bodies.[10]

Newman wrote to the Revd S. Rickards, 30 July 1834, trying to take an overview in a similar way.

> Blessed is he who is not corrupted by his age . . . ! Even Hooker, I should think (I speak under correction), but gradually worked his way out of his Puritanic education, but he *did* do so. The spirit of Puritanism has been succeeded by the Methodistic. (Of course, I do not use the word reproachfully, but historically.) We, the while, children of the Holy Church, whencesoever brought into it, whether by early training or afterthought, have had one voice, that one voice which the Church has had from the beginning.[11]

In this discovery of pattern, things Newman had thought new or recent proved to be equally phenomena of the ancient Christian world, or of other centuries:

> Two things are very remarkable at Chalcedon – the great power of the Pope . . . and the marvellous interference of the civil power, as great almost as in our kings. Hence when Romanists accuse our Church of Erastianising, one can appeal to the Council, and when our own Erastians appeal to it, one can bring down on them a

counter-appeal to prove the Pope's power, as a *reductio ad absurdum*.[12]

There are seen to be 'generations or centuries of degeneracy or disorder, and times of revival . . . one region might be in the mid-day of religious fervour, and another in twilight or gloom'.[13]

Development

I want to concentrate next in this section on negative aspects of this historical process in reception, the ways in which it has gone wrong for a time, its failure to remain a concerted endeavour. This is the first step towards the consideration of 'revisionism' we must come to after this, the 'picking-up of the story' after division. The principle laid down in the earliest Christian centuries and crisply formulated by Vincent of Lérins was that the faith is always and everywhere the same for everyone. We have seen various stresses arising in contexts since then, and various ways in which the principle has been tested. It became obvious quite early that it could not always and everywhere by affirmed in the same words by everyone. Language changes, and the association of words with a given set of ideas shifts. Moreover, the topics on which *formulae* have been needed have become more numerous over time.

The most acceptable way of explaining this, and containing it within the existing 'deposit of faith', was to talk of unfolding or making explicit what had been at first merely implicit. But however it is handled, the enlargement and revision of the corpus of *formulae* must appear to place the earlier and briefer accounts in an inferior position. This seems to be what is happening, for example, in this Roman Catholic text: 'Yesterday, the theme of the church seemed to be confined to the power of the Pope . . . Today, it is extended to the episcopate, the religious, the laity and the whole body of the Church.'[14] So to speak of development can appear to make the faith at a later time somehow an advance on what went before. But that might suggest that a Christian of a later date had some sort of 'advantage' in the faith.

'Development' is a term adopted by Newman in an attempt to purify from the negative trappings of this debate the case which had to be made for some form of revision or enlargement over time in which 'the faith which is always the same' remains a constant. Concern to maintain this delicate balance of sameness and difference is everywhere in his exploration of the seven 'notes' or 'tests' of right development he identifies:

> if it retains one and the same type,
> the same principles,
> the same organisation;
> if its beginnings anticipate its subsequent phases,
> and its later phenomena protect and subserve its earlier;
> if it has a power of assimilation and revival,
> amid a vigorous action from first to last.

Overall there has undoubtedly been in the history of Christian thought a shift from a static to a dynamic model, taking place decisively perhaps as late as the period of these debates of the last century. For most of the Christian centuries the motif has been of a fixed quantity of faith essentially given once and for all; and the *desideratum* has been adherence to it. When it seemed that there had been a departure from it, talk was of the need for a return to the primitive faith. As a rule, reform has always been thought of in terms of a return to an ideal state of things obtaining in the primitive Church, which has somehow been lost.

Reciprocally, it has been argued that new is bad. 'Antiquity then was ever the test of truth; novelty of error,' comments Pusey.[15] In the Lollard debates Johannis Purvey says in his *Ecclesiae Regimen*, that the insistence of the Fourth Lateran Council that all persons of either sex must make confession once a year is an innovation 'and full of hypocrisy, pride and blasphemy'.[16] The same suspiciousness of addition or innovation recurs everywhere in Reformation and post-Reformation circles.[17] 'Innovation' is a judgemental term. It is characteristically deemed to be the work of 'others', and others who are in some sense enemies.

That is the tension which naturally and repeatedly arises. A useful example of an attempt to resolve it is to be found in Newman's own time in the framing of the Roman Catholic dogma of the Immaculate Conception (1854):

> All are aware with how much diligence this doctrine of the Immaculate Conception of the Mother of God has been handed down, proposed and defended by the most outstanding religious orders, by the more celebrated theological academies, and by very eminent doctors in the science of divinity. All know, likewise, how anxious the bishops have been to profess openly and publicly, even in ecclesiastical assemblies, that the Most Holy Mother of

God, the Virgin Mary, because of the merits of Christ our Lord, the Saviour of mankind, which were foreseen, was never subject to original sin . . .'[18]

The text goes on to cite the past comprehensively after this, with an emphasis that here is no case of innovation, but the mere formulation of something already accepted.

FALSE DEVELOPMENT

What I have been describing is a highly complex processing of the faith over time, which has taken place on the general theological presumption that the whole is somehow held secure in its ultimate working out by the action of the Holy Spirit. Is it possible that things can go wrong, even for a time, so that at a given point there are actually errors in the faith as understood or formulated, errors which subsequently have to be rectified?

The antithesis between a 'wrong' or 'false'; and a 'right' development, is strong in the sixteenth-century Martin Chemnitz. He takes it for granted that that is the pattern, and his has been a common assumption in most ages when authors have addressed themselves adversarially to schismatics, heretics, dissidents, or those who have simply disagreed with their own position. There is a further idea which we must look at here, and one integral to the treatment of error as something which occurs over time, and that is that error may be a serial process. In his *Examen Concili Tridentini*, Chemnitz expresses his conviction that it is possible for the reception process to be sequentially skewed. A false sequence of development might be the result of simple human error, even perhaps non-culpable, though that has all the difficulties of the implication that the Holy Spirit could let the Church go astray. Martin Chemnitz prefers to see it as a result of deliberate falsification or conspiracy (as 'fabricated').[19] 'This is the real reason why they contend about the sacrament of penance, that they may make reconciliation and remission of sins dubious and uncertain.'[20]

Chemnitz allows that it will not always be possible to trace the sequence of a (true or false) development in the reception process. He thinks it desirable that the result be tested directly against an ultimate standard, which he would identify as simply that of Scripture. 'In my booklet against the Jesuits I had noted down certain very inappropriate sayings of Justin, Clement and Epiphanius on this question which most manifestly conflict with the Scripture . . .'[21]

Nevertheless, Chemnitz is keen to try to explore sequences of reception. His usual pattern is to go chronologically through the evidence. He thus takes it that there is indeed a *serial* process by which things, once they have begun to go wrong, will progressively get worse. For example, he places at the beginning of one 'false trail' Peter Lombard, twelfth-century author of the *Sentences* which became the standard theological textbook throughout the Middle Ages: 'Now because Lombard had first of all made a sacrament of repentance, the scholastics afterward began to inquire what is the material and what the form from which repentance could have the nature of a sacrament and could support the definition.'[22] This was, Chemnitz contends, demonstrably an innovation for the reason that nothing coming earlier in time gave warrant for it.

So he can argue that the scholars who came after that had no secure anchorage for their attempts at explication; and they disagreed with one another because there were no common points of reference which were equally authoritative or compelling for all:

> Therefore also, as in a new thing, since no statements were found with the Fathers, the scholastics debated in various ways what in penance might be such a material which would become a sacrament when the Word came to it. In order to retain the peculiar nature of a material, some taught that the sins themselves are the material of this sacrament. Others said that the sinner himself, confessing, is the material.[23]

Chemnitz thought that, once begun on, a trail like this could lead further and further into error. 'Afterward a transformation was made, and they changed the element or material from the quality of a substance into the quality of an action and argued that the actions of penance could be the material of this sacrament.'[24] The doctrinal position thus established can then be consolidated, as Chemnitz holds to have happened in the work of the Council of Trent:

> This is the teaching of the scholastics, for the strengthening of which this decree was made, which will be more correctly understood from this comparison of the scholastic doctrine, namely, that we should be taught that pardon for sins and reconciliation with God are obtained in repentance on account of our love, not by faith on account of the merit of Christ.[25]

A problem presents itself about the reception of such questioned sequences. We must ask how a development will appear to commentators who may be suspicious of the results. Chemnitz was very suspicious. 'The men of Trent', that is, the Fathers of the

Council of Trent, 'say that the universal consensus of the Fathers and of the Catholic Church from the beginning understood the kind of sacrament of penance such as they themselves teach'. But he would contend this is not true. He can identify among their arguments some 'unknown to all of antiquity'.[26] But he thinks he *can* follow the process by which a false tendency has indeed led by a traceable sequence to the present Roman Catholic formulation of doctrine. 'Indeed, it is useful to observe in the history of antiquity from what beginnings, once the tendency has been started, little by little things finally progressed to the papalist arguments and opinions about the sacrament of penance.... Little by little ... superstitious opinions began to be patched on, to the effect that these ceremonies merited and produced forgiveness.'[27]

So when a negative reception, or rejection, takes place in the minds of part of the Christian community (here the Lutheran), after the fact of a positive reception by another (the Roman Catholic), evidences which persuaded the first group in one direction are disallowed by the other. There then arises the need for re-reception (to which we shall come in a moment).

The 'true or false development' model, with its built-in sequencing, has proved unsatisfactory. It is obvious that we are dealing with a far more complex process, in which the same contributors can be cast in different roles and opposing constructions be put upon the same events by the parties involved in them.

In the early Church the *consensus fidelium* was sharpened and clarified by challenges, some of which were eventually declared unorthodox when the Church had discussed them. Sometimes it discussed them for a long time. (Naturally we tend to hear more about the persistent cases. 'Heresy' is by definition a matter of persistence in error.) Arius (c. 250–c. 336), a priest of Alexandria, began to popularize the view that Christ was in some way a subordinate in the Trinity, being created by the Father and not coequal and coaeval with him. The thing quickly escalated to confrontation, with a synod held at Alexandria excommunicating him. He was not silenced, and that meant that it was eventually deemed necessary to convene a general council to settle the matter. This council, at Nicaea in 325, framed the Nicene Creed, which has been almost universally in use ever since. Here a challenge was more or less contained, although something like Arianism recurs spontaneously in every generation.

If the challenge continues, two things happen. One is polarization and the forming of camps, with accompanying acrimony: 'Contention has taken the place of love; suspicion, of trust; outcry against man, of prayer to God . . . the very desire to love one another, seems well nigh gone amid this ceaseless strife.'[28] The other is that issues and aspects not perceived at the outset come into view. Now it could be argued that it is better to know about these than not, for they are likely to be perceived eventually in any case. But on the negative side, there can be a sense that things are deteriorating. At the end of the twelfth century Alan of Lille in his book *Against the heretics* describes in the strongest language the way things have got worse and worse. There used to be different heresies which arose at different times, he says, which were condemned by the Church. But in his own time these have all fused together into one 'general heresy' at the hands of heretics who are at the same time old and new. This sense that a single issue has become a sea of troubles is the other face of the 'multiplication of detailed concerns'.[29]

Separated reception: the processes of being drawn into controversy

A controversy between two Englishmen, William Cole and John Jewel (1522–71), Bishop of Salisbury, illustrates graphically the kinds of force which were at work in creating and maintaining for many generations two contradictory pictures of the same events at the Council of Trent. Dr Cole made what seems to have been a frank offer to conduct a discussion open-mindedly with Jewel 'upon occasion of a sermon that the said bishop preached before the Queen's majesty and her most honourable Council, 1560'. He was discomfited to get back a harsh piece of polemic which made it plain that Jewel regarded him as an enemy. Cole wrote a second letter, by way of an explanation of what he had intended by his first.

> I heard by report of many that . . . ye openly wished that one man thinking otherwise than you do would charitably talk with you, whom you would with like charity answer, and endeavour to satisfy . . . with which cause I was moved to write as I did, intending, if I might, to learn of you that I knew not, and that could by learning persuade a man not wholly unlearned to yield thereunto. . . . But I find not this meaning in your writing sent to me.[30]

Cole thought he had been invited to respond to an offer on terms he understood. He found the terms were otherwise. This is a common pattern in controversy because the adversarial stance is by definition hostile to rapprochement and concerned with gaining submission and compliance.

When he discovered his mistake, Cole was anxious that no further harm should come of the affair:

> I pray you that of all this encounter there grow no further breach of amity or harm other ways. . . . I am not nor will be against any article that learning or reason can shew I ought to believe, being ready without malice to hear and take what may be alleged to drive me that ye teach; and desiring you herewithal to construe my sayings by the intent I had in them.[31]

But for Jewel it continued to be a matter of conducting a war against an enemy. So although Cole seems to have glimpsed the possibility of discussion tending towards the framing of a common view, it appears that Jewel did not. He speaks outright of 'our Adversaries'.[32]

The tendency to give contrasting or contradictory accounts of theological positions taken in the past is to be found widely in the Reformation and post-Reformation West, and it is accompanied by many forms of both disingenuousness and self-deception of the sorts exemplified by the Cole and Jewel letters. To give one more example, Pusey's Sermon on the Eucharist, 'A comfort to the Penitent', was preached in Christ Church Cathedral, Oxford, in 1843,[33] as the first of a series of University Sermons. It puts forward a strong 'real presence' line on the question of what happens to the bread and wine of the Eucharist after consecration. In a preface he remarks:

> It is with pain that the following sermon is published. For it is impossible for any one not to foresee one portion of its effects; what floods, namely, of blasphemy against holy truth will be poured forth by the infidel or heretical or secular or anti-religious papers with which our Church and country is at this time afflicted. It is like casting with one's own hands that which is most sacred to be outraged and profaned. Still there seem to be higher duties, which require even this.

This flood he sees to be now let loose not by, but in spite of, his own words. 'Nothing, throughout the whole Sermon, was further from my thoughts than controversy.'

This is an especially difficult area of reception to get a grip on. There is a wealth of polemical theological literature in which the two sides take a frankly adversarial stance. But a good deal of that must represent the failure of mutual reception and the arrival of exasperation, where one party cannot get the other to listen. In 1865

Pusey wrote an attack on 'extravagances' current among Roman Catholics, which he saw as barriers to reunion. He calls the book *Eirenicon*.[34] It is one of the central paradoxes of theological controversy that war can inadvertently be made in the name of peace. It is not of course quite so simple as that in the case of this book of Pusey's, and as in the Cole and Jewel example, it is the complexity of motivation and action which makes it a useful illustration for our purposes.

How should the would-be peacemaker respond to the provocation to controversy? One can seek to stay outside it, as Cole had tried to do, and as Newman attempted at first in the *Eirenicon* affair. Newman wrote to Pusey, on 5 September 1865,

> For myself, I don't think I have written anything controversial for the last 14 years. Nor have I ever, as I think, replied to any controversial notice of what I have written. Certainly, I let pass without a word the various volumes that were written in answer to my Essay on Doctrinal Development, and that on the principle that Truth defends itself, and falsehood refutes itself, and that, having said my say, time would decide for me, without my trouble, how far it was true, and how far not true.

He wants to avoid having to reply to the *Eirenicon*: 'I can't conceive I could feel it in any sense an imperative duty to remark on anything you said in your book.' He goes so far as to try to enter into the debate on the combatants' side, so as to underline his own unprejudiced position. 'I daresay there is a great deal on which I should agree. Certainly I so dislike Ward's way of going on, that I can't get myself to read the *Dublin*.'[35]

Newman tried at this early stage to establish a stance perhaps especially Anglican, that diversity of opinion is perfectly acceptable within the limits of orthodoxy, and that there must be no intrusion on others' right to hold their own different views. 'But while I would maintain my own theological opinions, I don't dispute Ward the right of holding his, so that he does not attempt to impose them on me.' He would, however, disapprove 'did authority attempt to put them down while they do not infringe on the great catholic verities'.[36]

But he was not able to keep to this. What he felt to be at stake when he had read Pusey's book was not mere diversity of view but actual misrepresentation, and the use of argument to persuade falsely. On 32 October 1865, he wrote to Pusey: 'It is true, too true, that your book disappointed me. It does seem to me that "Eirenicon" is a misnomer; and that it is calculated to make most Catholics very angry. And that because they will consider it rhetorical and unfair.'[37]

One of the ways in which it is unjust is that it juxtaposes as though they were all equally evidences an assortment of authorities Newman judges to be incompatible. It was a conscious wish of Newman's at this time to see all authorities harmonize, as indeed Pusey himself thought.

> I will quote the language not of one, two, or three, not from one age or one school, but the uniform teaching of the Fathers of every Church and of every variety of mind; in every sort of writing.[38]

> Discordant voices . . . cannot be the one voice of truth.[39]

> This body of faith ['the deposit'] is spoken of by different names, from the very earliest times, as a recognized whole. . . . It is called 'the Faith of the Church', 'the preaching of the Church', 'the truth of the Churches', 'ecclesiastical teaching' . . .[40]

But here he cannot accept that a common case is made by the authorities Pusey judges to be at one. 'How is it fair to throw together Suarez, St. Bernardine, Eadmer and Faber?'[41]

This tendency to see coherence where it does not exist extends in Newman's view to portrayal of the position of a few people as that of the Roman Catholic Church, moreover of a position they themselves did not consistently hold. The opinions Pusey criticizes are 'the opinions of a *set* of people, and not even of them permanently'.[42]

So Newman's entry into the controversy was on grounds of misuse of evidence. Whether that was intentional or not was irrelevant to the need to set the records straight.

In the end Newman did decide to publish a reply to Pusey. He wrote to him to warn him, and to try to lay down ground-rules which would exonerate him from any suggestion of malpractice in controversy on his own part:

> You must not be made anxious that I am going to publish a letter on your 'Eirenicon'. I wish to accept it as such, and shall write in that spirit. And I write, if not to hinder, for that is not in my power, but to balance and neutralize other things which may be written upon it. It will not be any great length. If I shall say anything which is in the way of remonstrance, it will be because, unless I were perfectly honest, I should not only do no good, but carry no one with me, but I am taking the greatest possible pains not to say a word which I shall be sorry for afterwards.[43]

This was not mere caution about putting himself in the wrong. Newman understood that.[44]

The winning of minds is not achieved by confrontation, and he was treading a tightrope between showing Pusey where he was wrong and winning his goodwill towards Newman's case. Thus was Newman drawn, as Cole had been, into a battle he had not wanted to be adversarial.

If that is the kind of thing that can happen at the personal level, despite mutual goodwill, the problems at the level of communities are clearly exponentially greater. Separated reception occurs when communities divide and as a result stop thinking with universal intention, although they may deem themselves to be the whole remaining true Church, and deem themselves to preserve the principle of universal intention in that way. Their concern then typically becomes to maintain their own faith.[45]

Then a long historical process can ensue, when for many centuries the communities which have become separated struggle to come to sufficiently common terms to make it possible for them to proceed with reception together. There may be retelling of a common past so as to disown it.

This perception of deliberate collective misrepresentation on the part of the other side has proved poisonous. But even in a gentler mood resentment of one group by another can be hard to shift. On 25 March 1661 in England, a commission was appointed to meet at the Savoy.[46] Its object was to find means by which the 'Presbyterian' could be reconciled with the 'episcopal' polity. This had been an issue throughout the Reformation period in the British Isles and it threatened division still. The hope in which the commission met was that both sides had maintained a common faith. A committee appointed by House of Lords in 1641 on innovations in doctrine had expressed this aspiration:

> In an humble conformity to this your Majesty's Christian design, we, taking it for granted that there is a firm agreement between our brethren and us in the doctrinal truths of the reformed religion, and in the substantial parts of divine worship, and that the differences are only in some various conceptions about the ancient form of church-government, and some particulars about liturgy and ceremonies . . .[47]

In the debates the Presbyterians were to say what they objected to. The Puritan Richard Baxter, who certainly wanted peace, found the bishops disappointing in their leadership.

The bishops were not strong enough to employ the language of authority ... they gave their answers, not as if the matter were under joint discussion, but as if each question were submitted to them for their decision; alleging as their reason, that according to the terms of the warrant, no alterations could be adopted, unless they were shown to be necessary, and were approved by both parties.[48]

The result was a change of mood, a resentment in Baxter, which set up new barriers. 'The rejoinder ... composed by Baxter ... seems to have been intended ... to leave on record a sense of injury and an expression of indignation, which ... were lamentably out of place in an attempt to bring two parties of opposite sentiments to a mutual understanding.'[49] There was a rescue-attempt to achieve equality of treatment and mutual respect. 'The nonconformists entreated that before their powers expired, an attempt might be made to hold a personal conference, and to conduct a disputation on terms acceptable to both parties' (with three from each side, which was done).[50] But there was now too much bad feeling.

At length Bishop Cosin produced a paper, *as from a considerable person*, which greatly narrowed the field of controversy, and might possibly at an earlier period have opened a way for some permanent arrangement. It was proposed that the complainers should distinguish between what they charged as sinful, and what they opposed as inexpedient. But the issue was now inevitable.[51]

'And so,' says Bishop Kennet, 'ended this conference without union or accommodation.'[52] Thus and thus the growth of misunderstanding.

CHAPTER TWELVE

COMING OUT OF CONTROVERSY

Toleration

Toleration sits uneasily with reception, because it allows the other to continue in his or her opinion without real acceptance of the view tolerated, without moving position, without seriously considering whether it may not be possible that the two views are one. That approach is exemplified here:

> In the mean time, out of compassion and compliance towards those who would forbear the cross in baptism, we are content that no man shall be compelled to use the same, or suffer for not doing it; but if any parent desire to have his child christened according to the form used, and the minister will not use the sign, it shall be lawful for that parent to procure another minister to do it; and if the proper minister shall refuse to omit that ceremony of the cross, it shall be lawful for the parent, who would not have his child so baptised, to procure another minister to do it, who will do it according to his desire.
>
> No man shall be compelled to bow at the name of Jesus, or suffer in any degree for not doing it, without reproaching those who out of their devotion continue that ancient ceremony of the Church.[1]

Pusey thought reunion with Rome might be achieved on equal terms. At this date, that seemed to Newman Utopian. 'Yet he believed that a better understanding might be promoted and some approximation won by the attempt on either side to do justice to the other.'[2] This is clearly a stage further than mere toleration:

> We all desire to know and to teach *the* Faith; we all believe that we have it; I do trust that, if we could understand one another, we might meet in one truth. But this cannot be the sound and healthy and normal state of a Church, which we have been wont thankfully to call pure and Apostolic, that we should be

contradicting one another: this is not like the time of Apostles, when all were of one heart and one mind. . . . Why, instead of this endless strife, casting out one another, will we not seek one another, be at pains to understand one another, harmonize what all believe truly, not by abandoning any truth, but by affirming together all which is the truth.[3]

The hypothesis of uneven development

Can we take it that if a sequence can go wrong it can be got right? Holding what not all Christians can hold, and holding it in a divided-off group, is intrinsically separative, and cannot therefore meet the 'Vincent of Lérins' criteria to which what is 'common' is central. 'Separated' reception results, and that can maintain division and hostility. But it is also possible for it to result in the particular insights or emphases of a given community being able to develop within it in a special way. Notions that have thus been growing in the comparative isolation of separated communities, can now perhaps be brought back together again.

But reception can take place unevenly in different communities, might that imply that some are more 'advanced' than others and must 'lead' them into the truth? Or does the 'unevenness' take the form of special angles of view, so that each comes to have a developed understanding of part of a greater whole which is the totality of the faith? In the late twentieth-century climate the first possibility, which would have seemed self-evident in, for example, missionary contexts in the nineteenth century, is unacceptable because we place stress on mutual respect of equals. The unevenness is now more readily regarded as a legitimate diversity. It reflects the diversity of the gifts of the Spirit, and therefore must be regarded as a richness.

The drawback to any other model than that of equality is that the result of condemnation of dissent by one community of the views of another has been largely negative. This is neither a helpful nor a truthful model if we are to go forward into a future united Church. If there is to be acceptance of the value of diversity we have to postulate something different, a complementarity. That is to argue that some communities or groups or even individuals have historically had one insight, some another. There is hope that they will all fit together ultimately in reception (though not necessarily without further modification), at the level where reception is truly the activity of the whole Church. There is a web or network of ideas as well as of minds at work in the reception process. This was something Newman came to see clearly. 'Every part of the Truth . . . seen detached from the whole, becomes an objection,' he points out.⁴ On this view, the truth is a complex of interdependent elements in which the interdependence is as important as the individual elements themselves.

Revisionism

'Revisionism' has not had a good press. It can mean a 'retelling' of past events designed to deny that something happened, which new interests now would not want to admit took place. An example of such clear going against the facts is the attempt to deny that the Nazi holocaust ever happened. But that does not mean that there is not a 'good' revisionism. That would be a 'rewriting' more accurately of what had originally been a false picture. It requires both the 'infinitely patient collective reflection' we have already mentioned, and openness to seeing where the story has been wrongly told before.

In a letter of Newman's, written in 1826, he begins by suggesting that it might be put to the test whether the Anglican divines from the sixteenth century onwards, if read so as to eliminate the adversariality of the polemic in which many of them had been engaged, had amongst them set out an account of their beliefs which formed a coherent and harmonious whole.

> My dear Rickards, In our last conversation I think you asked me whether any use had occurred to my mind to which your knowledge of our old divines might be applied. Now one has struck me, so I write. Yet very probably the idea is so obvious that it will not be new to you, and . . . I begin by assuming that the old worthies of our Church are neither Orthodox nor Evangelical . . . now it would be a most useful thing to give a kind of summary of their opinions. . . . If, then, in a calm, candid, impartial manner, their views were sought out and developed, would not the effect be good in a variety of ways?⁵

Here he began to feel his way towards a principle perhaps fully explicated only in our own day, when (within certain limits) diversity tends to be seen as a theological good. He perceives that variety can be complementary, that theology forms a system on the model of a jigsaw puzzle, where pieces of many different shapes make one picture, as well as on the model of a catalogue which is to include all truths which it is necessary to salvation to believe.

> I would advise taking them *as a whole* . . . stating, indeed, *how far* they differ among themselves, yet distinctly marking out the

grand, bold, scriptural features of that doctrine in which they all agree. They would then be a band of witnesses for the truth, not opposed to each other (as they now are), but one – each tending to the edification of the body of Christ, according to the effectual working of His Spirit in everyone, according to the diversity of their gifts, and the variety of the circumstances under which each spake his testimony. [Newman's emphasis.]

Rickards replied less enthusiastically. 'I do not quite agree with you in thinking that much can be done in these times of ours, through the weight of old authorities.'[6] Newman proved to be right in general, that the result of studying earlier Christian authors in their contexts would be to show that they are a band of witnesses to the same truth. He was also right that readers would be captured by the exercise because it would show them the earlier Church (and the Church in other places), as a living community.

So one significant area where 'revisionism' is clearly needed concerns 'the nature and impact of the Reformation's confessional divisions'.[7] Felicity Heal suggests that the 'Protestant thesis', with its stress on the acculturation of popular reforming to state action, provided a promising focus for argument and research. 'Its hint of confessional determinism was seldom explicitly discussed,' she notes. The present 'revisionist' line is broadly that 'the English people did not expect a Reformation, that most of them resented its coming, and that it impoverished them spiritually, ritually and materially'.[8] It is striking that the same evidences which previously pointed one way can now been made to lead in the other direction. Wills and accounts of churchwardens 'that had previously been used to emphasize the impact of reform' are now read so as to show (for wills) 'a continuing commitment to the cults of catholicism' and (for accounts) 'compliance with the central government, but a strong desire to protect parish traditions and worship'.

The Orthodox are the most prominent example of an ecclesial community, or group of communities, which would tend to deny the possibility of development on the grounds that the decisions of the early Ecumenical Councils stand for all time, with tradition fixed and completed. Their fear is quite straightforwardly that development may mean change. But that resolution is tested overtime by what can only be seen as 'the torrent of the day',[9] when events make it necessary to say something about a new situation. But the Orthodox, like every Christian community, have been brought up against events which have made it necessary to review the underlying principles of that assumption, and to be open to 'revision' of their historical assumptions. *The Confession of Dositheus* (1672) was produced by a synod convened in Jerusalem in 1672 to deal with the problems posed by the 'protestantizing' influence of Cyril Lucaris, elected Patriarch of Alexandria in 1602 and of Constantinople in 1621. Rapprochement with Protestants was actively sought from the Protestant side in every century after the sixteenth; the common bond was dislike of Rome. Sometimes real goodwill was achieved between Orthodox and Protestants by this unlikely (and today ecumenically undesirable) route. But his *Confession of Dositheus* attempts to define Orthodoxy over against Protestantism. It does so by stressing the imperative of faithfulness to tradition and denying even the possibility of development.

> We believe to be members of the Catholic Church all the Faithful, and only the Faithful who, forsooth, having received the blameless Faith of the Saviour Christ, from Christ Himself, and the Apostles, and the Holy Oecumenical Synods, adhere to the same without wavering; although some of them may be guilty of all manner of sins.[10]

This approach of defending a faith which must be the same in every age not only in its content but also in its formulation, could not work in the same way over the lifting on 7 December 1965 of the mutual anathemas of 1054 which formally separated the Roman Catholic and Orthodox communions. Here something had to give. It was essential to admit that something had gone wrong and had to be put right.

> We come together . . . to make a common study of a particular subject – those events of the year 1054 which took place between the sees of Rome and Constantinople. . . . We are to explore together some ways of rectifying from either side what can be rectified, with the aim of removing an obstacle to the further development of brotherly relations and the dialogue between our Churches.[11]

Among the obstacles along the way, as these brotherly relationships of trust and esteem are developed, there looms the memory of the decisions, actions and painful incidents which came to a head in 1054 in the sentence of excommunication passed on the patriarch Michael Cerularios and two other persons by the legates of the Roman See, led by Cardinal Humbert, which legates were then themselves the object of corresponding sentence on the part of the Patriarch and the Synod of Constantinople. . . . Nothing can be done to change the fact that these events were what they were in that particularly disturbed period of history. But now that a calmer and fairer judgement has been made about them, it is important to recognise the excesses by which they were marked, and which brought in their train consequences which, as far as we can judge, went beyond what was intended or foreseen by those responsible. Their censures bore on particular persons and not on the Churches, and were not meant to break the ecclesial communion between the sees of Rome and Constantinople.[12]

Accordingly, the lifting of anathemas which was achieved as a result of these efforts accepts that mistakes have been made and that rectification can be necessary. But that can be argued to be no concession to a doctrine of development. For rectification is not development. Nevertheless, it is an acknowledgement that the tradition may have been for a time imperfectly preserved or transmitted. That is certainly something it has been possible for the Orthodox to say in dialogue with Old Catholics:

> Journeying through history, the Church of Christ has become divided into many churches which disagreed with each other because the faith and doctrines handed down from the Apostles were debased. . . . This led among other things to the false and unacceptable theory that the true visible Church . . . no longer exists today, but that each of the individual Churches retains only a portion, greater or less, of the true Church and that none of them, therefore, can be regarded as a genuine and essentially complete representation of the true Church.[13]

This fits in well with the notion of a Church *in via*. The picture of a pilgrim community in which perfection and consummation are yet to be realized is scriptural. But it is also in tension with talk of fixed tradition and resistance to development. 'At the Council [Vatican II], the Church is looking for itself. It is trying, with great trust and a great effort, to define itself more precisely and to understand what it is.'[14]

There is another option, but one found only in comparatively recent Christian centuries. One community of twentieth-century Baptists have been able to say of their own articles: 'We do not regard them as complete statements of our faith, having any quality of finality or infallibility. As in the past so in the future Baptists should hold themselves free to revise their statements of faith as may seem to them wise and expedient at any time.'[15] This seems to reverse the principle with which we began, that the faith is always and everywhere the same, and with it many of the concomitant notions of completeness and permanence and universality. It takes development to be something which can take place piecemeal, both in the sense that one community or group of Christians may have it before or independently of another; and in the sense that it can be short-term, for a period only. This is not a line many communities would want to follow, but it comes usefully here as a reminder that revision of historical prejudices is not necessarily permanent or universally applicable.

Conclusion

Where accounts refer to the same events it must in principle be possible to tell a single story. But this telling of a single story cannot be achieved by minds at enmity (or even suspicious of one another), and therefore unable to listen sympathetically to one another's concerns. In such circumstances the past is always seen from a vantage-point over against that of others. It is only very recently indeed that any systematic consideration has been given to the need to repossess these events and reconcile the accounts. The rewriting of history could then be a less urgent need, if a given community did not feel bound by its past. The realization is very recent indeed that the history of theology is not ultimately an account of the triumph of one view over another, but of the infinitely patient collective reflection of the whole people of God upon the sometimes seemingly opposed views of spokesmen and parties, which must in the end – however long that takes – result in a *consensus fidelium* in one truth.

V
THE MODERN ECUMENICAL MODEL

CHAPTER THIRTEEN

WHAT IS 'ECUMENICAL RECEPTION'?

We the undersigned have voted against the report 'Toward Full Communion Between the Episcopal Church and the Evangelical Lutheran Church in America' and the proposed 'Concordat of Agreement....'

We, the undersigned ELCA members of the Lutheran-Episcopal Dialogue III, respect the right of our dissenting colleagues to interpret the report and the agreement for full communion as they choose. However, we cannot recognize their interpretation as correct.[1]

This is clearly not consensus. These assenting and dissenting reports appended to the end of the 'agreement' of the early 1990s arrived at in the USA between Lutherans and Episcopalians (Anglicans) fall short of that. Throughout the Assenting Report there are expressions of 'regret', but these can have a tone of reproof: 'We regret the fact that they no longer endorse the conclusion of the Lutheran Council in the USA report on "The Historic Episcopate", which both of them helped to formulate in 1984.'[2] So what we have in this example is a very incomplete reception, even within this document and by the people who wrote it. That is in fact a very rare occurrence in such 'agreed statements'. They are mostly unanimous. But I give it as an example because it underlines the fact that there are special difficulties in trying to 'receive' a formulation when churches are divided. For that is the present worldwide situation.

In the early Church 'ecumenical reception' would have meant the reception, by the whole community of Christendom, of a point of faith or order, which might or might not be in the shape of an actual doctrinal formula. It was essentially a shared, 'universal' activity of the local churches acting together; that is after all what 'ecumenical' primarily implies.

In the present situation of separation, where there is lingering pride in the differences between the divided churches,[3] and even sometimes a residual mutual mistrust, reception has to begin with a process undertaken by each ecclesial community for itself on the assumption that the primary task is to answer to the wishes of that separated community. It is, moreover, a community defining itself as a self-governing ecclesial entity, even, in some cases, as the only such entity about whose true ecclesiality its members can have no doubt.

As the authors of the agreement just quoted acknowledge, this is a complex business, which is likely to take time and have to find its own pathway

> of careful study and evaluation of the work and recommendations of . . . dialogue. . . . This will require some years for both churches and should not be done precipitously. They will need to consult with the Lutheran and Anglican communions internationally and with other ecumenical partners.[4]

If, when each community has enquired within itself, they all prove to agree, the point can perhaps be deemed in the future a belief of all Christians. But even if the same universality of consensus is the aim, the agreement is arrived at in different ways from that of the early Church.

The difference is important because the assumptions we are seeing are radically other than those of the early Church. It would then have been inconceivable that in matters of faith any community could be free to make a decision independently, and still call itself 'Church' if it opted to believe differently from other churches. Yet in a divided Christendom we are in a position where, at least for the moment, decisions can only be made independently. There is no other machinery.

So the fundamental problem of modern ecumenical reception is that it does not start from the presumption that there is only one faith in the one Church, although it looks to that as the goal. Even here, the ground is not quite level, for many would want to add 'only one faith in essentials' and press for diversity in some other respects. This is an important issue and one which I have tried to develop elsewhere. Perhaps it merely shows by its more conspicuous awkwardness the incompleteness of what seemed on the face of it a more unified process in the early Christian centuries. There was a higher degree of papering over cracks in the early process than was easily acknowledged. (For instance Western bishops were not always as fully represented as those from the East in early 'ecumenical councils'.) It may turn out when the picture is more complete that the visible shortcomings of modern 'ecumenical reception' at its present stage are not so far removed as they appear from those of that earlier process. But the obvious contrasts of principle are consciously-felt and therefore important.

We have to go back before we can go forward here, and look into the hinterland of this pattern of ecclesially independent decision-making.

Official statements of autonomy in separated churches

It is characteristic of the churches of the sixteenth-century Reformation and after in the West that they make central to their own traditions documents which have become 'official' especially for them. The primacy of Scripture is apparent, as we should expect. It is usual to distinguish between Scripture as foundation and these other texts as exposition. It is also common to mix what might be called 'universal' documents (such as Scripture and, in another way, the Nicene Creed), and documents particular to the tradition in question. Consistently there is an intention to persevere with the texts thus assembled, and to take them as a kind of 'canon' for the church which is listing them as its 'official' texts. Here are some examples where that is visibly happening:

> The Church of Ireland doth receive and approve the Book of the Articles of Religion, commonly called the Thirty-Nine Articles, received and approved by the archbishops and bishops and the rest of the clergy of Ireland in the synod holden in Dublin, A.D. 1634; also, *The Book of Common Prayer and Administration of the Sacraments, and other Rites and Ceremonies of the Church, according to the use of the Church of Ireland* . . . as approved and adopted by the synod holden in Dublin, A.D. 1662, and hitherto in use in this Church. And this Church will continue to use the same, subject to such alterations only as may be made therein from time to time by the lawful authority of the Church.[5]

> The Church of Denmark takes as its confessional basis the Apostles' Creed, the Niceno-Constantinopolitan Creed, the Athanasian Creed, the Augsburg Confession of 1530, Luther's Small Catechism.[6]

> The Evangelical-Lutheran Church of Finland confesses that Christian faith which, having its basis in the Holy Word of God,

the Prophetic and Apostolic books of the Old and New Testament, is articulated in the three main creeds of the ancient Church and in the unchanged Confession of Augsburg and the other confessional books of the Lutheran Church which are included in the Book of Concord, and holds as the highest law of the confession that unshakeable truth, clearly declared in these confessional books, that the Holy Word of God is the only rule by which all doctrine must be examined and judged in the Church.[7]

The Church of Norway has as its confessional basis by a law of 1687 the Apostles' Creed, the Niceno-Constantinopolitan Creed, the Athanasian Creed, the Augsburg Confession of 1530, Luther's Small Catechism.[8] The Declaration of the Foundation Documents of the Church of Sweden concerning Faith, Confession and Doctrine, 30 September 1992, says:

> The faith, confession and doctrine of the Church of Sweden which is manifested in its worship and life, is founded upon God's holy Word, as given in the prophetic and apostolic scriptures of the Old and New Testaments; is summarised in the Apostolic, Nicene and Athanasian creeds and in the original text of the Augsburg Confession of 1530; is affirmed and acknowledged in the Resolution of the Uppsala Assembly of 1593 and is explicated and elucidated in The Book of Concord and other documents approved by the Church of Sweden.[9]

> The Evangelical Lutheran Church of Lithuania, as a community organized of Christ and his Gospel, confesses as the only basis of her teaching and life the canonical books of the old and the New Testament, and in explaining the Holy Scripture keeps to the Apostolic, Nicene and Athanasian Creeds, the unchanged Augsburg Confession, the Catechisms of Martin Luther and other writings gathered in the Book of Concord, as they came into being in the flow of the history of Christianity.[10]

The family resemblances in this series of Lutheran lists are obvious, and they raise the question of the principles which lie behind the differences they also display. Here each church takes as official nearly but not quite the same list of texts as another. They are consciously Lutheran, but also consciously different from one another.

An 'official' declaration made by churches together in Germany in the frightening circumstances of 1934 expresses the paradoxes of the situation with some sharpness. It brought Lutheran and Reformed together in those conditions of crisis:

According to the introductory words of its constitution of 11 July 1933, the German Evangelical Church is a federal union of confessional churches which grew out of the Reformation, of equal rights and parallel existence. The theological premise of the association of these churches is given in article 1 and article 2, paragraph 1 of the constitution of the German Evangelical Church, recognized by the national government on 14 July, 1933:
Article 1. The impregnable foundation of the German Evangelical Church is the Gospel of Jesus Christ, as it is revealed in Holy Scripture and came again to the light in the creeds of the Reformation. In this way the authorities, which the church needs for her mission, are defined and limited.
Article 2, paragraph 1. The German Evangelical church consists of . . . territorial churches.

We, assembled representatives of Lutheran, Reformed and United churches, independent synods, Kirchentage and local church groups, hereby declare that we stand together on the foundation of the German Evangelical Church as a federal union of German confessional churches. We are held together by confession of the one Lord of the one, holy, universal and apostolic church.

We declare . . . that the unity of this confession . . . is severely threatened . . . the theological premise on which the German Evangelical Church is united is constantly and basically contradicted and rendered invalid . . . by means of strange propositions. If they obtain, the church – according to all the creeds which are authoritative among us – ceases to be the church.[11]

By contrast, two kinds of official statement made in division have been consciously provisional or partial. The first have stressed that what is decreed is 'just for now'; the other that it is 'just for us'. 'Just for us' may amount to the taking of an ecclesial position, as it does for Baptists, where the individual congregation is the supreme exemplification of the Church and can act for itself. 'Just for now' is a principle stressing openness to the Spirit. Both are in play in the following passage:

> Your committee recognize that they were appointed 'to consider the advisability of issuing another statement of the Baptist Faith and message, and to report at the next Convention'.[12]
>
> . . . your committee have decided to recommend the new Hampshire Confession of Faith,[13] revised at certain points, and

with some additional articles growing out of present needs, for approval by the Convention, in the event a statement of the Baptist faith and message is deemed necessary at this time.

The present occasion for a reaffirmation of Christian fundamentals is the prevalence of naturalism in the modern teaching and preaching of religion. ... We repudiate every theory of religion which denies the supernatural elements in our faith. ... Baptists approve and circulate confessions of faith with the following understanding, namely:

1. That they constitute a consensus of opinion of some Baptist body, large or small, for the general instruction and guidance of our own people and others concerning those articles of the Christian faith which are most surely held among us. They are not intended to add anything to the simple conditions of salvation revealed in the new Testament, viz., repentance towards God and faith in Jesus Christ as Saviour and Lord.

2. That we do not regard them as complete statements of our faith, having any quality of finality or infallibility. As in the past so in the future Baptists should hold themselves free to revise their statements of faith as may seem to them wise and expedient at any time.

3. That any group of Baptists, large or small, have the inherent right to draw up for themselves and publish to the world a confession of their faith whenever they may think it advisable to do so.[14]

This sort of thinking contrasts strikingly with the intention in some other communities that nothing shall be deemed official which is not in intention permanent and universal, at least for that community itself. But that proviso, at least for the community itself, that assumption that a separated community may make rules for itself, not only in the domestic details of its common life but also in matters of faith, is the problem.

Repair work

Two kinds of repair work or 're-reception' are necessary to achieve again today something like harmony with the 'by all', 'at all times' and 'in all places' which Vincent of Lérins in the early fifth century thought were the three basic tests of right reception. Those tests may need some nuancing today, especially in view of the claims of legitimate diversity and inculturation. But something like them

WHAT IS 'ECUMENICAL RECEPTION'?

must logically be required if it is to be possible to unite again in one faith.

The first repair needed is the rethinking by separated communities of attitudes to one another, and of their duty of ecclesiological respect for one another. This involves a kind of 'reception of one another', or 'mutual reception'. Only when that is achieved can Christians think in terms of making decisions as one body. The second is the rethinking of the acceptance sometimes found in separated communities, that the faith can be 'confessional' in the sense that it may legitimately differ from one community to another.

CHAPTER FOURTEEN

MUTUAL RECEPTION

The problem of entrenched positions

In climbing out of separate positions churches and ecclesial communities have recognized that it cannot be done all at once. They have tended to look to a series of 'stages'. One such list runs from 'ecumenical cooperation, through bilateral and multilateral dialogue, preliminary recognition (defined as 'eucharistic sharing and cooperation, without exchangeability of ministers') to full communion. In this list, full communion is seen as involving a common confession of faith, mutual recognition of baptism and a sharing in the Lord's Supper, mutual recognition and availability of ordained ministers, a common commitment to evangelism, witness and service, a means of common decision-making, a mutual lifting of any existing condemnation between the two churches.[1] Other dialogues have explored other series of steps, but all have in common the recognition that there are existing positions from which it will be possible to climb back to unity only with a good deal of patience and perseverance. In these circumstances, reception becomes fragmentary, jerky, episodic, laborious.

How did it come about that it is so difficult to bring churches together that we have to think in this way? Turid Karlsen Seim says 'for a Norwegian Lutheran of my generation to grow into ecumenical commitment is almost a conversion'. She grew up in a post-war Norwegian society of almost total homogeneity of 'devoted Lutheran confessionalism'; with a 'lack of awareness about the presence of other Christian communities in the country'.[2] Over the centuries this problem of a separation of thinking, of every world-view, growing out of a division which keeps Christians from knowing one another, became entrenched until the comparatively recent ecumenical experiences which have made rethinking possible.

It goes back a long way. Christianity began in the late Roman world. The relative homogeneity of the intellectual culture there was created and held in being by political forces which formed a single Empire. But at the collapse of that Empire in the fifth century into a 'Greek' East and a 'Latin' West a cultural division began. The language difference was increasingly separative from the sixth century, when few remained bilingual. By 1054 the two communities had self-images so distinct that it became possible for them to fall formally apart into schism. The immediate trigger was both theological and political. But behind this lay centuries of mutual alienation. It was that which began to carry with it differences of style and understanding.

At a later stage ecclesial life became further subdivided, especially in the West, into all the variformity of the Reformation. Again there was anger and hostility. This sixteenth-century phenomenon gave rise to confessionalism or 'denominationalism', which carried with it a mass of fine differences in the way the churches saw themselves, and in their 'ecclesial culture'.

The separated reception processes which take place as communities cease to communicate, enhance and encourage the incipient differences of style, approach and character which we now tend to think of in terms of 'culture'. These are naturally occurring (and not necessarily by any means undesirable) phenomena in ecclesial communities. They are a bad thing only when they take a community away from others and make it consider itself 'better' or even 'the only true Christian community'. There may come to be limited or no contact, as in the Seim experience cited above. Or there may be encounters, but encounters which result in a build-up of hostility and rejection. When that happens the checks and balances of comparison cannot continue to be made as time goes on. The result tends to be the emergence of a 'mindset' in each community, which subsequently colours the reception process for the community, and can keep it inward-looking. Seim comments:

> The battle was about the right interpretation of the confessional tradition and much less about the exclusiveness of this tradition itself. To some extent any debate was a competition for excellency in being fully and truly Lutheran. Such was the climate of my theological upbringing.[3]

Even where in today's ecumenical environment communities are striving hard to free themselves of such constraints of attitude and assumption, their effects linger. They are observable in the responses to the *Baptism, Eucharist and Ministry* text of the World Council of Churches (the 'Lima' text of 1982). These responses were collected by the World Council of Churches in the first systematic and extended exercise since the Second Vatican Council, in the twentieth-century sort of 'ecumenical reception'. The responses came in with great variation of tone. Many of the responding churches had to think in ways they had not been asked to think before. They found it difficult to do. Many of them realized for the first time that they lacked the structures for common decision-making even within their own communities, and certainly had no means of recognizing agreement with other churches formally or informally. Almost all found it hard to 'think as one Church' with other churches. They tended to cling to their own tradition as the touchstone they could trust.

There are determined adherences to broad standpoints in what they have to say for themselves. (In one response 'the Reformation emphasis' is described as 'essential'.)[4] There are straightforward references to denominational preferences: 'As Methodists we miss . . .'[5] or: 'The document aids Lutherans by reminding them of the nature of their tradition. In a Church Catholic, Lutherans want to say the Gospel. In a Church Evangelical they want to say a word catholic.'[6] There is insistence upon points traditionally of especial importance to a given community: 'More work is needed to make clear that ministry must not be built on a hierarchical model.'[7] There are even lingering expressions of resentments. 'We try to overcome the superior mentality of those churches which . . .'[8] These responses have not yet made for themselves Seim's discovery: 'What I had believed to be the full picture, was a fragment of a mirror long broken.'[9]

Perhaps two types of such fixity of 'mindset' in the attitude of one community to another tend to stand in the way of mutual recognition more forcefully than any other. The first is the 'churchmanship' or 'style of ecclesial community', which can create or reflect differences of 'ecclesial identity'. These make Christians in a given community identify themselves first and foremost as (for example) 'Baptist' or 'Orthodox' or 'Anglican', or even as 'Southern Baptists', 'Russian Orthodox', 'High Anglicans', rather than as Christians. The sense of a special identity can be strong. It can encourage a sense that one group of Christians is uniquely the Church, or define 'true Church' in a way which places a heavy emphasis on certain characteristics peculiar to a given community or communities. It may generate rejection of others as communities or Christian individuals, as in the condemnation by the seventeenth-century Calvinist Helvetic Consensus Formula: 'We can by no means approve the opinion of those . . .'[10] A separatism derived from such rejection was easily encouraged at the time the separation happened, and it remains so:

> We are agreed . . . on separation . . . from the evil and from the wickedness which the devil planted in the world; in this manner, simply that we shall not have fellowship with them [the wicked] and not run with them in the multitude of their abominations. . . . Since all who do not walk in the obedience of faith and have not united themselves with God so that they wish to do his will, are a great abomination before God, it is not possible for anything to grow or issue from them except abominable things.[11]

This sort of thing is relatively familiar ground historically, and innumerable illustrations could be marshalled. It is crucially different from the condemnation of heresy, in that those who 'separate' are seeing themselves as a 'remnant', a small group in whom the truth is preserved, and are condemning all the rest of those who call themselves Christians.[12] The early councils' condemnation of heretics came from a consciousness that here were dissenters from an otherwise united and single-minded body, the one Church of all faithful people. Once that self-image of the Church is lost, and replaced by one of a community in pieces, the pieces begin to locate their sense of ecclesial identity in what is peculiar to them, and to reject one another's ecclesiality.

The second category of fixity of ecclesial mindset – consciously perceived and labelled as such only in relatively recent decades, but now vigorously clamouring for attention – is 'cultural' mindset.[13] I shall be using 'cultural' in two ways. I am first concerned with the political, ethnic and other 'secular' dimensions of a community's life, as a legitimate and necessary part of its 'being itself'. In this connection there has been a realization by the West that it has been proceeding on an arrogant assumption of its own superiority, of having thought in terms of what has been described as 'the white peoples' duty to provide the proper faith for the rest of the world'.[14] But we have to ask what this concept of 'culture' means ecclesiologically. It is frequently taken in contemporary discussion, as in the quotations here, to refer especially to the cultures of the Third World whose survival has seemed threatened by Western political and cultural dominance. This is the kind of preoccupation we see in this 'Response to BEM' by the Methodist Church in New Zealand:

> As we seek to discover appropriate responses to the gospel as Maori, and Pakeha (European) in Aotearoa (New Zealand) and as we relate to Polynesian people and are involved with the Asian church, we are led to ask questions about the 'Northern' and 'Western' nature of the text (1.3). This has to do, in part, with

language, but also with imagery and concept. We recognize that a document prepared for worldwide use will inevitably have to be general, and will arise out of a particular tradition and style. . . . We note that Northern Hemisphere cultural perspectives dominate the text, and we are concerned that other cultural perspectives and heritages may not readily relate to the way Christian faith is expressed in this text. We also consider that a rather institutional view of the Church permeates the document, and, out of our New Zealand Methodist history, the definite place given to bishops may be uncomfortable for some people.[15]

The Christian missions of the nineteenth century certainly took with them the presumption that the education and values of the society from within which the mission was sent out were themselves superior to those of the societies being converted to the faith; and that it would be good for those societies to be presented with that culture along with the Christian faith. There has been a backlash against what was patronizing, arrogant and destructive in this practice, and lasting resentments persist in many societies which now consider themselves to have been damaged by it. Others are simply asserting themselves constructively:

Faith and Order debates are not ecumenical debates until those of us from outside the West have theological substance of our own to put on the table for reflection and discussion. . . . An ecumenical body such as the World Council of Churches now has much more to learn from theological development in Asia and elsewhere than the latter from the former.[16]

The *Catechism of the Catholic Church* is consciously open to 'the adaptation of doctrinal presentations and catechetical methods required by the differences of culture, age, spiritual maturity, and social and ecclesial condition among all those to whom it is addressed'. It recognizes these to be 'indispensable adaptations'.[17]

Underlying this call for a rebalancing of attitudes is a profoundly radical question:

What do Athens and Rome have to do with Egypt, Ethiopia, West Africa, East Africa and South Africa? Likewise, what do Wittenberg, Geneva, Zürich, Canterbury, Edinburgh, Richmond (Virginia), and New York have to do with sub-Saharan Africa and the Afro-Caribbean come of age?[18]

The foundations of the Christian theological tradition were laid in a world of Greek philosophical thought in the Roman Empire; it took many of its continuing modern preoccupations in the West from ideas which came to the surface in the divisions of the sixteenth century and after (those of Lutheran thinkers at Wittenberg, Calvin at Geneva and so on). Should these now be set aside by Christians coming into a 'sense of themselves' appropriate to the modern 'two-thirds world'? Latin America in particular has spoken out, in favour of rejection of the 'academic type of theology that is divorced from action' which Europe has, it argues, fostered as 'one form of cultural domination'.[19] But similar thinking is being heard elsewhere.

This is to argue that the totality of the culture in which a church grows up ought to shape it to so substantial a degree that it should feel free not to 'receive' whatever it chooses of order and even faith elsewhere. It is obvious enough that there could be, as a result, a body calling itself 'Church' in which almost nothing was shared or commonly received with others.

There is also a danger in such attempts to redress the balance that redress will go too far and overbalance into a new tyranny. That can perhaps be seen to happen in present trends in 'political correctness'.[20]

At the same time, and despite conscious attempts at eliminating it, a lingering legacy of the 'old' world's influences is not hard to see in the pronouncements of 'young' churches. It is not easily removed, because of the way it penetrated their foundations through mission from the West. The Confession of Faith of the Protestant Sumatran/Indonesian Huria Kristen Batak was framed independently of the help of Western theologians, but is certainly not uninfluenced by them in its hostility to reception of other communities. It reflects at an early stage (1951), something of the reaction against the West, but at the same time it shows a continuing dependency on the heritage of Western preoccupations with which Christianity arrived in that culture. There is an insistence at the beginning of the document that:

> This Confession of Faith is the continuation of existing confessions of faith, namely the three confessions of faith which were acknowledged by the Fathers of the Church: (1) the Apostles' Creed, (2) the Nicene Creed, (3) the Athanasian Creed.

But each clause has an explanation of what it rejects, at the end of its affirmation of the positive point it seeks to make. For instance, Article 2 has what certainly seems to be a universal intention. It explicitly rejects a 'subordinationist' view of the relationships of the Persons of the Trinity, as the early Church did. Yet in Article 3 we find an attack on Roman Catholicism because that was regarded with hostility by the Western Protestantism to which these Christians were first converted. So Article 2 will 'reject and refute the doctrine of the Roman Catholics'. It selects topics and adopts positions accordingly. For example, it condemns the view 'That Mary, the mother of the Lord Jesus, or, as they call her, the Blessed, may intercede for us with God . . . the doctrine of the Roman Catholics which teaches that the priest can sacrifice Christ in the Mass.' It speaks of: 'The false doctrine of the Roman Catholics which teaches that the Pope in Rome is the Vicar of Christ on this earth.'[21] It is clear from all this that the old mutually alienating 'mindsets' and the newer 'culturally determined' ones can and indeed must overlap substantially. It is also apparent how deeply entangled in old hostilities their roots can be.

All this is relatively well-trodden ground, and I have therefore only sketched it in. But it has to be noted at the outset if we want to explore what is involved in mutual reception by estranged communities of Christians.

Changing assumptions

The *liveness* of reception can be alarming. Attitudes and assumptions shift imperceptibly all the time. New or changing agendas repeatedly emerge. So although the 'mindset' can remain adversarial, there can also be a constantly shifting ground, on which the processes of mutual reception of communities is struggling to take place. That attracts anxious comment about the apparent impossibility of knowing where to begin and how to proceed now: 'In recent decades philosophical pluralism and cultural diversification have undermined [the common conceptual] framework. New discoveries in the fields of semantics, linguistics and sociology of knowledge have raised doubts as to the possibility of drafting doctrinal statements akin to the Chalcedonian definition.'[22]

A new undercurrent noticeable in the texts of the World Council of Churches' 1993 Faith and Order Conference at Santiago[23] is something very close to an acceptance of the value, if not the validity, of continuing disagreement. To say that 'conflicting perspectives often each express significant elements of truth'[24] is to suggest not only the now generally accepted notion that each community has preserved with special clarity some elements of the fullness of Christian truth, but that the truth in those elements may in the end have to be taken to be compatible with their being in conflict. 'There is a cheap unity which avoids contested issues because they disturb the peace of the church. Costly unity will not be afraid of legitimate conflict,'[25] takes the line that contested issues may have to be settled by real contests. The texts are able to speak of the need for 'the courage to struggle for truth when necessary *even at the expense of comfort and peaceful unanimity*' (Gal. 2.5) [my italics].[26]

If this is really what is meant, it represents a huge shift away from the 'convergence' and 'harmony' ecumenism which has been taken as basic since the Second Vatican Council, in which diversities are seen as the many faces of a single truth. There is arguably a movement to the view that *koinonia* may prove to be partial or complete *also* in the sense that there will continue within it to be differences about the faith. So we find the statement that 'a test of our *koinonia* is how we live with those with whom we disagree'. There is thus a paradox in the assertion at Santiago: 'We are confident we are being led through such tensions into a deeper and broader *koinonia* in the Spirit.'[27] For 'broader' can be read as 'containing the unreconciled' where 'deeper' surely cannot.

Those with an ecumenical ear to the ground will have picked up the vibrations of a number of other movements of the troops in recent years,[28] of which this return to the defence of ecclesial and confessional identities, of a diversity not complementary with unity but testing it, is one of the most obvious. Another has been the threat of conflict between those for whom the 'ethical commitment' to issues of peace and justice and ecology has had a higher priority than the continuance of the slow process of theological rapprochement through the multilateral and bilateral dialogues which have been going on throughout the century, but especially since the Second Vatican Council. This assumes that the two may in some way indeed be in conflict, and there are real issues of priority and preference between them.

So the issues ecumenism must address appear different in each community, and they can be seen to be changing over time on the worldwide ecumenical scene. Context, both ecclesial and temporal, affects them, to the point where some theologians have argued that we should take context as our starting-point, recognize the living community as 'Church where it is'. That would all seem to place the task of mutual reception in a quicksand, because it becomes hard to get a firm foothold.

Unity and diversity: the new context

A main underlying reason for this wish would seem to lie in the continuing shift in the ecumenical balance of the claims of unity and diversity, and those of the universal and local. The ecumenical theological enterprise has up to now been a drive for 'unity in unanimity' without compulsion or compromise but in the expectation that all Christians everywhere will ultimately be able to recognize their own faith and order in the one. The recent 'contextual' enterprise puts the local, particular, specific first, and is prepared, if necessary, to let that be at the expense of unity.[29]

The Santiago texts of the 1993 World Council of Churches Faith and Order meeting have a good deal to say about context on understandings of this kind. 'Koinonia . . . will be marked by diversity in its forms of witness.'[30] There is a recognition that diversity is now becoming a much more complex phenomenon, indeed perhaps a phenomenon of a new order. There is an awareness that we have not yet come to the end of the multiplication of diversity, and must not close the door while any remain outside the ecumenical process in their attitude to difference.[31] And it is no longer a case of the kind of diversity between churches or confessions which has been traceable throughout the centuries of division, but of a newly conscious political, ethnic, cultural, contextual diversity.[32] There is a special concern here, arising quite properly from a deep vein of Christian tradition, to protect the weak and minorities; and give them a proper place in the ecclesial scheme of things.[33]

A certain amount can readily be said, and is said in the Santiago texts, to reassure us that this shift is ultimately not destructive of unity.

> The inter-dependence of unity and diversity which is the essence of the churches' *koinonia* is rooted in the Triune God revealed in Jesus Christ.[34]

> Unity and diversity are safeguarded within the structure of the church. Both unity and diversity are expressive of *koinonia*.[35]

> The *koinonia* of the church is also universal. One community cannot be isolated from the rest.[36]

But the detailed effort entailed in working out how the new order of diversity, and its renewed assertiveness, is to be held in a right balance with unity in the Church barely begins to be addressed in the Santiago documents, although the need is recognized. ('As we travel the way of pilgrimage, we will need to be able to understand each other's theological language and cultural ethos.')[37]

The texts sound warning notes about the direction of such work. Let me take two areas of especial concern. The first is language. We find familiar understandings:

Koinonia in faith does not imply a uniformity which eliminates diversity of expression. The fact that God's revelation in Christ is addressed to all human beings of every time and place requires that it find expression in a variety of linguistic, cultural and theological forms.[38]

But there is a hint of something more. 'All language, even that in Scripture and creed, is inculturated,' although with the stricture that inculturation must not have it all its own way. ('But the revelation in Christ and the work of the Spirit may challenge some of our culture and concepts.')[39]

A second is confessional identity. Here the Santiago texts are open-eyed about the dangers of the contextualization which divides and narrows and is inward-looking, and points to the desirable direction of change:

As we strip ourselves of false securities, finding in God our true and only identity, daring to be open and vulnerable to each other, we will begin to live as pilgrims on a journey, discovering the God of surprises who leads us into roads which we have not travelled, and we will find in each other true companions on the way.[40]

This is a recognition that a clinging to confessional identity as to a familiar and secure place will not do, if it prevents openness to one another and willingness to change in whatever way God leads. The whole is set in the context of the 'call to metanoia and kenosis' and the need for Christians to see themselves in their churches as 'penitent pilgrims'.[41]

All this has implications, some of which are set out in the lists of suggested tasks to be found in the Santiago documents. There is a listing of 'steps on the way' (used as a heading). Here again, there is a clear recognition of the importance of attention to context:

In relation to faith, the churches must continue to explore how to confess our common faith in the context of the many cultures and religions, the many social and national conflicts in which we live.
In relation to life, the churches must dare concrete steps toward fuller koinonia, in particular doing all that is possible to achieve a common recognition of baptism, agreement on a common participation in the eucharist, and a mutually recognised ministry.

In relation to witness, the churches must consider the implications of koinonia for a responsible care for creation, for a just sharing of the world's resources, for a special concern for the poor and outcast, and for a common and mutually respectful evangelism that invites everyone into communion with God in Christ.[42]

There is evidently no intention in the Santiago texts to depart from the methodology of 'theological study through agreed texts'. Nevertheless, this is beginning to be envisaged as an exercise itself to be contextualized:

> We ask the churches to take advantage of the ecumenically elaborated explication, *Confessing the One Faith*, as an appropriate instrument for the process of better understanding of our common faith within and among the churches. They are also invited to concretize the Explication within their own contexts.[43]

> We recommend that the Standing Commission of Faith and Order take responsibility for producing a Study Guide of this explication.[44]

Contextualization is thus seen as a necessary task, but not one to be undertaken on its own, because discussion needs to look out to the universal as well as inward to the local context, as Santiago elsewhere recognizes in the passage just touched on.[45]

There is further discussion of future ecumenical methodology, which indicates some remaining uncertainty of direction on these unity-diversity problems.

> We must reflect further on the fact that our different traditions give differing levels of priority to various criteria; but if we can arrive at recognition of the same ensemble of criteria, even if they are being used in different ways, we shall have taken a step forward.[46]

Two issues are juxtaposed here unresolved: the question of particular differences of emphasis in different traditions; and the question of different readings of the same 'set' of principles taken as a whole. Other comments in the same area also feel their way to 'new ways of doing theology which provide more adequate tools to express community on the way to God in visible unity'.[47]

So we are not at the end of changing assumptions, nor likely to be. That makes it difficult to gauge where the ground may be firm to walk on, on the way to mutual reception of one another's communities.

CHAPTER FIFTEEN

SHARED RECEPTION – YOUR FAITH OR MINE?

A crucial question even in the early Church was what each local church could legitimately decide 'officially' for itself. There was early acceptance of the principle that in matters of faith only the universal will do. That was never the case for rites.

Any notion that different communities can have different faiths is a different matter. (The absurdity of that is encapsulated in the medieval oxymoron 'the comoun sect of god'.[1] Sectarianism cannot share.) But the underlying (and often unconscious) assumption on which articles of faith peculiar to themselves have been framed and kept to by divided churches is undoubtedly that differences of faith can be legitimate. For example, the Methodist Articles of Religion of 1784 were a revision of the Anglican Thirty-Nine Articles, made by John Wesley and adopted by the Methodist Conference in Baltimore in 1784.[2] That was done for good practical reasons, for the Anglican Articles would not quite do, and Methodists needed to be clear about their own special needs. So there is a sense in which such 'articles of faith' are unavoidably tokens of a failure or breakdown of reception of a common faith.

Inherent in such article-making is a tendency to seek out particular points as most important, most sure – frequently because they are thought to have been neglected or misrepresented elsewhere. Or articles condemn opinions held in another community. They may do this with no sense of a separative intention – indeed even in the name of unity in the truth, as does this text of 1527:

> Dear brethren and sisters, we who have been assembled in the Lord at Schleitheim on the Border, make known in points and articles to all who love God that as concerns us we are of one mind to abide in the Lord as God's obedient children. . . . In this we have perceived the oneness of the Spirit of our Father and of our

common Christ with us. For the Lord is the Lord of peace and not of quarrelling, as Paul points out.[3]

> Dear brethen and sisters in the Lord: these are the articles of certain brethren who had heretofore been in error and who had failed to agree in the true understanding, so that many weaker consciences were perplexed, causing the Name of God to be greatly slandered. Therefore there has been a great need for us to become of one mind in the Lord, which has come to pass.[4]

This is nobly put. Yet it plainly cannot go along with the desire 'that all can act and speak together' in the whole of Christendom.[5] In the ecumenical climate of the late twentieth century such a text would have to speak quite differently if it were to claim to have a unitive purpose.

We might take for illustration here a set of articles from the Anabaptist community which made the above assertions: 'The articles which we discussed and on which we were of one mind are these: 1. Baptism; 2. The Ban; 3. Breaking of Bread; 4. Separation from the Abomination; 5. Pastors in the Church; 6. The Sword; and 7. The Oath.'[6] The Mennonites adopted the Dordrecht Confession (1632), which is a mature expression of such Anabaptist thought. Their range of articles is similar but not identical:

> 1. Of God and the creation of all things; . . . 2. Of the fall of man; . . . 3. Of the restoration of man through the promise of the coming of Christ; . . . 4. Of the advent of Christ into this world, and the reason of his coming; . . . 5. Of the Law of Christ, which is the holy Gospel, or the New Testament; . . . 6. Of repentance and amendment of life; . . . 7. Of holy Baptism; . . . 8. Of the Church of Christ; . . . 9. Of the election, and offices of teachers, deacons, and deaconnesses, in the Church; . . . 10. Of the Lord's Supper; . . . 11. Of the Washing of the Saints' Feet; . . . 12. Of matrimony; . . . 13. Of the office of civil government; . . . 14. Of defence by force; . . . 15. Of the swearing of oaths; . . . 16. Of the ecclesiastical ban or excommunication from the Church; . . . 17. Of the shunning of those who are expelled; . . . 18. Of the resurrection of the dead and the last Judgement.[7]

The danger therefore is that a selection of key points which happen to have been controversial at a time of division may come to be thought of as definitive, even complete, and above all as a basis for unity when they must in fact exclude others from that unity, even others of very closely similar opinion, as is the case in these two instances.

There are several related issues, which I have dealt with elsewhere and which we can only touch on here.

Legitimate diversity

Unanimity is now sometimes seen as being in conflict with respect for legitimate diversity, and therefore a threat to it. There are important definitional tasks here, not least for the term 'legitimate' itself. Defining how Christians differ (or legitimately may differ) and how they are (or ought to be) the same is a new task of ecumenical reception in the late twentieth century, when it is possible to survey all these confessional positions side by side as legitimate expressions of the faith in various communities.[8] But it takes place in its turn against a varying background of assumptions about the desirability of the diversity, which has been consolidated in differentiated 'confessional identity'. In the first half of the century a diversity now often a matter of sectarian pride was frequently seen as a ground of shame. That the Faith and Order Conference at Edinburgh in 1937 should say, 'We humbly acknowledge that our *divisions* are contrary to the will of Christ,'[9] is not perhaps remarkable. In comparison the *Message* of the First Assembly of the World Council of Churches (1948) is startling. '[God] has brought us here together in Amsterdam,' it begins. 'We are one in acknowledging Him as our God and Saviour. We are divided from one another not only in matters of faith, order and tradition, but also by pride of nation, class and race. But Christ has made us his own, and he is not divided. . . . We intend to stay together.' That is a frank acknowledgement that diversity may be culpable, a matter of pride. Similarly, for the Lund meeting in 1952 to say

> We affirm that throughout Christendom there is, despite divisions, a unity already given by God in Christ. . . . Concerning the fact of this unity and of the participation in it of every Christian we have no doubt. The co-operation in the Ecumenical Movement is one practical proof that this unity is here

is a straightforward expression of faith and hope. More tormented, because it seeks to express the tangled relationship of diversity and unity, is the following:

> We differ, however, in our understanding of the relation of our unity in Christ to the visible holy, Catholic and Apostolic Church

... in consequence, we differ in our understanding of the character of the unity of the Church on earth for which we hope. ... Yet our differences in the doctrinal and sacramental content of our faith and of our hope do not prevent us from being one in the act of believing and of hoping.[10]

The Roman Catholic Directory for the Application of Principles and Norms in Ecumenism underlines the tension all this points to: that all churches and ecclesial communities display in their ecumenism a sense of the need to keep faith with the fullness of understanding to which their own tradition has come in its faith and life; but this inevitably affects their willingness to go forward boldly into a union which will make Christ's one Church a visible reality. This is the common experience and it is nothing new. The desire to be 'united not absorbed' underlies the current debate about the balance of unity and legitimate diversity which is going on in all the churches. In its own wrestling with this problem the revised *Directory* confronts squarely the need to face realistically the inadequacy of mere co-operation and sharing, and the imperative to make the commitment to real unity.[11] Because this is a pioneering exercise, and one on which no other community has said so much as yet, it is useful to dwell on it again here at some length.

The *Directory* follows the teaching of the Second Vatican Council in saying that

> the fullness of the unity of the Church of Christ has been maintained within the Catholic Church while other Churches and communities, though not in full communion with the Catholic Church, retain in reality a certain communion with it. ... This unity ... subsists in the Catholic Church as something she can never lose, and we hope that it will continue to increase until the end of time.[12]

This seems to understand the ecclesiology of 'subsisting in' rather conservatively, by locating the indefectible unity of the Church not only fully but also specially in one of the existing churches. So the term 'Catholic Church' is being used here in a double sense. It refers both to the universal Church and to the Church of Rome.[13] To be in communion with that (Roman) Church is then to enter into that unity (universality), and degrees of communion with it can be said to reflect degrees of unity.

Now there can be no objection to that model if it can also be held that other churches are both universal, and historically and uniquely themselves, so that communion with them, too, is union in the universal. But that is not really what this document seems to intend. To say that would be to take a step beyond Vatican II's recognition of the ecclesiality of the Churches of the East and (in a different way) of the 'ecclesial Communities' of the Western Reformation: 'Ecumenical formation makes concern for the unity of the Catholic Church and concern for communion with other Churches and ecclesial Communities inseparable.'[14] This must, it seems, be read as placing these 'others' to some degree outside full catholicity at present.

The confidence remains that communion exists, even if incomplete communion.[15] The *Directory* returns to the theme. 'The only basis . . . for sharing and cooperation is the recognition on both sides of a certain, though imperfect, communion already existing' (36). But this partial communion merely sets up a loving relationship between churches and ecclesial communities.[16] It does not constitute, as understood here, a full sharing in catholicity.

Rome is of course not alone in taking this position. The Orthodox churches take it too. Indeed, in their confidence that the true Church is in them almost all churches and ecclesial communities do so, and it is a substantial reason for the present ecumenical impasse that when it comes to commitment to one another all find it so difficult to trust themselves to the catholic in one another; to be open to 'truth wherever it is found' (57); to follow through to its natural and logical end the 'mutual striving to understand and esteem what is good in each other's theological traditions' (61e); to go on together to the consequences of the fact that 'dialogue has created new relationships' (61e).

The *Directory* reveals a sensitivity to the implications of this partly equivocal use of 'catholic' throughout the text.[17] Everywhere in the *Directory* there is a desire for openness coupled with a caution which requires Roman Catholics always to look carefully for conformity with their own church's traditions:

> Ecumenical openness is a constitutive dimension of the formation of future priests and deacons (76). . . . But discussions can usefully be organized with other Christians, at the universal and the local level, while observing the relative norms of the Catholic Church (82).[18]

The depth of the difficulty all this reflects shows up best perhaps in the highly condensed and not entirely clear paragraph 74:

> Students must learn to distinguish between on the one hand revealed truths, which all require the same assent of faith, and on

the other hand the manner of stating those truths and theological doctrines [which by implication do not].[19]

The text goes on to explain that

> from the beginning the dogmatic formularies of the magisterium have always been appropriate for communicating revealed truth and . . . remaining unchanged, they will always communicate it to those who interpret them properly (ME, 5).

Two distinctions are being made. The first is between that which is unchanging in the Church's tradition and the re-expression of the faith in language and even concepts appropriate for each age.[20] This is the familiar pairing of continuity and change with which all churches and ecclesial communities grapple. The second is the distinction between the truth (which cannot vary) and the expression of the truth (which can).[21]

The ecumenically positive (though not logically clearly warranted) deduction made is that 'it follows that different theological formulations are often more complementary than contradictory'. That seems to imply that catholicity subsists in the formularies of the Roman Catholic Church but it also embraces legitimate diversity of conception and language (in the traditions of other churches?) because these converge with and are alternative expressions of the one truth. The entailments are not fully spelt out, and the resulting ambivalence seems to reflect the genuine impossibility, at the present stage of the ecumenical process, of saying whether catholicity may be truly in other churches beside the Roman Catholic, even while communion is imperfect.

The persistence of this difficulty about catholicity, which it cannot be too often stressed is shared (in various forms) with other churches and ecclesial communities, should not be allowed to mask the scale of the Vatican II reorientation of the Roman Catholic Church with regard to other churches which is reflected here. But it has to be taken seriously because upon its solution in that and other communities ultimately depends the success of the ecumenical endeavour.

Despite the inherent difficulty with which it is struggling, a significant feature of the Roman Catholic *Ecumenical Directory* is its wholehearted commitment to the principle that Christian theology should always be done ecumenically, that: 'An ecumenical dimension should permeate all theological formation.'[22]

But again and again the tension is there between openness to other traditions and careful adherence to Catholic tradition as Rome defines it.

> [Catholics] should know their own Church and be able to give an account of its teaching, its discipline and its principles of ecumenism. The more they know these, the better they can present them in discussions with other Christians and give sufficient reason for them. They should also have accurate knowledge of the other Churches and ecclesial Communities with whom they are in contact (24).[23]
>
> Knowledge of the history of divisions and of efforts at reconciliation, as well as the doctrinal positions of other Churches and ecclesial Communities will make it possible to ... discern what is legitimate diversity and what constitutes divergence that is incompatible with Catholic faith (57b) [again the ambivalence].
>
> [Catechesis] should expound clearly, with charity and with due firmness the whole doctrine of the Catholic Church, respecting in a particular way the order of the hierarchy of truths[24] and avoiding expressions and ways of presenting doctrine which would be an obstacle to dialogue (61a).

As before the natural tension is clearly causing difficulties which are potentially theologically stimulating because they force us to confront the issue of risk-taking under the Spirit and the commitment to one another in Christ that goes with it.

We can see a little further into this by examining what is proposed by way of content for ecumenical teaching. This brings us back to the issues at the heart of this study, of the ways in which the faith is received by all Christians both individually and collectively. Thus we read of

> 79. a. the notions of catholicity, of the visible and organic unity of the Church ... from their historical origins to the present meaning from the Catholic viewpoint;
> b. the doctrinal basis of ecumenical activity with particular reference to the already existing bonds of communion between Churches and ecclesial Communities;
> c. the history of ecumenism, which includes that of the divisions and of the many attempts during the ages to re-establish unity, their achievements and failures, the present state of the search for unity;
> d. the purpose and method of ecumenism, the various forms of union and of collaboration, the hope of re-establishing unity, the conditions of unity, the concept of full and perfect unity.[25]

> 76. In each subject ... the following aspects may be suitably emphasised: a. the elements of the Christian patrimony of truth and holiness which are common to all Churches and ecclesial Communities, even though these are sometimes presented according to varying theological expressions ...
> c. points of disagreement on matters of faith and morals which can nonetheless encourage deeper exploration of the Word of God and lead to distinguishing real from apparent contradictions.
>
> 77. The teacher should instil in his students fidelity to the whole authentic Christian tradition in matters of theology, spirituality and ecclesiastical discipline. When students compare their own patrimony with the riches of the other Christian traditions of east and West, whether in their ancient or modern expression, they will become more deeply conscious of this fullness.

The point does not need to be laboured further. The crucial difference – and much hangs on whether or not it proves in practice to *be* a difference – is between teaching the (Roman) Catholic faith and teaching the Catholic faith as it is slowly beginning to be understood ecumenically. It is encouragingly possible here for the *Directory* to say that 'ecumenism calls for renewal of attitudes and for flexibility of methods in the search for unity' (56).

Rome's profound concern to go carefully in this area of difficulty is apparent in the emphasis throughout the document on 'direction' ('directives or orientations' (42)), with its implications of caution[26] and control; on catechesis; and on systematic 'formation' of both pastors and the ordinary faithful. The whole of Chapter III is devoted to this theme:

> 23. Catholics are invited to respond according to the directives of their pastors, in solidarity and gratitude with the efforts that are being made in many Churches and ecclesial Communities....
>
> 24. Catholics need to act together and in agreement with their bishops. ...
>
> 30. The initiatives of the faithful in the ecumenical domain are to be encouraged. But there is need for constant and careful discernment by those who have ultimate responsibility for the doctrine and discipline of the Church.[27] It belongs to them to encourage responsible initiatives and to ensure that they are carried out according to Catholic principles of ecumenism. They must reassure those who may be discouraged by difficulties and moderate the imprudent generosity of those who do not give

SHARED RECEPTION – YOUR FAITH OR MINE?

sufficiently serious consideration to the real difficulties in the way of reunion.

29. It belongs to the College of Bishops and to the Apostolic See to judge in the final instance about the manner of responding to the requirements of full communion.[28] It is at this level that the ecumenical experience of all the particular Churches is gathered and evaluated; necessary resources can be coordinated for the service of communion at the universal level and among all the particular Churches that belong to this communion and work for it; directives are given which serve to guide and regulate ecumenical activities throughout the Church. . . . It is often to this level of the Church that other Churches and ecclesial Communities address themselves when they wish to be in ecumenical relation with the Catholic Church. And it is at this level that ultimate decisions about the restoration of communion must be taken.

Paragraph 193 speaks of 'norms' and 'rules'. No one could wish to dispute the importance of having rules and keeping them, and of ecumenical faithfulness to the most exacting standards. But there must be a question whether such rules can be formulated unilaterally and still be ecumenical. We have to ask whether they should not be agreed ecumenically.

It deserves to be underlined here that the *Directory*'s emphasis on guidance and direction is balanced by an acknowledgement that 'concern for restoring unity pertains to the whole Church, faithful and clergy alike. It extends to everyone, according to the potential of each, whether it be exercised in daily Christian living or in theological and historical studies' (55). 'Formation of all the faithful' is the heading for paragraph 58. 'The objective of ecumenical formation is that *all* Christians be animated by the ecumenical spirit' (58).

This is rightly coupled with taking the local as the starting-point and moving out from there to the universal. 'The particular local context will always furnish the different characteristics of the ecumenical task' (34). The people of God in each place are shown gathered about their bishop in this work. 'In the diocese, gathered around the bishop, in the parishes, and in the various groups and communities, the unity of Christians is being constructed and shown forth day by day.'[29] There is a strong awareness of the need for ecumenical teaching to be related to the 'concrete' situation and to go at a pace which allows for the time it takes for attitudes to change.

'The method of teaching should allow for the necessity of progressing gradually' (57g). 'Ecumenical formation requires a pedagogy that is adapted to the concrete situation of the life of persons and groups, and which respects the need for gradualness in an effort of continual renewal and of change in attitudes' (56).[30]

This is caution rightly exercised. It is in keeping with the recognition of the huge importance of the exercise of the utmost rigour in ecumenical theology.

> Catechesis will have an ecumenical dimension if it arouses and nourishes a true desire for unity and still more if it fosters real effort, including efforts in humility to purify ourselves, so as to remove obstacles on the way, not by facile doctrinal omissions and concessions, but by aiming at that perfect unity which the Lord wills and by using the means that he wills.

This starting from where we are locally and within a given tradition must be right, but it must run in harness with an awareness of catholicity as something which may already in God's eyes extend beyond the Roman Catholic communion.

This principle is clearly expressed in paragraph 58:

> 'The grace of unity', is of primary importance. This unity is first of all unity with Christ in a single movement of charity extending both towards the Father and towards the neighbour. Secondly, it is a profound and active communion of the individual faithful with the universal Church within the particular Church to which he or she belongs.[31] And thirdly it is the fullness of visible unity which is sought with Christians of other Churches and ecclesial communities (58).

In the relation between the second and the third lies an area of vast importance and huge difficulty for all Christians. The *Directory* makes a contribution of inestimable importance in revealing the honest endeavour of the Roman Catholic Church to get it right. I have dwelt on it because it pioneers. Other Christians and ecclesial communities are beginning to make their own contribution to the discussion as generously.

NOTES AND REFERENCES

Preface

1. Faith and Order Paper (Louvain, WCC, 1971), p. 137.
2. G. Tavard, 'A Catholic Reflection on the Porvoo Statement', *Midstream* (1994), p. 356.
3. A. Houtepen, 'Reception' in N. Lossky *et al.* (eds.), *Dictionary of the Ecumenical Movement* (Geneva, WCC, 1991).
4. Cf. Apostolic Constitution, *Fidei Depositum*, 2, CCC, p. 4.
5. *Fidei Depositum*, 3, CCC, p. 5.
6. E. H. Schillebeeckx acknowledges that 'divergent views truly existed' at Vatican II, and yet we are able to speak now of 'the mind of the Council'. *A Struggle of Minds* (Dublin, 1963). F. M. Bliss, *Understanding Reception: A background to its ecumenical use* (Rome, Vatican, 1991), p. 138.
7. Vincent of Lérins, *Commonitorium*, ed. G. Moxon (Cambridge, 1915).
8. *Fidei Depositum*, 2, CCC, p. 4.

1. Divine pedagogy: the role of revelation

1. 'We believe not by natural reason but because God reveals truths of faith. But that means faith is certain because it is founded on the word of God, who cannot lie.' CCC, 156–7, p. 39.
2. CCC, 52, p. 19.
3. CCC, 52, p. 19.
4. 'Yet even if Revelation is already complete . . . it remains for Christian faith gradually to grasp its full significance over the course of the centuries.' CCC, 66, p. 22.
5. That is in itself a highly complex and technical 'reception' story which has been told elsewhere. Useful is H. W. Howarth, 'The influence of Jerome on the Canon of the Western Church', *Journal of Theological Studies*, 10 (1908–9), pp. 481–96.
6. A. Hudson, ed., *English Wycliffite Sermons* (Oxford, 1983) I, p. 466.
7. Cecil M. Robeck, William R. Barr and Rena M. Yocom, eds., *The Church in the Movement of the Spirit* (Grand Rapids, Michigan, 1994), p. 31.
8. 'Messenger formulas such as "Thus saith the Lord," or "The Lord told me to tell you" can be incredibly intimidating to those who are confronted by them.' Robeck, Barr and Yocom, p. 35.

9. Robeck, p. 35.
10. Robeck, p. 36.
11. *The Acts and Decrees of the Synod of Jerusalem, Sometimes Called the Council of Bethlehem*, tr. J. N. W. B. Robertson (London, 1899), Decree IX, 'Creeds of the Churches', p. 491.
12. William R. Barr and Horand Gutfield writing on 'The Spirit in the institutional life of the Church', in Cecil M. Robeck, William R. Barr and Rena M. Yocom, eds., *The Church in the Movement of the Spirit*, p. 93.
13. It is also 'a reality which finds its place in the hierarchical communion and bears its stamp', L.-J. Suenens, *Co-responsibility in the Church*, tr. Francis Martin (London, 1968), p. 204.
14. Barr and Gutfield in *The Church in the Movement of the Spirit*, p. 95.
15. Robert Barclay, *An Apology for the True Christian Divinity being an Explanation and Vindication of the Principles and Doctrines of the People called Quakers* (New York, 1832), pp. 1–14; *Theses Theologicae* (1675), Second Proposition 'Concerning immediate revelation'.
16. Barr and Gutfield in *The Church in the Movement of the Spirit*, p. 98.
17. Barr and Gutfield in *The Church in the Movement of the Spirit*, p. 99.
18. This is a matter to which Augustine gave considerable attention throughout his writings, and notably in his *Harmony of the Gospels*. Augustine is able to see it as providentially arranged for our good. The Gospels are complementary. Matthew wrote on the royal lineage and the account of Jesus' life, as they stood in relation to the present life of men, and Mark follows him closely and looks like his attendant and epitomizer. Luke seems to follow up the priestly lineage. Moreover, Scripture makes patterns. John writes on the contemplative, and other evangelists on the active life. *De Consensu Evangelistarum* I.v.8.
19. See my *The Language and Logic of the Bible* (Cambridge, 1984–5), Vol. I, ch. 1.
20. B. Smalley, *The Study of the Bible in the Middle Ages* (3rd edn, Oxford, 1983); H. de Lubac, *Exégèse médiévale* (Paris, 1959).
21. 'It even happens that this sense of the faithful . . . can precede theological work and provide it with a fundamental intuition.' Suenens, *Co-responsibility*, p. 205.
22. Alexander Murray, 'Confession before 1215', *Transactions of the Royal Historical Society*, 6th Series, 3 (1993), pp. 51–82.
23. Bede, *Ecclesiastical History*, IV.9.
24. Bede, *Ecclesiastical History*, IV.7.
25. Bede, *Ecclesiastical History*, V.22.
26. William of Canterbury, *Miracula S. Thomae Cantuarensis*, *Materials for the History of Archbishop Thomas Becket*, ed. James C. Robertson, 7 vols., Rolls Series (1875–85), I.282–3; and see Benedicta Ward, *Miracles and the Mediaeval Mind* (Aldershot, 1982), p. 31.
27. Quoted by Baldric of Dol, *Historia Ierosolymitana* 4.13, in Ward, *Miracles*, p. 121.
28. Bernard of Clairvaux, *De Consideratione*, 3.412–13, tr. Ward, *Miracles*, p. 182.
29. C. R. Cheney, *Selected Letters of Pope Innocent III*, pp. 27–8, and Ward, *Miracles*, p. 186.

30. Orderic Vitalis, *Historia Ecclesiastica*, ed. M. Chibnall (Oxford, Oxford University Press, 1969–78), 9.190.
31. Peter Damian, Sermo 2.4, *Sermones*, ed. J. Lucchesi, CCCM, 57 (1983), p. 4.
32. William Newburgh, *Historia Rerum Anglicarum* in *Chronicles of the Reigns of Stephen, Henry II and Richard I*, ed. R. Howlett, 2 vols, London, Rolls Series (1884–9), 27.82–4, and Ward, *Miracles*, p. 207.

2. Mater et Magistra: 1 Mater

1. See D. de Soujeole, '"Societé" et "Communion" chez S. Thomas d'Aquin', *Revue Thomiste*, 90 (1990), 587–622, p. 587.
2. A useful list of New Testament texts is given in the agreed text of the Second Anglican–Roman Catholic International Commission, *Church as Communion*.
3. *Koinon, quippe Graeci commune dicunt; unde et communicantes quod communiter, id est pariter, conveniant.* Isidore, *Etymologies*, ed. W. M. Lindsay (Oxford, 1911), 20.14, and D. de Soujeole, '"Societé" et "Communion",' p. 603.
4. CCCM, 84 (1988), p. 44.32.
5. *Unitas fidei et in actionibus pietatis communio in scripturis . . . autenticis.* D. de Soujeole, '"Societé" et "Communion",' p. 604. Cf. thirteenth-century examples from the same source.
6. For a recent survey, see my *The Church and the Churches*; for a study of the issues, see, especially, J. M. R. Tillard, *Église des Églises*.
7. F. M. Bliss, *Understanding Reception: A background to its ecumenical use* (Rome, 1991), p. 136.
8. Apostolic Constitution, *Fidei Depositum*, CCC, p. 5.
9. I shall normally employ the word *laos* for a 'whole-community' laity (which stresses that the ordained remain members of the *laos*), and 'laity' in the context of the first option, where the laity are seen as a section of the community.
10. It is important that the 'priesthood of all believers' does not mean that each believer is a priest, but rather that all believers share in Christ's one priesthood.
11. Vatican II, *De Ecclesia*, IV.30, Tanner, II, pp. 874–5.
12. 'This distinction is involved in the choice and commission of the Apostles: and its continuance is implied in our Lord's words to them connecting their work with his second coming.' Report, *The Position of the Laity*, 62.
13. This placing of the hierarchy in one camp and common clergy and laity in the other was already an irritant in nineteenth-century England. Froude wrote to Newman, 31 July 1835, 'in spirituals each bishop is absolute in his own diocese, except so far as he may have bound himself by ordination oaths to his Primate—so that not only the laity but presbyters are cut out. Froude to Newman, 31 July 1835, Mozley, Vol. 11, p. 117.
14. L.-J. Suenens, *Co-responsibility in the Church*, tr. Francis Martin (London, 1968), p. 203.
15. Suenens, *Co-responsibility*, p. 30.
16. Suenens, *Co-responsibility*, p. 193.

17. Konrad Raiser, 'Laity in the Ecumenical Movement', *The Ecumenical Review*, 45 (1993), p. 376.
18. Vatican II, *De Ecclesia*, IV.30, Tanner, II.874-5. See too 'The leaven of society: the worldly vocation of the laity', General Audience of 3 November, *Catholic International*, 5 (1994), 10-11. There is a similar thrust in the new *Catechism*, CCC, para. 873.
19. Vatican II, *De apostolatu laicorum*, Tanner, II.988.
20. Vatican II, *De ecclesia in mundo*, 43, Tanner, II.1097.
21. Vatican II, *De apostolatu laicorum*, Tanner, II.988.
22. Werner Simpfendörfer, 'Intercultural living; ecumenical learning', *The Ecumenical Review*, 45 (1993), p. 397.
23. Suenens, *Co-responsibility*, p. 196.
24. Suenens, *Co-responsibility*, p. 210.
25. Suenens, *Co-responsibility*, p. 188.
26. Bliss, *Understanding Reception*, p. 145.
27. Nélida Ritchie, 'Laity and Contextual Theology', *The Ecumenical Review*, 45 (1993), p. 385.
28. See Brian Stock, *The Implications of Literacy* (Princeton, 1983).
29. Council of Ephesus, 431, Second letter of Cyril to Nestorius, Tanner, I. 40-1.
30. Ritchie D. Kendall, *The Drama of Dissent: The Radical Poetics of Nonconformity, 1380-1590* (Chapel Hill, 1986), p. 70.
31. Alvin Kernan, *The Cankered Muse: Satire of the English Renaissance* (Yale, 1959), pp. 14-30.
32. MS Rawl, C. 208, fols. 53r-54r, A. W. Pollard, *Fifteenth Century Prose and Verse* (New York, 1903), pp. 138-9; Kendall, *The Drama of Dissent*, p. 60.
33. Keith Thomas, *Religion and the Decline of Magic* (London, 1971), pp. 177ff.
34. Thomas, *Decline of Magic*, pp. 283ff.
35. *The Workes of . . . Mr William Pemble* (3rd edn, 1635), p. 559 and Thomas, *Decline of Magic*, pp. 163-4.
36. J. Norden, *The Surveyors Dialogue* (1607), p. 107.
37. Oliver Heywood, *Diaries*, ed. J. Hosfall Turner Brighouse, 1881, 4.24.
38. Thomas, *Decline of Magic*, pp. 166ff.
39. Vatican II, *De Libertate religiosa*, I.4, Tanner, II.1104.
40. John Jewel, Defence of his *Apologia*, *Works*, ed. J. Ayre (Parker Society, 1845-50), Vol. IV, p. 911.
41. Jewel, *Apologia*, 3.iii, *Works*, IV, p. 909.
42. Jewel, Defence of the *Apologia*, VI.1, *Works*, III, p. 207, but cf. *Works*, IV, p. 913.
43. Paul VI, address to International Congress on the Theology of Vatican II, quoted in Suenens, *Co-responsibility*, p. 205.
44. See *The Doctrine of the Russian Church*, tr. R. W. Blackmore (Aberdeen, 1845), p. 159-60.
45. C. Walton, *Notes and materials for an adequate biography of . . . William Law comprising an elucidation of the scope and content of the writings of Jacob Böhme and of his great commentator Dionysius Andreas Freher* (London, 1854), p. 4. A comparison with George Eliot's closely contemporary Mr Casaubon in *Middlemarch* is irresistible.

46. Preface to Pusey's sermon on 'Entire Absolution of the Penitent', preached First Sunday in Advent, 1846 (*Nine Sermons*, 4th edn, London, 1891), p. x.
47. Mozley, Vol. 11, p. 4.
48. Also in the background here is the question who is to 'count' in the Church. 'Can you tell me whether the poor are invited to sign the lay petition, or those only who have some sort of property?' asks Newman in connection with the marshalling of support for his own enterprise within the 'Oxford Movement'. Mozley, Vol. 11, p. 27.
49. Walton, *Notes and materials*, p. 644.
50. Raiser, 'Laity in the Ecumenical Movement', pp. 376–7.
51. Ritchie, 'Laity and Contextual Theology', p. 386.
52. Ritchie, 'Laity and Contextual Theology', pp. 384–5.
53. Ritchie, 'Laity and Contextual Theology', p. 387.
54. Simpfendörfer, 'Intercultural living', p. 398.
55. Gert Rüppell, 'Following Christ in a World of Anguish', *The Ecumenical Review*, 45 (1993), p. 393.
56. T. Clarke, 'Communities for justice', *The Ecumenist*, 19 (1981), pp. 17–25.
57. Konrad Raiser points to the recent development within the ecumenical movement of 'special interest groups' among the laity, notably in the women's movement. 'Laity in the Ecumenical Movement', p. 375.
58. See, too, my *The Church and the Churches*, Chapter 2.
59. Michael Ramcharan, 'Consciousness of the People of God', *The Ecumenical Review*, 45 (1993), p. 403.
60. Rüppell, 'Following Christ', p. 393.
61. Simpfendörfer, 'Intercultural living', p. 398.
62. G. Baum, 'Three theses on contextual theology', *The Ecumenist*, 24 (1986), pp. 49–59.
63. Discussed in Russell Barta, ed. *Our Sunday Visitor* (Indiana, 1980).
64. Kendall, *The Drama of Dissent*, p. 15.
65. Rüppell, 'Following Christ', p. 394. 'All God's people' seems here to exclude the class of experts.
66. Rüppel, 'Following Christ', p. 392.
67. Summarized in Raiser, 'Laity in the Ecumenical Movement', p. 381.
68. Ritchie, 'Laity and Contextual theology', p. 387.
69. As Newman himself did for a time against the Pope.
70. Mozley, Vol. 11, p. 40.
71. Mozley, Vol. 11, p. 62.
72. Mozley, Vol. 11, pp. 129–30.
73. Mozley, Vol. 11, pp. 129–30.
74. (III.10) Vatican II, *De apostolatu laicorum*, Tanner, II.988.

3. Mater et Magistra: 2 Magistra

1. *Professio Fidei Tridentina*.
2. D. Fenlon, 'The Tridentine profession of faith', in C. S. Rodd, ed., *Foundation Documents of the Faith* (Edinburgh, 1987), pp. 54–5; and see F. M. Bliss, *Understanding Reception*, p. 61.
3. *Creeds of the Churches*, p. 440. The *Catechism of the Catholic Church* speaks

of the link between motherhood and teaching in these terms: 'because she is our Mother she is also our teacher in the faith'. CCC, para. 169.
4. Vatican II, *De divina revelatione*, II. 10, Tanner, II.975.
5. David Thompson, 'History, Scripture, the Church and Ecumenism', in G. R. Evans and M. Gorgues, eds., *Communion et réunion, Essays in Honour of Jean Tillard* (Louvain, 1995).
6. The work of George Tavard is particularly important here. For a bibliography, see the recent Festschrift, *The Quadrilog*, ed. K. Hagen (Minnesota, 1994).
7. The Council of Florence speaks of the *occidentalis sive orientalis consuetudo* in connection with the use of leavened or unleavened bread in the Eucharist. The Second Vatican Council groups 'traditions' with 'institutions, liturgical rites, and the *vita Christiana disciplina*' of individual churches in speaking of the Eastern Catholic churches (the uniate churches) which, while remaining in communion with the See of Rome, nevertheless historically preserve traditions of the Greek East.
8. *Decretum de Ecclesiis Orientalibus Catholicis*, 1, Tanner, I.900.
9. *De Oecumenismo* (*Unitatis Redintegratio*), 14. Tanner, I.916.
10. *De Presbyterorum Ministerio et Vita* (*Presbyterorum Ordinis*), Tanner, I.1062.
11. *De Oecumenismo* (*Unitatis Redintegratio*), 14, Tanner, I.917.
12. Choan-Seng Song, in *Encounters for Unity*, pp. 32–42.
13. Defined as that 'by which faith is brought to maturity and the disciple of Christ is formed through deeper and more orderly knowledge of Christian doctrine and through daily closer loyalty to the Person of Christ'. *Codex Canonum Ecclesiarum Orientalium* (Vatican, 1990), Canon 617.
14. CCC, 13, p. 9.
15. William J. Levada, Archbishop of Portland, Oregon, Address to Symposium, February 1994, *Catholic International*, 5 (1994), 333–40, p. 335.
16. CCC, 22, p. 11.
17. CCC, 24, p. 11.
18. *Codex Canonum Ecclesiarum Orientalium*, Canon 617.
19. *Codex Canonum Ecclesiarum Orientalium*, Canon 604.
20. On Augustine's catechesis see also the short study by Eugene Kevane, *Catechesis in Augustine* (Villanova, 1983). See, too, G. R. Evans, 'St. Augustine on knowing what to believe', *Augustinian Studies*, 24 (1994), pp. 7–26.
21. *De Cat. Rud.* i.1.
22. *De Cat. Rud.* ii.3.
23. *De Cat. Rud.* v.9.
24. *De Cat. Rud.* vi.10.
25. *De Cat. Rud.* iii.5.
26. *De Cat. Rud.* iii.6.
27. *Confessiones*, III.5.
28. *De Cat. Rud.* ix.13.
29. *De Cat. Rud.* vii.11.
30. *De Cat. Rud.* x.14–15.
31. *De Cat. Rud.* xiii.18ff.
32. *De Cat. Rud.* xv.23.

33. See Levada, Address, p. 336.
34. See *The Doctrine of the Russian Church*, tr. R. W. Blackmore (Aberdeen, 1845), pp. viff.
35. Blackmore, p. 32. This point is illustrated by a quotation from Cyril.
36. Blackmore, pp. 34–5.
37. Blackmore, p. 145, using the edition of 1833.
38. Blackmore, p. 164.
39. *Codex Canonum Ecclesiarum Orientalium*, Canons 627–30.
40. Vatican II, Decree *De Institutione Sacerdotali*, II.2, Tanner, II.948.
41. Vatican II, *De Episcoporum Munere*, III.iii. 30.2, Tanner, II.933.
42. Vatican II, *De Episcoporum Munere*, II.14, Tanner, II.925.
43. CCC, 193.
44. CCC, 18, p. 10.
45. Levada, Address, p. 337.
46. It is noted that hagiographical sources are intended to enrich the doctrinal presentations, CCC, 21, p. 11.
47. Benedictus XV, Ep. Apost. *Communes Litteras*, 10 Apr. 1919, AAS 11 (1919), p. 172; Pius XI, Ltt. encycl. *Divini Illius Magistri*, 31 Dec. 1929, AAS 22 (1930), pp. 49–86; Pius XII, *Allocutio ad iuvenes*, A.C. I., 20 Apr. 1946, *Discorsi e Radiomessaggi*, VIII, pp. 53–7.
48. Vatican II, *De educatione Christiana*, 8, Tanner, II.965.
49. Levada, Address, p. 339.
50. Cardinal Ratzinger, 'The Catechism and the Optimism of the Redeemed', quoted in Levada, Address, p. 339.
51. Levada, Address, p. 340.
52. Levada, Address, p. 336.
53. Levada, Address, p. 338.
54. See *Episcopal Ministry*, Report of the Archbishops' Commission on the Episcopate (London, 1990), pp. 21ff.
55. The *Catechism of the Catholic Church* links episcopal responsibility for preaching to the duty to oversee who does it and where.
56. 'Eating' metaphors are very common in medieval discussions of the thoroughness with which the reading should be done, and the nourishment to be obtained.
57. Printed in PL 156.
58. J. J. Murphy, *A Bibliography of Mediaeval Rhetoric* (Toronto, 1971), is useful here.
59. Anti-Establishment, anti-clerical groups; and dualists, respectively.
60. On the early development of these, see my *Alan of Lille* (Cambridge, 1983).
61. Especially in the Late Middle Ages, where Masses were paid for to be said for the souls of dead relatives, for example.
62. See *Episcopal Ministry* on some of the resulting problems.
63. E. W. Brooks, ed. and tr., *Select Letters of Severus*, (London, 1903), Vol. II, p. 15, I.2.
64. i.e. the Pope. This sermon was a conscious continuation of 'my first Eirenicon'. E. B. Pusey, *Nine Sermons Preached before the University of Oxford and Printed Chiefly between 1843–1855* (London, 1891), 'The Rule of Faith', Fifth Sunday after Epiphany, 1851, Preface, p. xxv.

65. Otto Pfleiderer, *The Development of Theology in Germany since Kant and its Progress in Great Britain since 1825*, tr. J. Frederick Smith (London, 1890), pp. 315–16.
66. *Confessions* I.viii.
67. cf. *De Utilitate Credendi*, 26 and elsewhere.
68. *Confessions* III.iv.
69. *Confessions* III.v.
70. *Confessions* V.v.
71. *Confessions* VI.ii.
72. *Confessions* VII.xxi.
73. *Confessions* VIII.1.
74. *Confessions* VIII.xii.
75. Mozley, Vol. 11, pp. 129–30.
76. Mozley, Vol. 11, p. 49.
77. *Apologia*. I have used the text printed London, 1900, p. 11.
78. *Apologia*, p. 18.
79. *Apologia*, To the Year 1833, p. 7.
80. *The History of the Church of Christ* (1794–1809). The book was completed and published after Milner's death in 1797 by his brother Isaac. On Milner, see Isaac's memoir as a Preface to Joseph's *Practical Sermons* (London, 1800).
81. *Apologia*, p. 26.
82. *Apologia*, p. 25.
83. *Apologia*, p. 28.
84. Isaac Newton, *Observations on the Prophecies of Daniel and the Apocalypse of St. John* (posthumous, 1733). This millenarist work, loosely in the tradition of Joachim of Fiore, depends like the rest of its genre on the hypothesis that the Pope is Antichrist.
85. *Apologia*, p. 7.
86. William Beveridge (1637–1708), Bishop of St Asaph, author of an *Exposition of the Thirty-Nine Articles* (posthumous, 1710).
87. Mozley, Vol. 1, pp. 23–4.
88. John Bird Sumner published *Apostolical Preaching* in 1815.
89. *Apologia*, p. 9. This is ironic in view of the fact that Sumner denied in the Gorham case controversy in 1847 that baptismal regeneration is a fundamental doctrine in Church of England teaching.
90. *Apologia*, p. 9.
91. *Apologia*, p. 10.
92. *Apologia*, p. 12.
93. 1803–36, Newman's colleague at Oriel and a fellow-Tractarian.
94. *Apologia*, p. 24.
95. *Apologia*, p. 25.

4. Education of the ordinary clergy

1. Orderic Vitalis describes the young men at the monastery of Bec in this way during the years when Anselm taught them in the late eleventh century.
2. G. H. Moberly, *Life of William of Wykeham* (1887), pp. 106–8, 204.
3. *Register of Bishop John de Pontissara*, Canterbury and York Society, 1 (1915), p. xxxix.
4. *Reformatio Legum Ecclesiasticarum* (1850), pp. 105, 116.
5. Gilbert Burnet, *A Discourse of the Pastoral Care* (1692), i.i, p. 602.
6. A. Gibbons, *Ely Episcopal Records* (1891), p. 4.
7. *Works of Archbishop Whitgift*, Parker Society, 3 (1853), pp. 394–5 and 401, 403.
8. Strype, *Annals of the Reformation*, Oxford 1824, 7 vols., Vol. 3, p. 429.
9. E. Grindal, *Works*, Parker Society (1943), pp. 185–8.
10. *The Injunctions and other Ecclesiastical Proceedings of Bishop Barnes*, Surtees Society (1850), pp. 20–1, 44, 70.
11. E. S. Shuckburgh, *Emmanuel College* (London, Robinson, 1904), p. 23.
12. R. Sanderson, *Sermon ad Clerum* (1664 edn), p. 57.
13. *Visitation Articles*, ed. W. Frere, London, 3.42, 47.
14. *Works of Bishop Jewel*, Parker Society, 3 (1848), pp. 109–12.
15. This is echoed in the sixteenth-century Bidding Prayers still used at Oxford and Cambridge in University Sermons.
16. R. B. and J. N., *The Life of Dr. Thomas Morton* (1669), pp. 95–6.
17. E. F. Carpenter, *Thomas Tenison* (1948), pp. 142–6.
18. Burnet, *A Discourse*, especially Chapter 7 'Of the due preparation of such as may and ought to be put in orders'.
19. William Fleetwood, *Works* (1854 edn), 2.365.
20. Deryck Lovegrove, *Established Church, Sectarian People* (Cambridge, 1988), p. 17.
21. Lovegrove, *Established Church*, pp. 35ff. See too S. Greatheed, *General Union recommended to Real Christians in a Sermon preached at Bedford October 31, 1797. With an introductory account of an union of Christians of various denominations, which was then instituted to promote the knowledge of the Gospel; including a plan for universal union in the genuine Church of Christ* (London, 1798). J. D. Crosland, 'The Bedford Association: an early ecumenical movement', *Proceedings of the Wesley Historical Society*, 28 (1951–2), p. 95.
22. Lovegrove, *Established Church*, p. 44 gives the example of three meeting-houses in Bedford in 1798 sending out thirty into twenty or thirty villages. See, too, p. 50, on tight supervision.
23. Lovegrove, *Established Church*, p. 60, quoting Andover Church Minutes, 5 December 1817.
24. Bristol Education Society, Reports, Vol. 2 (1791–1806).
25. Lovegrove, *Established Church*, p. 71 and see C. E. Surman, 'Robey's Academy, Manchester, 1803–8', *Transactions of the Congregational History Society*, 13 (1937–9), 41–53.

26. Lovegrove, *Established Church*, p. 71, and Hampshire Congregational Association, Minutes, 22 April 1829.
27. Some examples are given by Lovegrove, *Established Church*, p. 73.
28. Vatican II, *De institutione sacerdotali*, V.16.
29. Vatican II, *De institutione sacerdotali*, V.16.
30. The Prologue to his *Summa Theologiae* stresses that theological teaching is best carried out in an orderly way.

5. Continuing education

1. R. Sanderson, *Sermon ad Clerum* (1664 edn), p. 57.
2. Peter of Waltham, *Remediarum Conversorum*, ed. J. Gildea (Villanova 1984), Prologue, p. 25.
3. Peter of Blois, *The Later Letters of Peter of Blois*, ed. Elizabeth Revell. (Auctores Britannici Medii Aevi, 13) (Oxford and London, 1993).
4. See B. Smalley, *The Study of the Bible in the Middle Ages* (3rd edn, Oxford, 1983).
5. Peter of Blois, *The Later Letters*, 36.1, p. 177.
6. Compare letters 19 and 78.
7. See *Disputatio cum Gentile*, *The Works of Gilbert Crispin*, ed. A. Abulafia and G. R. Evans (Oxford and London, 1986).
8. Peter of Blois, *The Later Letters*, 36.1, p. 177.
9. Peter of Blois, *The Later Letters*, 32.2, p. 165.
10. Peter of Blois, *The Later Letters*, 32.5-7, pp. 166-7.
11. John Jewel, *Apology for the Defence of the Church of England*, Works, Parker Society (1845-50), Vol. IV, p. 911.
12. Peter White, *Predestination, Policy and Polemic: Conflict and Consensus in the English Church from the Reformation to the Civil War* (Cambridge, 1992), pp. 87ff.
13. C. M. Dent, *Protestant Reformers in Elizabethan Oxford* (Oxford, 1983), p. 186.
14. Zacharias Ursinus, *The Summe of Christian Religion* (Oxford, 1591), pp. 241, 253.
15. 1795-1938, one of those involved in the developments of the years which led to the beginning of Tractarianism.
16. Mozley, Vol. 11, p. 122 (Newman's emphasis). He saw the problem dramatically. 'Yet does not every day's debate in Parliament show the importance of the thing, and tell us, trumpet-tongued, that as we sow we shall reap – that deserved ruin is the fruit of wilful negligence of the history of the Gospel?'
17. *Apologia*, p. 26.
18. Richard Hurrell Froude.
19. Mozley, Vol. 11, p. 156.
20. Mozley, Vol. 1, p. 238. He adds, 'I do not think there will be much to be gained for your object from German writers.'

6. Being official

1. Historically these have been most usually councils or synods.
2. CCC, 144, p. 36.
3. Vatican II, *De divina revelatione*, II.10, Tanner, II.975.
4. Council of Ephesus, 431, Second letter of Cyril to Nestorius, Tanner, I.40-1.
5. Council of Chalcedon, 451, Definition of the faith, Tanner, I.83.
6. Second Council of Constantinople, 553, 'Sentence against the Three Chapters', Tanner, I.108.
7. Second Council of Nicaea, 787, Definition, Tanner, I.136.
8. Tanner, I.30.
9. This is a reference to the sixteenth-century debate on the inclusion of the apocrypha.
10. The Constitution of the Church of Ireland, adopted by the General Convention in the year 1870: Preamble and Declaration, Porvoo, pp. 186-7.
11. See *Church and Churches*, Chapter 1.
12. That is one reason for the concern of those councils which did want to be thought of as ecumenical to make efforts to declare their universal authority when it had not in fact been the case that every bishop had been present.
13. Council of Ephesus, 431, Tanner, 1.65.
14. Constantinople, 868-70 is an example of a council not recognized by the East, Tanner, p. 137.
15. This is in contrast to summonings by Emperors in early centuries, and by 'princes' and 'magistrates' in the sixteenth-century Reformation.
16. The Constitution of the Church of Ireland, Porvoo, pp. 186-7.
17. Porvoo, pp. 189-90.
18. See Rowan Williams' recent study, *Arius* (London, Darton, Longman and Todd, 1987).
19. Tanner, I.31.
20. Third Council of Constantinople, 680-1, Tanner, I.125.
21. In the 'modern doctrinal writings which are held to be of authority in the eastern Church', *Answers of the Patriarch Jeremiah to the Lutherans*. This should be compared with Acts and XVIII Articles of the Synod of Bethlehem in relation to Calvinist teaching. The Eastern Churches had had no need to promulgate any new creeds from the time of John Damascene. See *The Doctrine of the Russian Church*, tr. R. W. Blackmore (Aberdeen, 1945), p. xv.
22. Philippe Labbe, *Concilia*, Florence, 1759-67, 56 vols., III.613.
23. The Constitution of the Church of Ireland, Porvoo, pp. 186-7.
24. Resolution of the Uppsala Assembly of 1593, Porvoo, p. 189.
25. See *Veritatis Splendor*, 'In addition, the Magisterium carries out an important work, of vigilance, warning the faithful of possible errors, even merely implicit ones, when their consciences fail to acknowledge the correctness and the truth of the moral norms which the Magisterium teaches. . . . Moral theologians are to set forth the Church's teaching and

26. Council of Constance, March 1415, Abbreviation read aloud by Cardinal Zabarella, Tanner, I.408.
27. That God cannot be bound by rules of human devising is a principle famously stressed by Gregory the Great in the sixth century.
28. Tanner, I.17–18.
29. F. M. Bliss, *Understanding Reception: a background to its ecumenical use* (Rome, 1991), p. 108.
30. And latterly representatives who are themselves lay people.
31. The Constitution of the Church of Ireland, Porvoo, pp. 186–7.
32. Under the leadership of one of their number who was senior by virtue of the 'metropolitan' character of the see he held. The calling of councils by emperors, princes and magistrates has a long history which there is not space to go into here. Such leadership has never by tradition interfered with doctrinal decision-making.
33. We have already noted that this was acted on in spirit rather than to the letter in the case of the great ecumenical councils of the early Church, where a rather unbalanced spread of bishops was actually present in each case, but where it was clearly intended that they should decide on behalf of the whole Church.
34. Mozley, Vol. 11, p. 110.
35. Chronicle of Convocation (1877, 1884, 1885, with resolutions agreed July 1885 (xxx, 244–65; xxxi, 270–4).
36. Even those within the 'official' process can feel they have no effect if they are not allowed to legislate. That is what happened when the Convocations were revived in England in the middle of the nineteenth century, but were not at first given the royal licence for revision of a canon. On 26 February 1861, Dr Tait said in the Upper House of Convocation, 'although we knew that it was very desirable that we should have the opportunity of meeting and expressing our opinions, and although we knew also that the opinions so expressed might often be of great influence on the country in general, yet still we did not feel that we were allowed to proceed with any real matter of business.' Chronicle of Convocation (1861), p. 346.
37. *The Archbishops' Committee on Church and State, Report* (London, 1916).
38. *Episcopal ministry*, pp. 101ff.
39. This was the theme of the Lambeth Conference of 1988.
40. Second Council of Constantinople, 553, 'Sentence against the Three Chapters', Tanner, I.108.
41. Tanner, I.406.
42. Tanner, I.313.
43. Tanner, I.17–18.
44. Constance, Tanner, I.438–9, Basle, Tanner, I.455.
45. On the issue of primacy there is a huge literature, and I have attempted here to trace only one thread. For a recent survey and bibliography, see *The Church and the Churches*.
46. Fourth Council of Constantinople, 869–70, Tanner, I.167.

47. See J. M. R. Tillard, *The Bishop of Rome* (Paris, 1982), tr. J. Satgé (London, 1983).
48. Council of Vienne, 1311–12, Decree 1, Tanner, I.360.
49. See the chapter on 'primacy' in my *The Church and the Churches*.
50. It was already so between Eastern Patriarchates and Rome in the Middle Ages and became more so within the West from the sixteenth century.
51. Bernard, *Letters* 190, PL 182.1053 and ed. J. Leclerq *et al.*, *Sancti Bernardi Opera Omnia* (Rome, 1957–78), Vols. 7–8.
52. Vatican I, 1869–70, OV, *De Romani Pontificis Infallibili Magisterio*, Tanner, II.815.
53. Vatican II, *De Ecclesia*, III.25, Tanner, II.870.
54. Vatican II, *De Ecclesia*, III.25, Tanner II.870.
55. Vatican II, *De Divina Revelatione*, 7, Tanner, II.974.
56. Vatican II, *De Ecclesia*, III.25, Tanner II.870, cf. *Si magisterium exercent Episcopi in Concilio Oecumenico coadunati, qui ut fidei et morum doctores et iudices pro universa Ecclesia doctrinam de fide vel de moribus ut definitive tenendam declarant, aut si per orbem dispersi communionis nexum inter se et cum sancti Petri successore servantes una cum eodem Romano Pontifice authentice res fidei vel morum docentes in unam sententiam tamquam definitive tenendam conveniunt. Codex Canonum Ecclesiarum Orientalium* (Vatican, 1990), Canon 597.
57. According to the Canon law for the Eastern Churches it is the Pope's role to strengthen his brother bishops in the faith and to proclaim doctrine on faith and morals definitively: '*cuius est fratres suos in fide confirmare, doctrinam de fide vel de moribus tenendam definitivo actu proclamat.*' 'Bindingness' is important, both to bind to believe and to bind not to believe: '*Fide divina et catholica ea omnia credenda sunt, quae verbo Dei scripto vel tradito, uno scilicet deposito fidei Ecclesiae commisso, continentur et simul ut divinitus revelata proponuntur sive an Ecclesiae magisterio sollemni sive ab eius magisterio ordinario et universali, quod quidem communi adhaesione christifidelium sub ductu cari magisterii manifestatur; tenentur igitur omnes Christifideles quascumque devitare doctrinas eisdem contrarias. Codex Canonum Ecclesiarum Orientalium* (Vatican, 1990), Canon 597, Canon 698. *Apostolic Constitution Fidei Depositum*, CCC, p. 5.
58. 'Thus it is clear that, by God's wise design, tradition, Scripture and the Church's teaching function are so connected and associated that one does not stand without the others, but all together, and each in its own way, subject to the action of the one Holy spirit, contribute effectively to the salvation of souls.' Vatican II, *De Divina Revelatione*, II. 10, Tanner, II.975.
59. *Fidei Depositum*, CCC, p. 4.
60. *Fidei Depositum*, CCC, p. 5.
61. CCC, paras. 80–1, p. 25.
62. CCC, para. 84, p. 26.
63. 'The Church's Magisterium exercises the authority it holds from Christ to the fullest extent when it defines dogmas, that is, when it proposes truths contained in divine Revelation or having a necessary connection with them, in a form obliging the Christian faithful to an irrevocable adherence of faith.'

There is an organic connection between our spiritual life and the dogmas. Dogmas are lights along the paths of faith; they illuminate it and make it secure. Conversely, if our life is upright, our intellect and heart will be open to welcome the light shed by the dogmas of faith.' CCC, para. 88, p. 26; para. 89, p. 27.
64. See *The Doctrine of the Russian Church*, tr. R. W. Blackmore (Aberdeen, 1845), p. 45. It is explained that the first and second councils were against Arius, 'who thought unworthily of the Son of God' and 'Macedonius, who thought unworthily of the Holy Ghost', so that the council can be seen to have a *raison d'être*.
65. 'The necessity for the Church to reach dogmatic decisions arises when the sound doctrine of the Church is threatened or when there is need for specific explanation and testimony to ward off heresy and schism, and in order to maintain the unity of the Church. It is clear that infallibility only applies to matters of salvation. ... The guidance of the Church by the Holy Spirit is therefore to be understood as one which is in correspondence with Scripture as well as transmitted apostolic teaching and is never without reference to these two (cf. Jn. 16.13).' *Koinonia: auf Altkirchlicher Basis*, ed. Urs von Arx, *Internationalen Kirchlichen Zeitschrift*, 79 (1989), pp. 197–8.
66. *Creeds*, pp. 572–3. 'With no one dissenting' seems arguably to have a different force from that of 'everyone agreeing'.
67. Vatican, *Ecumenical Directory*, para. 164.
68. Council of Ephesus, 431, Tanner, I.63.
69. CCC, para. 66, p. 22.

7. Defending the Faith

1. Mauritius Burdinus, the anti-Pope Gregory VIII (1118–21) is described as a Heresiarch by the First Lateran Council, but that is a rather different circumstance. Canon 5, Tanner, I.190.
2. Third Lateran Council, 1179, Tanner, I.224.
3. Fifth Lateran Council, 1512, Tanner, I.595.
4. Gilbert of Poitiers, *Commentaries on Boethius*, ed. N. M. Häring (Toronto, 1965), pp. 58–63.
5. Song of Songs 2.15 speaks of 'little foxes' and the theme of the tails tied together is explored by Bernard of Clairvaux in his sermons on the Song of Songs in the early twelfth century.
6. Fourth Lateran Council, 1215, Tanner, I.233.
7. Council of Trent, 1545, Tanner, I.560.
8. First Council of Constantinople, 381, Tanner, I.33.
9. Fourth Lateran Council, 1215, Tanner, I.233.
10. Fourth Lateran Council, 1215, Tanner, I.233.
11. Second Lateran Council, 1139, 30, Tanner, I.203.
12. First Council of Constantinople, 381, Tanner, I.33.
13. Council of Chalcedon, 451, *Epistula Papae Leonis ad Flavianum Ep. Constantinopolitanum de Eutyche*, Tanner, I.77.
14. Council of Basle, 1431, Tanner, I.456.

15. Council of Ephesus, 431, Second letter of Cyril to Nestorius, Tanner, I.40–1.
16. Council of Ephesus, 431, Second letter of Nestorius to Cyril, Tanner, I.49–50.
17. Council of Ephesus, 431, Tanner, I.67.
18. Council of Ephesus, 431, Tanner, I.74.
19. Tanner, I.31.
20. Council of Vienne, 1311–12, Tanner, I.380–1.
21. Council of Vienne, 1311–12, Tanner, I.382.
22. Council of Constance, 1414–18, Tanner, I.412. This is the council which condemned Wyclif.
23. Tanner, I.17–18.
24. Tanner, I.34.
25. Article XXI of the Church of England's Thirty-Nine Articles says that councils 'may err' . . .
26. The Constitution of the Church of Ireland, adopted by the General Convention in the year 1870: Preamble and Declaration, Porvoo, pp. 186–7.
27. Tanner, I.17–18.
28. E. J. Bicknell, *A Theological Introduction to the Thirty-Nine Articles of the Church of England* (London, Longman, 1991, 3rd edn revised by H. J. Carpenter, London, Longman, 1959) is a useful introduction to the framing of the Articles.
29. Bicknell, *A Theological Introduction*, pp. 20–1 summarizes the history of policies on subscription.
30. His Majesty's Declaration to all his loving subjects of his kingdom of England and dominion of Wales, concerning ecclesiastical affairs, 25 October, 1660, E. Cardwell, *A History of Conferences . . . from the year 1558 to the year 1690* (Oxford, 1840), p. 297.
31. *Letters and Correspondence of John Henry Newman during his life in the English Church*, ed. Anne Mozley (London, 1891), Vol. 11, p. 99.
32. Cardwell, *A History of Conferences*, p. 279.
33. Bicknell, *A Theological Introduction*, p. 21.

8. The anomalous

1. Bernard of Clairvaux, *Letter* 250.8.147, tr. Benedicta Ward, *Miracles and the Mediaeval Mind* (London, 1982), p. 184.
2. Gilbert of Poitiers is a case in point.
3. See my *Old Arts and New Theology* (Oxford, 1983).
4. John of Salisbury gives an account in his *Historia Pontificalis*.
5. *Codex Canonum Ecclesiarum Orientalium* (Vatican, 1990), Canon 606.
6. *Codex* Canons 640–50, esp. 647, 2.
7. *Codex* Canons 651–66.
8. Innocent III is important here. See too S. Menache, 'La naissance d'une nouvelle source d'autorité: l'université de Paris', *Revue Historique*, 268 (1982), 305–27.
9. Ian P. Wei, 'The Masters of Theology at the University of Paris in the late

Thirteenth and early Fourteenth Centuries: and authority beyond the schools', *Bulletin of the John Rylands University Library of Manchester*, 75 (1993), 37–63, p. 39.
10. Thomas Netter, *Fasciculi Zizaniorum*, ed. W. Waddington Shirley (London, 1858), pp. 312–14. Predictably to anyone familiar with the academic scene in any age, there resulted unjust suspensions and witch-hunts (p. 315).
11. Netter, *Fasciculi Zizaniorum*, p. 334.
12. *Ex confessionibus factis fratribus sequuntur lites, rapinae, discordiae, et aliae variae divisiones* (VII), also *fratres asserentes sibi confessos non iterum confiteri eadem peccata suis propriis sacerdotibus sunt haeretici* (VIII). Netter, *Fasciculi Zizaniorum*, p. 346.
13. Paul VI, address to International Congress on the Theology of Vatican II, quoted in L.-J. Suenens, *Co-responsibility in the Church*, tr. Francis Martin (London, 1968), p. 205.

9. Sharing a common mind

1. As the Orthodox-Roman Catholic Statement on *Faith, Sacraments and the Unity of the Church* (Bari, 1987), puts it, 'faith is inseparably both the gift of God who reveals himself and the response of the man who receives this gift.' Text in Paul McPartlan, ed., *One in 2000? Towards Catholic-Orthodox Unity*, (Slough, St. Paul's Publications, 1993), p. 54.
2. On 'We believe, I believe', cf. CCC, para. 167.
3. A version of some of this material was given as the Villanova Lecture on Augustine, 1993, and published in *Augustinian Studies*, 24 (1994), pp. 7–25.
4. And to make it in terms to which (it is of the essence of the declaration also to believe) all Christians always and everywhere have been able to assent. That remains broadly true, even though there are now communities which deliberately avoid using any creed. The *Dictum* of Vincent of Lérins needs nuancing today, as we shall see in the course of this study.
5. Lewis Bayly, *The Practice of Piety* (1648), p. 1.
6. *Opinare, scire, credere.* N. M. Häring, 'Two redactions of a commentary on a Gallican Creed by Simon of Tournai', *Archives d'histoire doctrinale et littéraire du moyen âge*, 41 (1974), 39–112, p. 45.
7. *Fides . . . est perceptio veritatis uniuscuiusque rei cum assensione sine causa cognitione.* Häring, 'Two redactions', p. 46, para. 11.
8. *Fides est certitudo rerum absentium supra opinionem et infra scientiam constituta.* Hugh of St Victor, *De Sacramentis* I.x.2, PL 176.331A.
9. On the history of consent, see K. Oehler, 'Der Consensus Omnium', *Antike und Abendland*, 10 (1961), pp. 103–29. The following material appears with modification, in my *Authority in the Church: a challenge for Anglicans* (Norwich, Canterbury Press, 1992, pp. 91–3, and *Problems of Authority in the Reformation Debates* (Cambridge, 1992), pp. 256ff.
10. Boethius, *De Hebdomadibus*, ed. H. F. Stewart *et al.* (Loeb edn, Heinemann, London, 1973), p. 40.
11. *Summa Theologiae* I q.2 a.1–3.
12. Anselm links the two in his *Proslogion*, Proemium, *Anselmi Opera Omnia*, ed. F. S. Schmitt (Rome and Edinburgh, 1938), p. 93.

13. Robert Barclay, *An Apology for the True Christian Divinity being an Explanation and Vindication of the Principles and Doctrines of the People called Quakers* (New York, 1832), pp. 1–14, *Theses Theologicae* (1675), Second proposition, 'Concerning immediate revelation'.
14. CCC, para. 165.
15. ARCIC AI E (3); cf. A II (27), *Growth*, p. 113.
16. Augustine, *Contra Faustum*, II.2. Isidore in the sixth century speaks of *consentire in unum*, *Etymologiae*, ed. W. M. Lindsay (Oxford, 1909), VI.xvi.12–13. Hincmar of Rheims in the ninth century sees it as a sign of the unity of the Church that there should be consent and *consonantia*. *De Praedestinatione*, 38.1, PL 125.419.
17. More, *Responsio, Complete Works*, ed. J. M. Headley (London and Yale, 1963), V.198.27; Erasmus, *Epistolae*, ed. P. S. Allen *et al.* (Oxford, 1906–58), 6.206. See, too, my *Problems of Authority in the Reformation Debates* (Cambridge, 1992), p. 256.
18. *Methodist Hymn Book* (1877 edn) 916, *Hymns and Psalms*, 374.
19. John Henry Newman, *On consulting the faithful in matters of doctrine*, ed. J. Coulson (Collins, 1961 and 1986), p. 55.
20. Urs von Arx, ed., *Koinonia: auf Altkirchlicher Basis, Internationalen Kirchlichen Zeitschrift*, 79 (1989), p. 196.
21. CCC, para. 84.
22. On Newman's definition, that 'certitude [is] a habit of mind, certainty . . . a quality of propositions'. If God is thought to impart the certainty to the content of the faith, believers may reasonably hold that they experience certitude. *Apologia*, p. 20.
23. *De Ut. Cred.* 16.
24. *De Ut. Cred.* 23.
25. The good leaders and teachers are those who have already found what they seek and are happy in it, or those who are on the way, but the right way, so that they are sure eventually to obtain what they seek. Augustine had second thoughts about the first class in his *Retractationes*, where he pointed out that no one truly knows God and has full happiness in him in his life (*Retr.* 1.xiv.2). Three other kinds of people are *not* to be trusted as witnesses and teachers, because their embracing of the faith rests on insecure foundations and that is affecting the soundness of what they hold or causing them to fail to hold properly anything at all. There are those who hold an opinion, in other words, think they know something which they do not know. There are those who know that they do not know, but do not seek to know. There are those who neither seek nor care that they do not know (*De Ut. Cred.* 25). In the case of religious faith, Augustine contends, those who tell us not to believe but to trust only to reason *least* deserve to be listened to. They are too arrogant to understand the limitations of human reason (*De Ut. Cred.* 27). Likewise, those who lay *claim* to be authoritative are not to be trusted, because such a one clearly lacks the humility of the truly wise man (*De Ut. Cred.* 28). Reception works, and only works, in openness and humility.
26. J. H. Newman, *Select Treatises of St. Athanasius in Controversy with the Arians* (London, 1903), Vol. 2.261, and see Samuel D. Femiano, *Infallibility*

of the Laity (New York, 1967, p. 23). Athanasius uses it, and it is pointed to with approval by Newman.
27. *Apostolic Constitution Fidei Depositum*, CCC.
28. William Whitaker, *Works*, Parker Society edition, p. 433.
29. *Works*, pp. 460–1.
30. John Henry Newman, *University Sermons*, Sermon V; 'Personal influence, the means of propagating the truth', ed. D. M. McKinnon and J. D. Holmes (London, 1970), 11–12, pp. 83–4 (12.2).
31. Newman, *University Sermons*, Sermon V; McKinnon and Holmes 19, p. 87.
32. 16, para. 11.
33. John Henry Newman to the Revd. A. P. Perceval on the *Tracts for the Times*. Mozley, Vol. 11, p. 57.

10. The ebb and flow of influence in the community

1. Konrad Raiser, 'Laity in the Ecumenical Movement', *The Ecumenical Review*, 45 (1993), p. 381.
2. Gerald J. Pillay comments in this connection that 'absence or presence of democracy' is not necessarily an indication of lay participation in the Church. 'The participatory principle and democracy in Church history: some observations', *Studia Historiae Ecclesiasticae*, 19 (1993), pp. 139, 141.
3. For a detailed discussion of one important example, see the next chapter.
4. Thomas More's *Supplication of Souls* is an example of an apologetic work of a type produced in this way in the climate of the earliest stirrings of the Reformation. *The Workes of Sir Thomas More* (London, 1557, repr. London, 1978). See too in *The Complete Works of St Thomas More*, ed. T. M. C. Lawlor and others (New Haven, 1981).
5. William Langland, *Piers the Ploughman*, Prologue, tr. J. F. Goodridge (London, 1959), p. 65.
6. Pardoners sold 'indulgences' which remitted part or all of the temporal penalty deemed to be due even when sin was forgiven, and which it was believed the soul must pay after death by spending a time in purgatory.
7. See John A. Yunck, 'The Lineage of Lady Mead', *Publications in Mediaeval Studies*, 17 (Notre Dame, 1963), p. 111 on the degree of stereotyping of this theme already apparent by the end of the twelfth century, and on the notion that this satire has its roots in a sense of intellectual superiority in those politically weak.
8. But see Thomas Netter, *Fasciculi Zizaniorum*, ed. W. Waddington Shirley (London, 1858), p. 294.
9. Netter, *Fasciculi Zizaniorum*, p. 378. The point at issue here is one well known in the West from at least Augustine's time. The unworthiness of a minister was not deemed to invalidate the sacraments.
10. Netter, *Fasciculi Zizaniorum*, pp. 280–2.
11. Netter, *Fasciculi Zizaniorum*, p. 367.
12. Netter, *Fasciculi Zizaniorum*, p. 293.
13. Netter, *Fasciculi Zizaniorum*, p. 374. *Quod non licet puerum baptizari cum argento in candela* (VI), p. 375.
14. Netter, *Fasciculi Zizaniorum*, p. 366.

15. Netter, *Fasciculi Zizaniorum*, pp. 280–2.
16. Netter, *Fasciculi Zizaniorum*, pp. 381–2.
17. The sentence of William of Barton Chancellor of the University of Oxford.
18. Netter, *Fasciculi Zizaniorum*, pp. 110–11.
19. Netter, *Fasciculi Zizaniorum*, p. 129.
20. *Et nonnullas propositiones et conclusiones infra scriptas haereticas, erroneas, atque falsas, olim ab ecclesia condemnatas, et determinationibus ecclesiae repugnantes, quae statum totius ecclesiae et tranquillitatem regni subvertere et enervare minuantur.* Netter, *Fasciculi Zizaniorum*, p. 276.
21. Netter, *Fasciculi Zizaniorum*, p. 293.
22. Netter, *Fasciculi Zizaniorum*, p. 272.
23. Netter, *Fasciculi Zizaniorum*, p. 270.
24. Netter, *Fasciculi Zizaniorum*, pp. 292–4.
25. Antoninus of Florence, *Summa Maior*, pars III.ii.4.13.
26. Thomas of Chobham, *Summa de Arte Praedicandi*, Corpus Christianorum Continuatio Medievalis, lxxxii (1988), p. 304.
27. *The Later Letters of Peter of Blois*, ed. E. Revell, Auctores Britannici Medii Aevi (Oxford and London, 1993), pp. 159–64, Letter 31, to unknown enquirers.
28. Commentary, I, c. 51 end.
29. De la Bigne, *Maxima Bibliotheca Patrum*, Paris, 1575–9, xxv, II, 83 and 86.
30. It is not inappropriate to ask how efficiently the theologically educated themselves were trained, but that must wait for another chapter.
31. Netter, *Fasciculi Zizaniorum*, pp. 375–6.
32. Aelred of Rievaulx, *Genealogia Regum Anglorum*, ed. R. Twysden, *Historiae Anglicanae Scriptores Decem* (London, 1652), col. 367.
33. Erasmus, *Collected Works* (Toronto, 1974–), Op. X.1208–9.
34. D. H. Green, 'On the primary reception of narrative literature in mediaeval Germany', *Forum for Modern Language Studies*, 20 (1984), pp. 290–1.
35. I omit consideration of the dualist heresies of the Middle Ages here, because they were going down an essentially non-Christian road. See, however, M. Barber, *The Trial of the Templars* (Cambridge, 1978).
36. See Barber, *The Trial of the Templars*.
37. A. Hudson, *Selections from English Wycliffite Writings* (Cambridge, 1978), p. 20.
38. Cf. Ritchie D. Kendall, *The Drama of Dissent: the Radical Poetics of Nonconformity, 1380–1590* (Chapel Hill, 1986), p. 19.
39. *Le Jeu d'Adam* (*Ordo Representacionis Ade*), ed. Wolfgang van Emden (Reading, 1994), pp. 21–2, 39, 41, 47.
40. *Nullus presbiter melius loquitur in pulpito quam ille liber loquitur*, as Richard Gilmyn of Coventry put it in 1486, Lichfield reg., Hales, f. 166v, Hudson, *Selections*, p. 187.
41. 'To Sir John Oldcastle AD 1415', *Minor Poems*, ed. F. J. Furnivall and I. Gollancz, J. Mitchell and A. I. Doyle, Early English Text Society, ES, 61, 73 (1970), no. 2/145ff., 156–8.
42. *The Later Letters of Peter of Blois*, p. 306, Letter 70, to unknown enquirers.
43. *Piers Plowman*, B VII and see whole of this passus.
44. 'The Lollard conceived the religious life to be a pilgrimage in which

religious enlightenment emerged from a continuous and unmediated intellectual struggle with the enemies of God's law.' Kendall, *The Drama of Dissent*, p. 49.
45. Kendall, *The Drama of Dissent*, p. 47.
46. Kendall, *The Drama of Dissent*, p. 59.
47. 'Awareness of Arundel's false witnessing and its ultimate powerlessness forces Thorpe to consider more closely the nature and sources of his own responses.' Arundel poses a question on the doctrine of Chrysostom. Thorpe cannot answer, so he turns to God and asks the Holy Spirit to help. Kendall, *The Drama of Dissent*, pp. 59–60.
48. Kendall, *The Drama of Dissent*, p. 66.
49. Bodleian MS Rawlinson C 208, f. 6v and see Kendall, *The Drama of Dissent*, p. 47.
50. Innocent III, *De Hereticis, Selected Works*, ed. Cheney. On the question of Lollard schools, see Anne Hudson, *The Premature Reformation* (Oxford, 1988), pp. 175ff.
51. *Rotuli Parl.* for 1382, iii.124–5.
52. *Calendar of Patent Rolls*, 1385–9, p. 427.
53. Pubic Records Office, C 54? 223.
54. *Chronicon*, ed. J. R. Lumby, Rolls Series (1889–95), ii.182. These examples are furnished by Hudson, *The Premature Reformation*, pp. 175–9.
55. *Seu scolas tenenti vel exercenti, aut talem librum facienti seu scribenti, vel populum sic docenti, informanti vel excitanti*, *Statutes of the Realm* (London, 1810–28), 10 vols., ii.127.
56. The Alnwick Court Book, see Hudson, *The Premature Reformation*, p. 181.
57. British Library, Egerton 2820, f. 116–116v, Hudson, *The Premature Reformation*, p. 184.
58. Hudson, *The Premature Reformation*, p. 182.
59. Hudson, *The Premature Reformation*, p. 183.
60. A. Gregory (London, 1877).
61. Gottfried Hamman, 'Ecclesiological motifs behind the creation of the "Christlichen Gemeinschaften"', in D. F. Wright, ed., *Martin Bucer*, (Cambridge, 1994), p. 129.
62. See, too, Werner Bellardi's foundational *Die Geschichte der 'Christlichen Gemeinschaften' in Strassburg (1546–50)* (Leipzig, 1934).
63. Hamman, 'Ecclesiological motifs', p. 133.
64. Hamman, 'Ecclesiological motifs', p. 139.
65. James Kittelson, 'Martin Bucer and the ministry of the church', in D. F. Wright, ed., *Martin Bucer* (Cambridge, 1994), p. 89.
66. F. W. B. Bullock, *Voluntary Religious Societies, 1520–1799* (St Leonards on Sea, 1963), p. 3.
67. David Carter, 'A Methodist Contribution to Ecclesiology', *One in Christ* (1994), pp. 161–75, concentrating on the contributions of Benjamin Gregory and J. H. Rigg, p. 162.
68. Henry D. Rack, *Reasonable Enthusiast: John Wesley and the Rise of Methodism* (London, 1989), p. 23.
69. Carter, 'A Methodist Contribution', p. 164.
70. J. H. Rigg, *The Methodist Class Meeting* (1865), p. 3.

71. Bullock, *Voluntary Religious Societies*.
72. Bullock, *Voluntary Religious Societies*, p. ix.
73. An exception is Methodism. Bullock, *Voluntary Religious Societies*, p. x.
74. Carter, 'A Methodist Contribution', p. 163.

11. Ideas in their context: histories of reception

1. David Thompson, 'History, Scripture, the Church and Ecumenism' in G. R. Evans and M. Gorgues, eds., *Communion et réunion, Essays in Honour of Jean Tillard* (Louvain, 1995).
2. Fourth Lateran Council, Constitution I, Tanner, I.230.
3. Tanner, I.230.
4. Constitutions, II.1, Tanner, I.314.
5. Porvoo, p. 194.
6. Mozley, Vol. 11, p. 117.
7. Mozley, Vol. 11, p. 126.
8. Mozley, Vol. 11, p. 286.
9. Mozley, Vol. 11, p. 287.
10. Pusey to Newman, 1829. Mozley, Vol. 1, p. 212.
11. Mozley, Vol. 11, p. 59.
12. Mozley, Vol. 11, p. 156.
13. *Apologia*, p. 23.
14. Cardinal Montini, speaking on 7 December, 1962, quoted by Y. Congar, 'Moving towards a Pilgrim Church', *Vatican II revisited*, p. 135. See too F. M. Bliss, *Understanding Reception: A background to its ecumenical use* (Rome, 1991), p. 140.
15. E. B. Pusey, *Nine Sermons Preached before the University of Oxford and Printed Chiefly between 1843 and 1855* (London, 1891), 'The Rule of Faith', Fifth Sunday after Epiphany, 1851, p. 25.
16. Thomas Netter, *Fasciculi Zizaniorum*, ed. W. Waddington Shirley (London, 1858), pp. 386–7.
17. Q. 1, 'Whether in the twentieth article these words are not inserted, "Habet ecclesia authoritatem in controversiis fidei".' E. Cardwell, *A History of Conferences . . . from the year 1558 to the year 1690* (Oxford, 1840), p. 270.
18. Creeds pp. 442–3.
19. Martin Chemnitz, *Examen Concilii Tridentini*, Locus IX, Section 1.vi, tr. F. Kramer (St Louis, 1978), p. 679.
20. *Examen*, VII.3.3, Kramer, Vol. II, p. 575.
21. *Examen*, Locus VI, Kramer, p. 391. Scripture is, however, notoriously not a simple or straightforward witness.
22. *Examen*, VII.3.2, Kramer, Vol. II, p. 572.
23. *Examen*, VII.3.2, Kramer, Vol. II, p. 572.
24. *Examen*, VII.3.3, Kramer, Vol. II, p. 572.
25. *Examen*, VII.4.7, Kramer, Vol. II, p. 586.
26. *Examen*, VII.1.18, Kramer, Vol. II, p. 565.
27. *Examen*, VII.1.18, Kramer, Vol. II, p. 565.

28. Pusey, *Nine Sermons*, 'The Rule of Faith', Fifth Sunday after Epiphany, 1851, pp. 61–2.
29. PL 210.307. See, too my *Alan of Lille* (Cambridge, 1983).
30. William Cole, in the *Works* of Jewel, Parker Society Series, Vol. I, p. 29.
31. Cole, Jewel, Vol. I, p. 29.
32. The papalists. *Examen*, Locus IV, Section II, Kramer, p. 346.
33. Pusey, *Nine Sermons*.
34. On all this see Wilfred Ward, *The Life of John Henry Cardinal Newman* (London, 1912), 2 vols., p. 91.
35. Newman to Pusey, 5 September 1865, Ward, II, p. 91.
36. Newman to Pusey, 5 September 1865, Ward, II, p. 92.
37. Newman to Pusey, 31 October 1865, Ward, II, p. 100.
38. Pusey, *Nine Sermons*, 'The Presence of Christ in the Holy Eucharist', Second Sunday after Epiphany, 1853, p. 47.
39. Pusey, *Nine Sermons*, 'The Rule of Faith', Fifth Sunday after Epiphany, 1851, p. 14.
40. Pusey, *Nine Sermons*, 'The Rule of Faith', Fifth Sunday after Epiphany, 1851, pp. 61–2.
41. Newman to Pusey, 31 October 1865, Ward, II, p. 100.
42. Newman to Pusey, 31 October 1865, Ward, II, p. 100.
43. Newman to Pusey, Feast of the Immaculate Conception, 1865, Ward, II, p. 102.
44. 'Even the *Month*, under the editorship of Father Coleridge, did not evince the degree of understanding sympathy with Pusey's book which Newman felt to be required in any reply which was to be at all convincing to the Puseyites themselves.' Ward, II, p. 99–100.
45. This is exemplified in some Lutheran Confessions.
46. Cardwell, *A History of Conferences*, p. 257.
47. 'The first Address and Proposals of the Ministers', Cardwell, *A History of Conferences*, p. 278.
48. Cardwell, *A History of Conferences*, p. 262.
49. Cardwell, *A History of Conferences*, p. 263.
50. Cardwell, *A History of Conferences*, p. 264.
51. Cardwell, *A History of Conferences*, p. 265 (emphasis in the original).
52. Cardwell, *A History of Conferences*, p. 266.

12. Coming out of controversy

1. His Majesty's Declaration to all his loving subjects of his kingdom of England and dominion of Wales, concerning ecclesiastical affairs, 25 October 1660, Cardwell, *A History of Conferences... from the year 1558 to the year 1690* (Oxford, 1840), p. 296.
2. Wilfrid Ward, *The Life of John Henry Cardinal Newman* (London, 1912), II, p. 104.
3. E. B. Pusey, *Nine Sermons Preached before the University of Oxford and Printed Chiefly between 1843 and 1855* (London, 1891), 'The Rule of Faith', Fifth Sunday after Epiphany, 1851, pp. 61–2. 'And while the shepherds are at

variance, the wolf cometh and scattereth the sheep'. 'The Rule of Faith', Fifth Sunday after Epiphany, 1851, pp. 61–2.
4. John Henry Newman, *University Sermons*, Sermon V, 'Personal influence, the means of propagating the truth' ed. D. M. McKinnon and J. D. Holmes (London, Longman, 1970), 19, p. 88.
5. 26 November 1926, Mozley, Vol. 1, pp. 143–5.
6. Mozley, Vol. 1, pp. 143–5.
7. Varying mythologies, and the sheer complexity of so long a period of religious change, have always ensured healthy controversy about Tudor religion. See Felicity Heal, 'Rewriting the History of the Reformation', *Church Times*, 13 May 1994, p. 8. See, too, Eamon Duffy, *The Stripping of the Altars* (Yale, 1992); Christopher Haigh, *English Reformations: Religion, Politics and Society under the Tudors* (Oxford, 1993); J. A. F. Thomson, *Early Tudor Church and Society* (Longman, 1993); C. Harper-Bill, *The Pre-Reformation Church in England, 1400–1530* (Longman, 1989); R. N. Swanson, *Church and Society in Late Mediaeval England* (Oxford, 1989).
8. See Heal, 'Rewriting the History', p. 8.
9. Mozley, Vol. 11, p. 60.
10. *The Acts and Decrees of the Synod of Jerusalem, Sometimes Called the Council of Bethlehem*, tr. J. N. W. B. Robertson (London, 1899), Decree XI, and *Creeds*, p. 495.
11. Address of Metropolitan Meliton of Heliopolis and Theira, 22 November 1965, Stormon, p. 118.
12. Common Declaration, 7 December 1965, Stormon, p. 127.
13. *Koinonia: auf Altkirchlicher Basis*, ed. Urs von Arx, *Internationalen Kirchlichen Zeitschrift*, 79 (1989), p. 192.
14. Cardinal Montini, speaking on 7 December 1962, quoted by Y. Congar, 'Moving towards a Pilgrim Church', *Vatican II revisited*, pp. 142–3. See too F. M. Bliss, *Understanding Reception: A background to its ecumenical use* (Rome, 1991), p. 140.
15. Report of Committee on Baptist Faith and Message, Southern Baptist Convention, 1925, Annual of the Southern Baptist Convention, 1925, pp. 71–6; *Creeds*, p. 345.

13. What is 'ecumenical reception'?

1. 'Toward Full Communion' and 'Concordat of Agreement', *Lutheran–Episcopal Dialogue*, Series III, ed. William A. Norgren and William G. Rusch (Minneapolis and Cincinnati, 1991), pp. 111, 112.
2. Norgren and Rusch, *Lutheran–Episcopal Dialogue*, p. 114.
3. Norgren and Rusch, *Lutheran–Episcopal Dialogue*, p. 111.
4. Norgren and Rusch, *Lutheran–Episcopal Dialogue*, p. 6.
5. Porvoo, pp. 186–7 (emphasis in the original).
6. Porvoo, p. 189.
7. Porvoo, pp. 189–90. The pastor being ordained is asked, 'Do you want to remain faithful to the pure Word of God, to avoid false doctrine, to preach fearlessly, and to administer the holy sacraments according to his ordinance?' Porvoo, p. 90.

8. Porvoo, p. 189.
9. Porvoo, p. 192.
10. Porvoo, p. 194.
11. Franklin Hamlin Littell, *From State Church to Pluralism*, (New York, 1960), pp. 184–8.
12. Report of Committee on Baptist Faith and Message, Southern Baptist Convention, 1925, Annual of the Southern Baptist Convention, 1925, pp. 71–6; *Creeds*, p. 345.
13. *The New Hampshire Confession* (1833, published with revisions by J. Newton Brown, 1853), *Baptist Confessions of Faith*, ed. William L. Lumpkin (Valley Forge, Pa, 1959) pp. 361–7 and *Creeds*, p. 334ff.
14. Faith, pp. 71–6; *Creeds*, p. 345.

14. Mutual reception

1. 'Toward Full Communion' and 'Concordat of Agreement', *Lutheran–Episcopal Dialogue*, Series III, ed. William A. Norgren and William G. Rusch (Minneapolis and Cincinnati, 1991), pp. 16–18.
2. See Seim's paper in G. R. Evans, Lorelei Fuchs and Diane Kessler, eds., *Encounters for Unity*, (Norwich, Canterbury Press, 1995), pp. 173–5.
3. Seim, *Encounters for Unity*, pp. 173–5.
4. *Churches Respond to BEM*, ed. Max Thurian, p. 87, Church of Scotland (Reformed).
5. *Respond*, p. 79, Methodist Church of New Zealand.
6. *Respond*, p. 36, Lutheran Church in America.
7. *Respond*, p. 80, Methodist Church of New Zealand.
8. *Respond*, pp. 83–4, Presbyterian Church in Cameroon.
9. Seim, *Encounters for Unity*, pp. 173–5.
10. The Helvetic Consensus Formula (1675), written by John Heidegger of Zurich at the request of the Swiss Diet, is a liberalized Calvinism. *Creeds*, p. 310.
11. Schleitheim Confession (1527), *Brotherly union of a number of children of God concerning seven articles*, *Creeds*, pp. 285–6.
12. See my *The Church and the Churches*, pp. 135–7.
13. The idea that a meeting of cultures is itself integral to the fullness of reception belongs in this very recent context. F. M. Bliss, *Understanding Reception: A background to its ecumenical use* (Rome, 1991), p. 122.
14. Margrethe Brown, *Encounters for Unity*, pp. 20–3.
15. *Respond*, pp. 78–9, Methodist Church of New Zealand.
16. Choan-Seng Song, *Encounters for Unity*, pp. 32–41.
17. CCC, para. 24, p. 11.
18. Mark D. Chapman, 'A Theology for Europe: Universality and Particularity in Christian Theology', *The Heythrop Journal*, 35 (1994), 125–40, p. 129.
19. Chapman, 'A Theology for Europe', p. 129.
20. See my article in *Journal of Ecumenical Studies*, 31 (1994), pp. 93–110.
21. Confession of Faith of the Sumatran/Indonesian Huria Kristen Batak, Protestant (1951), *Creeds*, pp. 555ff.
22. *Respond*, p. 55, Anglican Church of the Southern Cone.

23. A version of this material is published in *Midstream*, 33 (1994), pp. 253–64.
24. *Message*, 10.
25. Section III Report, 6.
26. Section I Report, 25.
27. *Message*, 10.
28. 'The ecumenical movement has changed over the past thirty years,' acknowledges the *Message* from Santiago (7), taking an overview of the shifts as they appear at present. I list its points (the numeration is mine):
    i. The voices of women and of those from beyond Europe and North America have joined the ecumenical conversation in strength, bringing new insights, new experiences, new diversities.
    ii. The significance for *koinonia* of common ethical commitment and action has been firmly placed on the Faith and Order Agenda.
    iii. The many positive movements of evangelical and charismatic renewal still need to be drawn into ecumenical partnership.
    There follows an acknowledgement that the transformation is still going on and is at times difficult and controversial. (Again the numeration is mine):
    i. Differences over the goals and methods of ecumenical work and theology have led to intense debates.
    ii. In these debates, conflicting perspectives often each express significant elements of truth.
    iii. We are confident we are being led through such tensions into a deeper and broader *koinonia* in the Spirit.
    iv. A test of our *koinonia* is how we live with those with whom we disagree.
29. Section II, Report, 4. Though not without a stress on sharing: 'While it is the churches in the local setting who are in a position to confess their faith in that context, their testimony should be shared with the wider ecumenical community.'
30. 'Further work', Section III Report, 22.
31. 'The invitation to participate in the pilgrimage provides an opportunity to invite others who have been hesitant hitherto to engage in dialogue.' Section I Report, 30.
32. 'The voices of women and of those from beyond Europe and North America have joined the ecumenical conversation in strength, bringing new insights, new experiences, new diversities.' *Message*, 10.
33. 'All members belong but not all are the same . . . thus difference is not a factor to exclude anyone from the *koinonia* of the church, especially when such differences are expressive of weakness or vulnerability.' Section I Report, 16.
34. Section I Report, 10.
35. Section I Report, 15.
36. Section I Report, 17.
37. Section I Report, 28.
38. Section II Report, 14.
39. Section II Report, 20.
40. Section I Report, 27.
41. Section I Report, 27.

42. *Message*, 10.
43. Section II Report, 5.2.
44. Section I Report, 28. I have been very selective here, for reasons of space. See too 'Further work', Section III Report, 22, on sacramental issues; 'Further work', Section III Report, 31, on joint structures; Section IV on mission also has practical tasks in mind.
45. A further suggestion is designed to help here. 'We would be assisted in our journeying by inter-contextual dialogues appropriately sponsored by regional Faith and Order study on hermeneutics.' Section I Report, 28. See too 'Further work', Section III Report, 22, on sacramental issues; 'Further work', Section III Report, 31, on joint structures; Section IV on mission also has practical tasks in mind.
46. Section II Report, 11.
47. Section I Report, 28.

15. Shared reception – your faith or mine?

1. Ritchie D. Kendall, *The Drama of Dissent: the Radical Poetics of Nonconformity, 1380–1590* (Chapel Hill, 1986), p. 43.
2. *Creeds*, pp. 354–60.
3. Schleitheim Confession (1527), *Brotherly union of a number of children of God concerning seven articles*, *Creeds*, p. 283.
4. Schleitheim Confession, *Creeds*, p. 291.
5. Phrase used by Faith and Order, St Andrews (1960) and also by WCC, New Delhi (1961), *Creeds*, pp. 582 and 583.
6. Schleitheim Confession, *Creeds*, p. 284.
7. *Creeds*, pp. 292–308.
8. See for example *Pluralisme et oecuménisme en recherches théologiques, Mélanges offerts à R. P. Dockx*, ed. R. E. Hoeckman (Louvain, 1976).
9. *Creeds*, pp. 572–3.
10. *Creeds*, pp. 577–8.
11. A version of this text was published in *The Tablet*, January, 1994.
12. 18 and UR. 4, 'Catholics hold the firm conviction that the one Church of Christ subsists in the Catholic Church' (17). 'Catholics hold the firm conviction that the one Church of Christ subsists in the Catholic Church "which is governed by the successor of Peter and by the bishops in communion with him" (LG, 8). They confess that the entirety of revealed truth, of sacraments, and of ministry that Christ gave for the building up of his Church and the carrying out of its mission is found within the Catholic communion of the Church' (17).
13. As in: 'At the level of the universal Church, the Pontifical Council for Promoting Christian Unity, a department of the Roman Curia, has the competence and the task of promoting full communion among all Christians' (53).
14. 57e.
15. 'A certain communion' is seen as helpful in paragraph 18 (already quoted).
16. 'Openness and mutual respect are the logical consequences of such recognition' (36).

17. It rests on *Unitatis Redintegratio* 24 in stressing that ecumenical activity 'has to be fully and sincerely Catholic, that is, faithful to the truth we have received from the Apostles and the Fathers and consonant with the faith the Catholic Church has always professed' (73).
18. Openness must not be entirely open-ended, for unforeseen situations can arise. 'The situations being dealt with in ecumenism are often unprecedented, and vary from place to place and time to time' (30). So 'careful note must be taken of the various prerequisites for ecumenical engagement that are set out in the Decree on Ecumenism of the Second Vatican Council' (24, cf. UR, 9–12, 16–18).
19. Cf. GS, 62.2, UR, 6; Congregation for the Doctrine of the Faith, *Mysterium Ecclesiae* (ME), 5.
20. 'Changing conceptions proper to a given age' and 'the truths which the Church intends actually to teach through its dogmatic formularies'.
21. Cf. 61e. 'the possibilities offered by the distinction between the truths of faith and their modes of expression'. 'From the time of their philosophical formation, students should be prepared to appreciate the legitimate diversity in theology which derives from the different methods and language theologians use in penetrating the divine mysteries.'
22. 'It is of particular importance that a course in ecumenism be given at an appropriate point in the first cycle. Such a course should be compulsory' (79). The idea and the possible content of 'a specific course in ecumenism' are developed in paragraphs 79ff.
23. 'With whom they are in contact' seems an unnecessary and perhaps unhelpful limitation, and one not imposed elsewhere in the document.
24. Cf. UR, 11, AG, 15.
25. I footnote the following not because they are less important but because they bear less directly on the present discussion:
    e. the 'institutional' aspect and the contemporary life in the various Christian Communities; doctrinal tendencies . . .
    f. some more specific problems such as shared worship, proselytism and irenicism, religious freedom, mixed marriages, the role of the laity and, in particular, of women in the Church;
    g. spiritual ecumenism, especially the significance of prayer for unity and other forms of tending towards the unity prayed for by Christ.
26. 'Catholics will act with honesty, prudence and knowledge of the issues. This readiness to proceed gradually and with care, not glossing over difficulties, is also a safeguard against succumbing to the temptations of indifferentism and proselytism, which would be a failure of the true ecumenical spirit' (23).
27. Cf. CIC, Can. 216 and 212; CCEO, Can. 19 and 15.
28. Cf. CIC, Can. 755.1, CCEO, Can. 902 and 904.
29. 27, cf. LG, 23; CD, 11; CIC, Can. 383.3 and CCEO, Can. 192.2.
30. On gradualness, cf. paragraph 194.
31. Cf. CIC, Can. 209.1; CCEO, Can. 12.1.

BIBLIOGRAPHY

Primary sources

The Acts and Decrees of the Synod of Jerusalem, Sometimes Called the Council of Bethlehem. Tr. J. N. W. B. Robertson, London, 1899.
Aelred of Rievaulx, *Genealogia Regum Anglorum.* Ed. R. Twysden, *Historia Anglicanae Scriptores Decem.* London, 1652.
The Archbishops' Committee on Church and State, Report. London, 1916.
Barclay, Robert, *An Apology for the True Christian Divinity being an Explanation and Vindication of the Principles and Doctrines of the People called Quakers.* New York, 1832.
Barnes, *The Injunctions and other Ecclesiastical Proceedings of Bishop Barnes.* Surtees Society, 1850.
Bernard of Clairvaux, *Sancti Bernardi Opera Omnia.* Ed. J. Leclercq, C. H. Talbot and H. M. Rochais, Rome, Vatican, 1957–78, 8 vols.
Burnet, Gilbert, *A Discourse of the Pastoral Care.* 1692.
Catechism of the Catholic Church. Latin text, Rome, Vatican, 1992. English text, London, Geoffrey Chapman, 1994.
Chemnitz, Martin, *Examen Concilii Tridentini.* Tr. F. Kramer, St Louis, Concordia, 1978.
Creeds of the Churches. Ed. John H. Leith, Virginia, Anchor, 1963, revised edn, 1973.
Crispin, Gilbert, *Disputatio cum Gentile. The Works of Gilbert Crispin.* Ed. A. Abulafia and G. R. Evans, Auctores Britannici Medii Aevi, Oxford, Oxford University Press and British Academy, 1986.
Ecumenical Formation: Ecumenical Reflections and Suggestions. A Study Document of the Joint Working Group between the Roman Catholic Church and the World Council of Churches. 20 May 1993.
Ely Episcopal Records. Ed. A. Gibbons, 1891.
English Wycliffite Sermons. Ed. Hudson, Oxford, Oxford University Press, 1983.
Episcopal Ministry. The Report of the Archbishops' Group on the Episcopate. London, Church House Publishing, 1990.
Fasciculi Zizianorum. Ed. W. Waddington Shirley, London, Rolls Series, 1858.
Grindal, E. *Works.* Parker Society Series, Cambridge, Cambridge University Press, 1943.
Innocent III, *Selected Letters.* Ed. C. Cheney, London, Mediaeval Texts Series, 1953.

Le Jeu d'Adam (Ordo Representacionis Ade). Ed. W. van Emden, Reading, Graduate Centre for Mediaeval Studies, 1994.
Jewel, John, *Apology for the Defence of the Church of England. Works*, ed. J. Ayre, Parker Society Series, Cambridge, Cambridge University Press, 1845–50.
Langland, William, *Piers the Ploughman*. Tr. J. F. Goodridge, London, Penguin, 1959.
More, Thomas, *The Works of Sir Thomas More*. London, 1557, repr. New Haven, Yale University Press, 1978.
More, Thomas, *The Complete Works of St Thomas More*. Ed. T. M. C. Lawler et al., Princeton, NJ, Princeton University Press, 1981.
Newman, John Henry, *Letters and Correspondence of John Henry Newman during his Life in the English Church*. Ed. Anne Mozley, London, 1891.
Peter of Blois, *The Later Letters of Peter of Blois*. Ed. Elizabeth Revell, Auctores Britannici Medii Aevi, 13. Oxford, Oxford University Press and British Academy, 1993.
Peter of Waltham, *Remediarum Conversorum*. Ed. J. Gildea, Villanova, Augustinian Institute, 1984.
Pusey, E. B., *Nine Sermons Preached before the University of Oxford and Printed Chiefly between 1843 and 1855*. London, 1891 and 1912.
Register of Bishop John de Pontissara, Canterbury and York Society, 1 (1915).
Sanderson, R., *Sermo ad Clerum*. London, 1664.
Smalley, B., *The Study of the Bible in the Middle Ages*. Oxford, Oxford University Press, 3rd edn, 1983.
Suenens, L.-J., *Co-responsibility in the Church*. Tr. Francis Martin, London, Burns & Oates, Herder & Herder, 1968.
Tanner, Norman P. (ed.), *Decrees of the Ecumenical Councils*. Georgetown, Sheed and Ward, 1990, 2 vols.
Thurian, Max, *Churches Respond to BEM*. Vol. I *Together in Mission and Ministry: The Porvoo Common Statement with Essays in Church and Ministry in Northern Europe. Conversations between the British and Irish Anglican Churches and the Nordic and Baltic Lutheran Churches*. London, Church House Publishing, 1993.
'Towards Full Communion' and 'Concordat of Agreement', *Lutheran–Episcopal Dialogue*. Series III. Ed. William A. Norgren and William G. Rusch, Minneapolis and Cincinnati, World Council of Churches 1991.
Vatican Council II: The Conciliar and Post-Conciliar Documents, I. (New Revised Edn,) ed. A. Flannery, Collegeville, Minnesota.
Whitgift, John, *Works of Archbishop Whitgift*. Parker Society Series, 3 (1853).

Secondary sources

Barber, Malcolm, *The Trial of the Templars*. Cambridge, Cambridge University Press, 1978.
Baum, G., 'Three theses on contextual theology', *The Ecumenist*, 24 (1986), 49–59.
Blackmore, R. W., tr., *The Doctrine of the Russian Church*. Aberdeen, 1845.
Bliss, F. M., *Understanding Reception: A background to its ecumenical use*. Rome, Vatican, 1991.

BIBLIOGRAPHY

Bullock, F. W. B., *Voluntary Religious Societies, 1520–1799*. St Leonards on Sea, Budd & Gillatt 1963.
Cardwell, E., *A History of Conferences . . . from the year 1558 to the year 1690*. Oxford, 1840.
Carpenter, E. F., *Thomas Tenison*. London, SPCK, 1948.
Carter, David, 'A Methodist Contribution to Ecclesiology', *One in Christ* (1994), 161–75.
Clarke, T., 'Communities for Justice', *The Ecumenist*, 19 (1981), 17–25.
Crosland, J. D., 'The Bedford Association: An early ecumenical movement', *Proceedings of the Wesley Historical Society*, 28 (1951–2), 95.
Dent, C. M., *Protestant Reformers in Elizabethan Oxford*. Oxford, Oxford University Press, 1983.
Duffy, Eamon, *The Stripping of the Altars*. Yale, Yale University Press, 1992.
Evans, G. R., *Old Arts and New Theology*. Oxford, Oxford University Press, 1983.
Evans, G. R., *Alan of Lille*. Cambridge, Cambridge University Press, 1983.
Evans, G. R., *The Language and the Logic of the Bible*. Cambridge, Cambridge University Press, 1984–5, 2 vols.
Evans, G. R., *Problems of Authority in the Reformation Debates*. Cambridge, Cambridge University Press, 1992.
Evans, G. R., *The Church and the Churches*. Cambridge, Cambridge University Press, 1994.
Fenlon, D., 'The Tridentine profession of faith', in C. S. Rodd, ed., *Foundation Documents of the Faith*. Edinburgh, T. and T. Clark, 1987.
Green, D. H., 'On the primary reception of narrative literature in mediaeval Germany', *Forum for Modern Language Studies*, 20 (1984), 290–1.
Haigh, Christopher, *English Reformations: Religion, Politics and Society under the Tudors*. Oxford, Oxford University Press, 1993.
Hamman, Gottfried, 'Ecclesiological motifs behind the creation of the "Christlichen Gemeinschaften"', in D. F. Wright, ed., *Martin Bucer*. Cambridge, Cambridge University Press, 1994, pp. 129–43.
Harper-Bill, C., *The Pre-Reformation Church in England, 1400–1530*. Harlow, Longman, 1989.
Houtepen, A., 'Reception', in N. Lossky et al., eds., *Dictionary of the Ecumenical Movement*. Geneva, World Council of Churches, 1991.
Howarth, H. W., 'The influence of Jerome on the Canon of the Western Church', *Journal of Theological Studies*, 10 (1908–9), 481–96.
Kendall, Ritchie D., *The Drama of Dissent: the Radical Poetics of Nonconformity, 1380–1590*. Chapel Hill, University of North Carolina Press, 1986.
Kernan, Alvin, *The Cankered Muse: Satire of the English Renaissance*. Yale, Yale University Press, 1959.
Lovegrove, Deryck, *Established Church, Sectarian People*. Cambridge, Cambridge University Press, 1988.
Lubac, H. de, *Exégèse médiévale*. Paris, Cerf, 1959, 2 vols.
Meyer, Harding, 'The ecumenical dialogues: situation-problems-perspectives', *Pro Ecclesia*, 3 (1994), 24–35.
Moberly, H., *Life of William of Wykeham*. London, 1887.
Norden, J., *The Surveyors Dialogue*. 1607.

Pfleiderer, Otto, *The Development of Theology in Germany since Kant and its Progress in Great Britain since 1825*. Tr. J. Frederick Smith, London, 1890.
Pillay, Gerald, 'The participatory principle and democracy in Church history: some observations', *Studia Historiae Ecclesiasticae*, 19 (1993), 139–56.
Rack, Henry D., *Reasonable Enthusiast: John Wesley and the Rise of Methodism*. London, Epworth, 1989.
Raiser, Konrad, 'Laity in the Ecumenical Movement', *The Ecumenical Review*, 45 (1993), 375–83.
Ramcharan, Michael, 'Consciousness of the People of God', *Ecumenical Review*, 45 (1993), 402–7.
Rigg, J. H., *The Methodist Class Meeting*. 1865.
Ritchie, Nélida, 'Laity and Contextual Theology', *The Ecumenical Review*, 45 (1993), 384–7.
Robeck, Cecil M., William R. Barr and Rena M. Yocom, eds.,*The Church in the Movement of the Spirit*. Grand Rapids, Michigan, Eerdmans, 1994.
Rüppell, Gert, 'Following Christ in a World of Anguish'. *The Ecumenical Review*, 45 (1993), 392–6.
Simpfendörfer, Werner, 'Intercultural living; ecumenical learning', *The Ecumenical Review*, 45 (1993), 397–8.
de Soujeole, D., '"Societé" et "Communion" chez S. Thomas d'Aquin', *Revue Thomiste*, 90 (1990), 587–622.
Stock, Brian, *The Implications of Literacy*. Princeton NJ, Princeton University Press, 1983.
Swanson, R. N., *Church and Society in Late Mediaeval England*. Oxford, Blackwell, 1989.
Tavard, G., 'A Catholic Reflection on the Porvoo Statement', *Midstream* (1994).
Tavard, G., For a bibliography, see the recent Festschrift, *The Quadrilog*, ed. K. Hagen (Minnesota, 1994).
Thomas, Keith, *Religion and the Decline of Magic*. London, Penguin, 1971.
Thompson, David, 'History, Scripture, the Church and Ecumenism' in *Communion et réunion: Essays in Honour of Jean Tillard*, ed. G. R. Evans and M. Gorgues, Louvain, Peeters, 1995, pp. 199–216.
Thomson, J. A. F., *Early Tudor Church and Society*. Harlow, Longman, 1993.
Tillard, J. M. R., *The Bishop of Rome*. Paris, Cerf, 1982, tr. J. Satgé, London, SPCK, 1983.
Tillard, J. M. R., *Église des Églises*, Paris, Cerf, 1984.
Tjørhon, Ola, 'The Porvoo Statement – a possible ecumenical breakthrough?' *Pro Ecclesia*, 3 (1994), 11–17.
Vincent of Lérins, *Commonitorium*. Ed. G. Moxon, Cambridge, Cambridge University Press, 1915.
von Arx, Urs, (ed.), 'Koinonia: auf Altkirchlicher Basis', *Internationalen Kirchlichen Zeitschrift*, 79 (1989).
Walton, C., *Notes and materials for an adequate biography of . . . William Law comprising an elucidation of the scope and contents of the writings of Jacob Böhme and of his great commentator Dionysius Andreas Freher*. London, 1854.
Ward, Benedicta, *Miracles and the Mediaeval Mind*. Aldershot, Scolar Press, 1982.

BIBLIOGRAPHY

Ward, Wilfred, *The Life of John Henry Cardinal Newman*. London, Longman, 1912.

White, Peter, *Predestination, Policy and Polemic: Conflict and Consensus in the English Church from the Reformation to the Civil War*, Cambridge, Cambridge University Press, 1992.

Williams, Rowan, *Arius*. London, Darton, Longman and Todd, 1987.

Yunck, John A., 'The Lineage of Lady Mead', *Publications in Mediaeval Studies*, 17, Notre Dame University Press, 1963.

INDEX

abbots 85
Abelard, Peter 103
Adam 131
adults 39
Africa 176
agreed statements 165
Alan of Lille 149
Albigensians 140
Ambrose of Milan 49, 52
Anabaptists 184
anathemas 159–60
Anglicans 12, 18, 151, 157, 166, 174
Antichrist 52
antiquity 76, 145, 148
Apollinarians 96
apostles 31, 159, 160, 168
   in *via* 160
Apostles' Creed 80, 168, 177
Apostolic See 191
apostolic Church 185
apostolicity xi
Aquinas, Thomas 63
Aristeri 95
Aristides of Athens 103
Arius, Arians 47, 95, 97, 98, 148
Asia 33
astronomy 167
Athanasian Creed 177
Athens 176
Augsburg Confession 80, 141, 167
Augustine 34–8, 41, 44, 47–51, 52, 53, 56, 113–15, 141
authority 6, 23
Aymara 43

Babel 115
Babylon 60
Babylonian captivity 27
Backster, Margery 129, 131
Bacon, Francis 60
Balaam 18
Baltimore 43
baptism 160
Baptists 168, 169, 174
Barnes, Richard 59
Basle 128
Basle, Council of (1431) 86
Baum, G., 23, 25
Baxter, Richard 153–4
Bede 7
Berengar 11
Bernard of Clairvaux 102, 152
Beveridge, Bishop 53
Bible, see Scripture
Bible-study 131
bilateral dialogue 172, 179
bishops 85
Blois, Peter of 65–8, 126
Bristol 61
Burnet, Gilbert 60

Calvin 177
Calvinists 174
Canada 25
Canon law 34, 83, 176
Caribbean 176
Carlyle, Thomas 47
Carthage 34
catechesis 33–4, 80, 190
catechumens 96

Cathars 95
ceremonies 148
Cerularios, Michael 159
Chalcedon, Council of (451) 79, 143
charismatic movements 4
Charlemagne 128
Chaucer 127
Chemnitz, Martin 146–7
children in the faith 15 ff.
Chobham, Thomas 126
Christ 30, 43, 114, 140, 158–9
Church, early 76
Church, local 77
Church of England 69, 83, 110
churches, divided 78
citizenship 10
Clement 146
clergy 55–64
Cole, William 149
Colet, John 55, 160
colonialism 24
community 10
conciliarity 82
confession 145
confessional identity 179, 181
conflict 22
consensus fidelium 16, 110–13, 148, 166
Constance, Council of (1415) 76, 86
Constantinople, Council of (381) 79
Constantinople, Council of (680–1) 79
consultation 84
contextualization 182
Convocation 58, 83
Cosin, John 154
Council, General 148
councils, 69, 70, 76ff.
 see synods
Councils, Ecumenical 55, 91, 158, 159
creation 181
Creeds 39, 75, 140
Cromwell, Oliver 99
culture 176, 180

Cyril Lukaris 159
Cyril of Alexandria 76, 96
Daniel, prophet 52
deacons 187
Declaration of Assent 100
defending the faith 94–101
degrees of communion 186
demagogues 46
Denmark 165–7
deposit of faith 31, 144, 152
development 144–9
Didymus the Blind 103
dissenters 45
diversity 179–80
doctrinal formulae 165
dogma 145
Dominicans 45
Dublin 82

Eadmer 152
East 78, 140
ecclesiolae 136
Edinburgh 92, 185
Egypt 81, 176
Ely 58, 61
Ephesus, Council of (431) 76
Epictetus 97
Epiphanius 146
Erasmus 55, 128
Eucharist 150
Eucharistic sacrifice 129
Eunomians 96, 97
Euyches 47
Evangelical 157
excommunication 11, 159
expert, expertise 27, 121

Faber Stapulensis, Jacobus 152
Faith and Order 176, 178, 180, 185
faith, primitive 145
Fathers 41, 147
Faustus the Manichee 49
Ferrara-Florence, Council of 78
Fidei Depositum, Apostolic Constitution 43
Finland 78, 167
Fleetwood, William 61
forgiveness 148

INDEX

formation 190
Francis of Assisi 45
freedom 22
Froude, Richard Hurrell 51, 54, 141

Geneva 176
Geoffrey of Nantes 67
Germany 169
Gospel viii
Greek 69, 173, 176
Gregory the Great 44, 75

Hadrian, Pope 86
harmony 115–19, 179
Heal, Felicity 158
Hereford, Nicholas of 125
heresy 94–101, 175
hierarchy 174
historic episcopate 165
Hoare, Henry 83
Hoccleve, Thomas 132
holocaust 157
Holy Spirit 4, 5, 31, 38, 77, 81, 88, 89, 110, 116–17, 140, 146, 158, 169, 170, 184
Houtepen, A. viii
Humbert, Cardinal 159
humility 36

ideology 24
Ignatius 52
Immaculate Conception 145
Ireland 80, 82, 98, 167
Irenaeus 143

Jacob 36
James, William 53
Jerome 130
Jesus 24, 155
Jewel, John 18, 68, 149, 150
Jews 36
Joachim of Fioere 141
John, Evangelist 52
John Paul, Pope 43
justice 179
Justin Martyr 52, 103, 146

Keble, John 51
koinonia 10, 180, 181

Lactantius 103
laity 11 ff, 28, 42, 144
Langland, William 122
language 144, 180, 181
Lateran Council III (1179) 94
Lateran Council IV (1215) 30, 140, 145
Lateran Councils 78
Latin 44, 59, 69, 130
Latin America 25, 177
law 123
Laymen, House of 83–4
legitimate diversity 156, 185, 188
Leo, St., 143
Lima 43
Lincoln 104
Lithuania 168
liturgy 13
Lollards 16, 123, 132
Lombard, Peter 66
London Missionary Society 61
Lord's Prayer, The 38, 39
Lund 185
Luther, Lutherans 80, 82, 148, 165, 166, 167, 168
Lyons, Council of (1274) 78, 85

Macedonians 95
magisterium 188
malice 150
Manichees 114, 115
Maoris 175
Mary, Virgin 39, 145–6, 178
Matthew, Evangelist 59
Mennonites 184
Methodism 82, 136, 174, 175, 176, 183
Middle Ages 54, 55, 66, 95, 104, 117, 120
Mildmay, Sir Walter 59
Milner, Joseph 52–3
Milton, John 103
miracles 8
mission 11, 32–3, 176
Monophysites 46, 143
morals 190
More, Hannah 135
More, Thomas 55, 112

mother Church 10–29, 30–53
multilateral dialogue 172, 179
mutual reception 172–82

narrative 35, 139–61
Nestorius 47, 76, 96
New Testament ix, 3 ff., 10, 59, 116
New York 176
New Zealand 175, 176
Newman, John Henry 20, 27, 50–54, 68–71, 83, 99, 112, 117–19, 142, 144, 150–3, 155, 157
Nicaea, Council of (325) 27, 76, 79, 81, 148
Nicaea, Council of (787) 76
Nicene Creed 139, 148, 167, 168, 177
Niceno-Constantinopolitan Creed 75
Nicholas, Pope 86
nonconformists 134, 154
Norway 80, 172
Novatians 95

obedience 86–92
officialness 75–93
Old Catholics 91, 113
Old Testament 114
Orthodox 3, 19, 31, 91, 113, 140, 157, 158, 160, 174
Oxford 104, 124, 150
Oxford Movement 19

parish priests 41
participation 86, 92
pastoral 12
Patriarch of Alexandria 159
Patriarch of Constantinople 159
patriarchs 85, 140
Paul VI, Pope 105
Paul, St 52
peace 179
penance 146, 148, 149
Pentecostalism 4
permanence 79
Peter, St., 88
Philippines 25
philosophers, philosophy 36, 48, 56

Platonists 50
Poitiers, Gilbert of 103
Polynesia 175
Pope 144
power 124
preaching 43–6
Presbyterians 153
primates 85
prophecy 52, 168
protestants 12, 98
Puritans 99, 143
Pusey 47, 145, 150–3, 155

Quartodecimans 86
Quechua 43

Radical Reformation 82
Raiser, Konrad 21
re-reception 148
real presence 150
Reformation 121, 145, 150, 153, 158, 173
Reformed 82, 98
remnant 175
revelation 3, 4, 5, 40, 93
revisionism 144, 157
Rickards, Samuel 143, 157, 158
rites 183
Roman Catholic Church x, 89–90, 98, 148, 177, 178
Roman Empire 114, 172, 173, 174, 176
Rome 159
Rose, Hugh James 69
Russia 19, 174

Sabbatarians 95
Sabellianism 28, 47
Salisbury 59
salvation 39
Sanderson, Robert 63
Santiago 178, 180, 181
Savoy Conference 153
Sawbridge, John 57
Scripture 3, 5, 6, 31, 32, 40, 48, 158, 160 and *passim*
sects 183
Seim, Turid Karlsen 172, 173

INDEX

Severus of Antioch 46
Sewell, W. 99
shared reception 183–91
shepherds 120
Socrates 38
South America 15, 43
Spanish 43
stages 172
Suarez 152
Sumatra 177
superstition 41, 148
Sutcliffe, Matthew 60
synods 39, 81
    see councils

teaching 3 ff.
Ten Commandments 39
Tenison, Thomas 60
Tetradites 95
Theodoret 142
Theophanes Procopovich 39
Thirty-Nine Articles 99, 100, 167, 183
Thorpe, William 133
Toulouse 94
tradition 31–2, 40, 158, 160, 186, 190
Trent, Council of 30, 83, 95, 149
Trinity 148, 177
truth 110–13
Turibio of Mongrevejo 43
tyranny 177

unanimity 76, 179, 180
united not absorbed 186
universality 4, 186
USA 165

Vatican Council, I 30, 47, 81, 87
Vatican Council, II 13, 14, 17, 30, 32, 33, 63, 160, 179, 186, 187, 188
Vatican Councils 78
Vicar of Christ 178
victimization 23
Vienne, Council of (1311–12) 87
Vincent of Lérins 144, 156, 170
visible Church 185
Voluntary Societies 136
Vulgate 130

Wesley, Charles 112
Wesley, John 183
West viii, 38, 78, 140, 175
Whately, Richard 51
Whitaker, William 117
White, Blanco 28
Wittenburg 176
World Council of Churches 92, 178, 185
Wyclif 104, 136
Wykeham, William of 56

York 83

Zürich 176

SPCK

The Society for Promoting Christian Knowledge (SPCK) has as its purpose three main tasks:

- Communicating the Christian faith in its rich diversity
- Helping people to understand the Christian faith and to develop their personal faith
- Equipping Christians for mission and ministry

SPCK Worldwide serves the Church through Christian literature and communication projects in over 100 countries. Special schemes also provide books for those training for ministry in many parts of the developing world. SPCK Worldwide's ministry involves Churches of many traditions. This worldwide service depends upon the generosity of others and all gifts are spent wholly on ministry programmes, without deductions.

SPCK Bookshops support the life of the Christian community by making available a full range of Christian literature and other resources, and by providing support to bookstalls and book agents throughout the UK. SPCK Bookshops' mail order department meets the needs of overseas customers and those unable to have access to local bookshops.

SPCK Publishing produces Christian books and resources, covering a wide range of inspirational, pastoral, practical and academic subjects. Authors are drawn from many different Christian traditions, and publications aim to meet the needs of a wide variety of readers in the UK and throughout the world.

The Society does not necessarily endorse the individual views contained in its publications, but hopes they stimulate readers to think about and further develop their Christian faith.

For further information about the Society, please write to:
SPCK, Holy Trinity Church, Marylebone Road,
London NW1 4DU, United Kingdom.
Telephone: 0171 387 5282